UNSTOPPABLE

Go the Distance with God

UNSTOPPABLE

Go the Distance with God

Patti Greene

Library of Congress Cataloging-in-Publication Data
Name: Greene, Patti, author.
Unstoppable: Go the Distance with God
Subjects: LCSH.
Inspiration — Religious aspects — Christianity.
Encouragement — Religious aspects — Christianity.
Success — Religious aspects — Christianity.
Description: *Greene Pastures Books*, 2025. Includes Endnotes

To: _____

From: _____

Date: _____

Dedicated to the Adult Children of John and Patti Greene

Jennifer Laura Greene Colley

John Rodman Greene, Jr.

James Charles Greene

Contents

Acknowledgements..i

Introduction 1

Translations and Versions of the Bible................................3

Chapter 1: Unveiling Christ-followers' Lack of Biblical Knowledge 7

Chapter 2: Understanding the Bible 10

Chapter 3: Recharge Your Bible Reading Habits 15

Chapter 4: Reading, Reflecting, and Studying...................19

Chapter 5: Experience his Love—On Shoes, Sin, and Savior.........24

Chapter 6: Ezekiel: When God says, "Enough is Enough!" 28

Chapter 7: Exploring Spiritual Gifts.................................35

Chapter 8: Discovering and Utilizing Spiritual Gifts...........47

Chapter 9: The Power of Discernment 52

Chapter 10: Discovering God's Call 56

Chapter 11: Amos: The Life of an Ordinary Man................60

Chapter 12: Lessons from the Good Samaritan 68

Chapter 13: The Power and Importance of Prayer 73

Chapter 14: Intercessory Prayer 76

Chapter 15: It: Isaiah and the Power of Prayer..................81

Chapter 16: Ten Tips for a Richer Prayer Life 88

Chapter 17: Praying for Your Children 91

Chapter 18: Habakkuk: A Model of Prayer and Worship...........97

Chapter 19: Hannah: A Biblical Character of Prayer and Worship.. 100

Chapter 20: Transformation Tips for Teaching and Preaching......... 103

Chapter 21: Revolutionizing Life through Prayer and Bible Study . 109

Chapter 22: Continuing to Serve God while Aging 113

Chapter 23: Solomon's Wisdom 119

Chapter 24: Choosing God's Path.................................. 125

Chapter 25: Crossing the Jordan: Embracing Change 128

Chapter 26: Embarking on the Journey of Pride 136

Chapter 27: Cultivating Humility 139

Chapter 28: Nurturing Kindness: Embracing the Spirit's Fruit 143

Chapter 29: Dealing with Imperfections and Regrets 150

Chapter 30: Learning from Life's Mishaps and Mistakes 153

Chapter 31: The Perils of Disobedience 158

Chapter 32: Exploring Motives and Intentions 164

Chapter 33: Purah: An Old Testament Servant 171

Chapter 34: Peter's Transformation:
From Hot-Headedness to Spiritual Maturity 176

Chapter 35: The Speck and the Log 180

Chapter 36: Barnabas: The Heart of New Testament Service 189

Chapter 37: Nehemiah: The Unlikely Leader Who Built Walls
and Hearts 195

Chapter 38: Exploring Leadership
through the Wisdom of Proverbs 203

Chapter 39: Dealing with a Crisis 213

Chapter 40: Navigating Accidents 218

Chapter 41: Loving Your Enemies 222

Chapter 42: Managing Stress 232

Chapter 43: Tests and Trials 242

Chapter 44: Navigating Suicide 248

Chapter 45: Coping with Grief: Minnie's Story 256

Chapter 46: Embracing the Inevitable 263

Epilogue 268

Endnotes 269

Bibliography 282

When All is Said and Done: Mom's Note to her Kids 292

About the Author 295

Other Books by the Author 297

NOTES 298

ACKNOWLEDGEMENTS

This book is the culmination of the support, encouragement, and contributions of many people, and I am deeply grateful to each one. Therefore, I would like to extend my heartfelt thanks to the following individuals:

John Greene, my loving husband, whose encouragement has been constant throughout our 46 years of marriage. He has supported every endeavor I've pursued, no matter how ambitious or unconventional and has been my rock through it all.

Ellsworth Johnson, whose unwavering belief in my potential has shaped every word I've written. Over the years, he has been my mentor and guide, offering invaluable help with vocabulary, punctuation, organization, and style. His persistence and constructive feedback have instilled in me the confidence to push beyond my limits.

Jennifer Greene Colley, our eldest child, whose loyalty, love, and joy have enriched our lives in countless ways. Her steadfast presence has been a source of strength and inspiration to us.

John Greene, Jr., our middle child, whose heart and character continues to fill us with love and gratitude. We are especially thankful for the ease in raising him from birth to adulthood.

Jimmy Greene, our youngest, has shown us that living life is an adventure, full of unexpected twists that sometimes become the moments to love and embrace the most.

Charles Londa, Sr., my father, imparted to me the value of reading. His example and passion for books instilled in me a lifelong love of learning.

Mafelda Izzo Londa, my mother, emphasized the significance of journaling and recording thoughts on paper. Her quiet wisdom and attention to detail have influenced my writing deeply.

Marla Moss, Bob Norman, Lynn Allen Paulsen, and my husband generously took the time to read my manuscript, offered their thoughtful feedback and helped me refine this book. Their insights, diligence, and unwavering support have made this book better in so many ways.

Finally, my deepest and most profound acknowledgment goes to Jesus Christ, whose guidance and presence in my life have been the foundation for everything I do. Without Him, this book would not have come to fruition.

To all of you, my sincerest thanks.

Patti Greene

INTRODUCTION

The title and subtitle of this book, *Unstoppable: Go the Distance with God*, is all about understanding one's purpose and how to endure through all the circumstances we encounters in life. Enduring one's life journey with God is why I authored this book. No matter what age the readers are, there will be hope that a life with God is attainable and that it is the best thing to strive for. YES, we can go the distance with God. YES, we can grow spiritually. YES, we can become resilient by enduring through tough times. And YES, we can leave a godly legacy to our friends, family, and those who know us.

Many Christians want to persevere with the Lord no matter what comes up, but they don't know how. Answering the how question is what this book is all about as it masters the depths of the Bible, unlocking the power of prayer, navigating the Christian life, pioneering leadership principles, and overcoming spiritual breaking points.

Most people wish to rise above challenges, disappointments, and doubts. They want to move forward, being strong and unstoppable in their faith. Believing you can do that is what unstoppable people do. People who are unstoppable have confidence and assurance that they are committed to their work, family, church, and more. They have the courage to "go the distance" to be the best person they can be in whatever they attempt to do.

Initially conceived as a legacy book for my children, this book expanded to benefit parents and adults seeking answers about the Christian faith. The topics included in this book were carefully selected for relevancy. Through my weaknesses and strengths, these narratives guide readers to embrace God's love.

I hope you, my readers, start or continue developing your faith in the power of God's Holy Spirit. Understanding those values, priorities, and coping with challenges can offer a prized spiritual inheritance. Written in a casual style, I attempt to inform and describe a life lived through faith in the Lord, not just for my family but as a heritage for all believers.

Scripture quotations are from the NEW AMERICAN STANDARD BIBLE ©1971,1977, 1995, 2020, unless otherwise noted in the text. The New American Standard Bible (NASB) is known for its meticulous word-for-word translation from the original texts. Since its inception in 1971, all later revisions have maintained their accuracy and readability. Therefore, I have integrated verses from all four versions throughout the book, making it a reliable source for everyone. Deity pronouns conform to the most popular versions of the Bible—the King James Version and the New International version—using a lowercase style. The exception being in quotations used from the New American Standard version which use a capital letter for the Holy Spirit, Jesus, and God.

In the course of reading this book, you will notice various words and phrases utilized to refer to specific concepts. For instance, the Bible is interchangeably referred to as Scripture, Scriptures, the Word of God, the Word of truth, God's Word, and Word of the Lord, all conveying the same meaning. Similarly, salvation is depicted through terms, such as accepting Christ or being born again. The term Christ-follower may be used synonymously with being a Christian or believer, while paradise may be used interchangeably with heaven. This repetition of terminology underscores the consistent message conveyed throughout the text.

As we embark on this journey exploring concepts rooted in the Bible, it is essential to establish short and simple definitions for key terms that will underpin our discourse taken from the *Elementary Bible Truths Handbook*.[1]

Bible: The holy, inspired Word of God.

Faith: Trust in God; a firm believing without proof; complete confidence.

Gospel: The good news of Christ's coming to earth, dying for our sins, and rising from the tomb on the third day.

Salvation: The redemption and forgiveness of sin through faith in Jesus Christ.

I have taken a bold step by revealing my vulnerabilities in this book. Even if you know me, you might be surprised by some of the personal anecdotes I have shared. However, I have done so because I believe that it is important for my adult children and yours to recognize that we are all flawed human beings who are striving to do better.

TRANSLATIONS AND VERSIONS OF THE BIBLE

ESV	English Standard Version
HCSB	Holman Christian Standard Bible
KJV	King James Version
LB	Living Bible
NASB	New American Standard Bible
NIV	New International Version
NKJV	New King James Version
NLT	New Living Translation

SECTION 1

Bible and
Biblical Characters

CHAPTER 1

UNVEILING CHRIST-FOLLOWERS' LACK OF BIBLICAL KNOWLEDGE

The Bible is not an end in itself,
but a means to bring men to an intimate and satisfying knowledge of
God,
that they may enter into Him, that they may delight in His Presence,
may taste and know the inner sweetness of the very God Himself
in the core and center of their hearts.

A.W. Tozer

"The story has been told about several famous preachers, but it actually happened to Joseph Parker, minister of the City Temple in London. An old lady waited on Parker in his vestry after a service to thank him for the help she received from his sermons. 'You do throw such wonderful light on the Bible, doctor,' she said. 'Do you know that until this morning, I had always thought that Sodom and Gomorrah were man and wife?'"[1] In case you are wondering, Sodom and Gomorrah were two cities, which were destroyed by God for their evil and wickedness. Similar instances like this make me wonder why do Christ-followers know so little about the Bible? My semi-short answer and thoughts follow. I have been a Bible teacher in church, homes, and outside venues, and I have been astonished to encounter people, even long-time Christ-followers, who know so little about the Bible, too.

However, I unequivocally include myself in that group. I'll never forget my first year of college, sitting in a New Testament class with my hand raised high, about to ask the professor, "So, what is circumcision?" Looking back, I can't believe I ventured down that path! Moreover, I thank God the professor never called on me; the thought of enduring that kind of embarrassment still makes me cringe. In this book, I aim to tackle your burning questions about the Bible, God, and related topics that you've been curious about but hesitant to ask.

As I considered this, I often find myself questioning why some people seem to have difficulty retaining knowledge from the Bible. Do Bible verses go in one ear and out the other? Do they never look at their Bible outside of Sundays? Do they have selective memories? Or is Satan wiping out what they have heard or learned? Alternatively, could it be that they have medical memory problems, or that some sin is blocking them from being involved with the Bible? Ultimately, I find myself wondering why some people don't take the Bible seriously, and whether or not they can truly consider themselves to be Christ-followers. These are tough questions to answer, but they are important ones to consider.

It baffles me that "so many know so little about the Bible" because since I accepted Jesus Christ 50+ years ago, I have taken the Bible seriously from the get-go. I say that with as much humility as I can muster, because I do not want it to come out prideful. "Lord, please forgive me if it is." That is not my intent. I am not perfect—just ask my husband! But what happened that was different?

To be effective in any Chistian ministry, we should have a good handle on God's Word. The desire to read the Bible and learn what God's will is and what he wants from us is one of the most beautiful ways we can show our love and devotion to him. If we are disciples of Christ, we should not neglect the Word, and I mean the entire Word, including the Old and the New Testaments. I believe the church should be used to lead people to Christ and then see them being transformed into Christlike individuals through training and discipleship. This will lead to their personal transformation.

However, some *choose not* to open their Bible. Some *choose not* to read or study their Bible. And some *choose not* to attend church, Bible studies, or discipleship classes. It is impossible to be an unstoppable believer without reading the Bible. People must make the Bible a priority in their lives!

For a Christ-follower, one act of kindness is to pray fervently for those who do not take the Bible seriously. Find out if they have a personal relationship with the Lord, encourage them to grow, and then stand by their side as they start the exciting life of knowing and loving God through his Word and Spirit.

Challenge

Consider setting aside dedicated time each day, not just Sundays— to immerse yourself in Scripture. Start by choosing a passage that resonates with you and commit to reading it, reflecting on its meaning, and applying it to your life. In addition to personal study, reach out to someone—a friend, family member, or fellow church member—who may also struggle with engaging in Scripture. Together, establish a regular time to discuss what you've read and how it impacts your walk with Christ. Remember, the journey of spiritual growth is not meant to be undertaken alone. By prioritizing the Bible and sharing that journey with others, you'll not only deepen your own understanding but also encourage those around you to seek a more profound relationship with God through His Word. Take this challenge seriously and watch how God begins to transform your mind and heart.

Be Unstoppable: Go the Distance with God,

And do not be conformed to this world, but be transformed by the renewing of your mind, so that you may prove what the will of God is, that which is good and acceptable and perfect.

Romans 12:2

CHAPTER 2

UNDERSTANDING THE BIBLE

> *Through the study of God's Word,*
> *we learn the deeper things of God.*
> *It is one thing to know He loves us,*
> *but it is entirely different to realize that*
> *He has a plan for our lives.*
>
> Charles Stanley

The *Guinness Book of World Records* asserts the Bible is the world's best-selling book. It has sold between five and seven billion copies since its earliest handwritten manuscripts over 1,500 years ago. It offers an account of creation and human history, from the beginning of time to the eventual end.[1] Comprising 66 books—39 in the Old Testament and 27 in the New Testament—the Bible presents a unified narrative. The Old Testament outlines creation, early history, and God's covenant with Israel, while the New Testament reveals the life of Jesus and the spread of his message. When we understand that the Bible is foundational to our Christian walk, we can go the distance with God.

Old Testament

The Old Testament includes:

- **Pentateuch:** The first five books of the Hebrew Bible, which detail creation, the Flood, and the journey of the Israelites from Egypt to the Promised Land. It is commonly known as the Torah.

- **Historical Books**: Twelve books chronicling Israel's history, including their conquest of Canaan and subsequent struggles.

- **Poetry and Wisdom**: Five books providing profound reflections on life, divine guidance, and human experience.

- **Major Prophets**: Five prophetic books highlighting themes of judgment and the hope of a coming Messiah.

- **Minor Prophets**: Twelve shorter books with similar messages of warning and the promise of restoration through the Messiah.

Some Bibles also feature the **Apocrypha**, which contain additional books that are not universally accepted as Scripture but are considered valuable for historical and moral instruction.[2]

New Testament

The New Testament contains:

- **Gospels and Acts**: Four books documenting Jesus' life, death, and resurrection, followed by the spread of the gospel through the Acts of the apostles.

- **Paul's Epistles**: Thirteen letters addressing issues in early churches and offering theological guidance.

- **General Epistles and Revelation**: Nine letters from other apostles and one prophetic vision of future events.

Who Reads the Bible and Why?

The Bible, the sacred text for Christians, is widely read by many for various purposes, including spiritual reflection and personal growth. It is considered the "go-to" book for Christ-followers. It is also read by many worldwide, religious and otherwise.

In a Huffington Post article titled "Who Reads the Bible—and Why?" contributor David Briggs states, "the top two reasons respondents said they read Scripture were for personal prayer and devotion and to learn more about their religion — with at least six in [ten] citing each factor. The third most popular reason was to seek guidance in personal decisions and relationships with spouses, parents, children, and friends... People no longer just open the pages of the Good Book. Thirty-one percent read it on the Internet and 22 percent used e-devices."[3]

The Bible serves as a roadmap for life, offering guidance, wisdom, and encouragement. It addresses every challenge humanity faces and serves as God's final word of authority. Regular reading strengthens faith and helps align our lives with God's purposes. Jesus said, *"The words that I have spoken to you are spirit and are life"* (John 6:63).

Enormous joy occurs when the Bible touches one's heart and guides them toward confession, repentance, and salvation. After acceptance of Christ, many continue to connect to the Bible to internalize God's truths and live accordingly. Even though there are various reasons to browse or study the Bible, many encounter a true and deep spiritual transformation, honoring and glorifying God through spiritual service to Him.

Outcomes of Reading the Bible

The late Pastor Adrian Rogers identified four key outcomes when believers seek understanding from God's Word:

1. Eyes will be opened (Psalm 119:18).
2. Understanding will be deepened (Luke 24:45).
3. Hearts will be stirred (Psalm 119:36), and
4. Minds will be enlightened (Psalm 119:73).[4]

Is the Bible Divinely Inspired?

Scripture itself and scholars, too numerous to name, affirm the Bible as divinely inspired. *"All Scripture is given by inspiration of God..."* (2 Tim. 3:16). It contains powerful, discerning thoughts, which guide us toward righteousness (Heb. 4:12).

Understanding God

The Bible reveals God's nature, goodness, and promises, guiding us to live a life worthy of him. It teaches us to imitate Christ and follow his example through stories, teachings, and parables. In 2 Timothy 2:15, believers are urged to study the Bible with intention and diligence. This process requires time, planning, and commitment. As we engage deeply with the Scripture, God's truths are progressively revealed and understood.

Applying Our Mind

Engaging thoughtfully with Scripture allows us to gain wisdom, strength, and clarity. A deeper study—whether it involves examining verses individually or exploring specific topics—can lead to transformative insights. Additionally, meditating on God's Word nurtures our spiritual growth, helping us align our desires with his will.

Powerful Discipline

Reading the Bible is a powerful spiritual discipline. My own journey began with a desire for guidance as I faced a difficult decision in my early 20s. Since then, Bible reading has become a daily source of joy, insight, and conviction.

I applaud you if you commit to read the Bible all the way through, and I encourage you to do so. However, it is not about doing it for external validation or to be able to claim how many times you have read the Word. Like the Pharisees, we must avoid reading the Word to impress others. God sees our heart and our motives, not just our actions.

Critics

The Bible has often been criticized, often by those who reject its authority or seek to justify their actions. Public figures like Jesse Ventura, Larry Flynt, and Ted Turner dismiss Christianity as a crutch for the weak. Jesse Ventura, former governor of Minnesota, once said, "Organized religion is a sham and a crutch for weak-minded people who need strength in numbers." Agreeing with him is Larry Flynt, producer of magazines such as Hustler and sexually graphic videos, who commented, "There's nothing good I can say about it [religion]. People use it as a crutch." Ted Turner once said, "Christianity is a religion for losers!" Ventura, Flynt, Turner, and others who think like them view Christians as being emotionally feeble and in need of imaginary support to get through life. They insinuate that they are strong and do not need a supposed God to help them with their lives.[5]

Unfortunately, this is a heartbreaking indictment against their denial of Jesus Christ, the One and only true God.

The Bible—Loved by Millions

Despite its critics, the Bible is cherished, read, and studied by millions worldwide. Baptist theologian Bernard Ramm encourages a lifelong commitment to Scripture, promising life-changing results. I urge you to engage with the Bible daily—it will transform your life.[6]

Be Unstoppable—Go the Distance with God,

This book of the law shall not depart from your mouth, but you shall meditate on it day and night, *so that you may be careful to do according to all that is written in it; for then you will make your way prosperous, and then you will have success. Be strong and courageous!*
Joshua 1:8-9

CHAPTER 3

RECHARGE YOUR BIBLE READING HABITS

The first thing that must occur if you want your prayers to be answered and you want your prayers to be powerful is to become a child of God.

Adrian Rogers

I am an expert on catalogs—at least, I feel like I am. Catalogs swamp my snail mail. I immediately take a fleeting look at the front cover, and I know whether a catalog ends up in the trash, in my bathroom, or on my coffee table. Many times, particular catalogs deserve my immediate attention! Marketing headlines entice me with their advertisements and sales. For example,

- Elegant Accents to Add to Your bathroom!
- Wrap Yourself in the Beauty of Authentic Irish Knits!
- Look for the Jumbo Almond Butter Crunch Buttery Toffee That's Twice as Thick, Ten Times as Tasty!
- Have a CHUCKLE—Then Try to Keep a Straight Face!
- Safari and African Home Decor Will Unleash Your Wild Streak!
- True Classics That Never Go Out of Style!
- September Classy Shopping Spree
- Guaranteed Forever![1]

If I like the color, layout, design, and uniqueness of memorable catalogs, I look forward to those special catalogs coming! When I open those kinds of magazines or emails, I anticipate feelings of joy and comfort from perusing the pages, whether I eventually purchase from that catalog or not.

Wouldn't it be wonderful to read the Bible with the same anticipation as our favorite catalog? What if we couldn't wait to sit down and pore over God's Word? What if we anticipated God's love, comfort, and support? The Bible is not a dull book. It is a book filled with God's love, guidance, and purpose for our lives. His Word also lays out how he wants to involve each of us in the lives of others.

How to Recharge Your Bible Reading Habits

1. Cultivate the habit of opening his Word regularly.

   But I, O LORD, cry to you; in the morning my prayer comes before you.
   Psalm 88:13 ESV

2. Find a quiet, distraction-free space to meditate upon his Holy Word.

   I will ponder all your work, and meditate on your mighty deeds.
   Psalm 77:12 ESV

3. Approach the Bible with anticipation, expecting a message from God each time you read.

   But, as it is written, "What no eye has seen, nor ear heard, nor the heart of man imagined, what God has prepared for those who love him"—these things God has revealed to us through the Spirit. For the Spirit searches everything, even the depths of God.
   1 Corinthians 2:9-10 ESV

4. Explore the subheadings within the Bible to gain knowledge and understanding.

   An intelligent heart acquires knowledge, and the ear of the wise seeks knowledge.
   Proverbs 18:15 ESV

5. Humbly ask for forgiveness and guidance from the Holy Spirit

to illuminate the meaning of the Scriptures.

But when He, the Spirit of truth, comes, He will guide you into all the truth; for He will not speak on His own initiative, but whatever He hears, He will speak; and He will disclose to you what is to come. He will glorify Me, for He will take of Mine and will disclose it to you. All things that the Father has are Mine; therefore I said that He takes of Mine and will disclose it to you.
John 16:13-15

6. Make intentional decisions to read the Bible and pray for specific needs.

   And this is the confidence that we have toward him, that if we ask anything according to his will he hears us. And if we know that he hears us in whatever we ask, we know that we have the requests that we have asked of him.
   1 John 5:14-15 ESV

7. Keep a journal to record insights and impressions from your study.

   Then the LORD answered me and said "Record the vision and inscribe it on tablets, that the one who reads it may run. For the vision is yet for the appointed time; It hastens toward the goal, and it will not fail. Though it tarries, wait for it; for it will certainly come, it will not delay."
   Habakkuk 2:2-3

8. Conclude your Bible reading with anticipation of its importance to your day.

   The steadfast love of the Lord never ceases; his mercies never come to an end; they are new every morning; great is your faithfulness.
   Lamentations 3:22-23 ESV

When I receive my Touch of Class catalog, I want to get away by myself, browse the catalog, dog-ear the pages, circle what I need, like, or buy.[2]

May we open the Bible with the same enthusiasm and reverence we reserve for our favorite catalogs, recognizing that it is a gift to explore and gain insights into God's truth, wisdom, and spirit.

Be Unstoppable—Go the Distance with God,

And He was saying to them all, "If anyone wishes to come after Me, He must deny himself, and take up his cross daily and follow Me."
Luke 9:23

Chapter 4

READING, REFLECTING, AND STUDYING

*Reading God's Word leads to study and tremendous insight.
Ask the Lord to reveal His truth to you concerning what you are reading.*

Charles Stanley

We must read, reflect, and study the Bible, as it is a divine gift tailored by God for us. This feat requires commitment and discipline, leading to deeper understanding and insight into God's truths and how to apply them to be "transformed by the renewing of our mind" (Rom. 12:2). Authored by God, using different authors and editors, the Bible is our manual for life — offering clear insights into his will. The Bible addresses substantial questions about us, yet many underestimate its relevance.

In life, we face many weighty decisions.

- Where will we go when we die?

- Why is there so much evil in this world?

- How do I know who to marry?

- What house should I buy?

- What ministries should I be involved in?

Furthermore, we encounter everyday concerns.

- How can I pass this test?
- Where should I go to college?
- Why didn't I make the basketball team?
- Where should I attend church?
- How can I stop sinning?

Men and women do not think it is right to "bother" God with small requests. But God desires us to communicate with him in all situations. A 2013 poll by Religion News revealed that "more than half of Americans think the Bible has too little influence on a culture they see in moral decline, yet only one in five Americans read the Bible on a regular basis."[1] This lack of perceived relevance might stem from a failure to engage with the Word of God. To truly benefit from biblical truths, we must distinguish between reading, reflecting, and studying the Word of God.

Reading the Bible

Reading the Bible for personal enlightenment occurs during a daily quiet time or devotional time. When reading leisurely, our reading is usually at an unhindered and comfortable pace focused on understanding his messages and deepening our relationship with him. However, it can easily become intense pleading or calling out to God for answers. As a rule, sitting around with many concordances, Bible dictionaries, or Christian theological books is not the preferred reading here. Reading to see what God is saying to us personally and getting to know God better should be the goal during this reading time. It is an occasion to learn more about God, his precepts and character, and how he desires to mature our faith. This time allows God to speak to us personally through his Word, although looking up words for meaningful clarification is helpful at times.

Tips for Your Devotional Time

- Be consistent in where your devotional time takes place,
- Use a Bible reading plan,

- Pray for the Holy Spirit's guidance,

- Focus on a relevant verse,

- Keep a journal.

I like to use a Bible without all the study notes and footnotes during my quiet time. The notes distract me from plain old reading God's Word. I want the Word of God to speak to me and not feel obligated to read what someone else has said about the verses I am reading, although I have had to look up a few things along the way. Personal preferences vary; some prefer a Bible without additional notes, and others prefer a more direct connection with the Word. There is no right or wrong way to have devotional time – personalize it to fit your likes, personalities, and time.

Reflecting on the Bible

While we will discuss this more in a later chapter, reflecting on God's Word is the time one spends contemplating, internalizing, and letting the Scripture shape our lives. Don't allow yourself to be hooked on any particular technique or program during this reflective time. These can quickly become so legalistic that you may have difficulty absorbing God's Word from them. Reflecting is quietly sitting before God, internalizing the Scriptures, thinking of God, and letting his thoughts and words become ingrained in our lives. This time serves many purposes: It provides wisdom, hope, understanding, illumination, answers, and more. 1 Chronicles 22:19a states, "Now devote your heart and soul to seeking the LORD your God."

I call this time "being in the zone," just listening to the Lord. By engaging with Scripture thoughtfully, we gain wisdom, strength, and clarity. Studying it in-depth—whether by looking at verses one by one or exploring specific topics—offers valuable insights. Meditating on God's Word helps us grow spiritually and align our desires with his will. During this time, you may be prompted to involve yourself in benevolent activities, such as calling someone residing in a nursing home, writing a letter, or offering time or service to someone in need. One's purpose and calling often stems from this time spent in his presence.

Comprehensive Study

Comprehensive study involves using commentaries, attending seminars, listening to sermons, or delving into historical events. Being organized is crucial. Through developing research skills, focus, and a commitment to prayer, we can gain a deeper understanding of theological doctrine and accurately interpret God's Word. Pastors and Bible study teachers spend hours studying and developing their sermons or classes like this. But laypeople should also become familiar with the Word by comprehensively studying this way. Do not leave your spiritual growth to only church pastors, Bible study teachers, or podcasts.

> *Study to shew thyself approved unto God, a workman that needeth not to be ashamed, rightly dividing the word of truth. (2 Timothy 2:15 KJV).*

Everyone's journey in studying the Bible is unique and develops over time. Customize yours to fit your interests, personality, and needs. When I was younger, I never wanted to write because I felt like there were so many good writers out there that I could never compare to them. Only through my devotional time and Bible study did I realize that God made us all different and our writing styles vary. You may like to sit outside on your back porch and read your Bible. You may want to participate in an in-depth Bible study at someone's home. You may like to reflect in the park. Whatever works for you, do it. Don't put off being taught by the Word of God. Get organized and get going.

For me, my serious Bible study takes place at my dining room table, but for my quiet and reflective time, you will find me on my mother's old, flowered couch in our downstairs library—of course, it is usually accompanied with my freshly brewed coffee. How about you?

Before moving on, let's understand some key facts about the Bible:

- *The Bible was in the beginning (John 1:1).*

- *The Bible will never pass away (Matthew 24:35).*

- *The Bible is right and true (Psalm 33:4).*

- *The Bible is what every man should live on (Matthew 4:4).*

- *The Bible judges the thoughts and attitudes of the heart (Hebrews 4:12).*

- *The Bible sustains all things (Hebrews 1:3).*

Moreover, we must realize that the Bible is profitable in many ways. It allows us to ask whatever we wish, and it will be done (John 15:7). It equips us to be used by God (Eph. 6:17) and gives us hope (Ps.130:5). It provides us with an understanding of the simple (Ps. 119:130) and is helpful for teaching, rebuking, correcting, and training in righteousness (2 Tim. 3:16). The Bible keeps us from moral filth and evil (James 1:21), makes us wise (Matt. 7:24), provides an understanding of the simple (Ps. 119:130), sets us free (John 8:31-32), shows us how much God loves us (1 John 4:19), and teaches us how to get to heaven (John 14:6).

Be Unstoppable—Go the Distance with God,

For I am confident of this very thing, that He who began a good work in you will perfect it until the day of Christ Jesus.
Philippians 1:6

CHAPTER 5

EXPERIENCE HIS LOVE—ON SHOES, SIN, AND SAVIOR

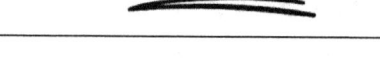

It's important to learn to walk in someone else's shoes. It helps to love people if we can look beyond who they are to who they can become.

Dr. John Bisango

My excitement began when I adorned my feet with a brand-new pair of high-heeled silver shoes! While I don't claim I am obsessed with shoes, most women [like me] feel confident slipping their feet into a new pair of sandals, wedges, boots, flats, heels, or tennis shoes. I am no exception. One day, I was psyched up to grace my feet in my new pair of shoes. My new silver shoes and I were going out on the town for the first time to Saks Fifth Avenue in Houston's Galleria to enjoy lunch with my good friend Dorothy. I stepped out of the house with my serotonin level bouncing high! As I pulled out of my driveway, I noticed my sanitation worker had come, and I needed to bring the garbage can to the back of the house. I exited my car and dragged the garbage can to its resting place. However, a stumble on my driveway marred the day as my new shoes bore a tear, leading me to ponder the significance of this mishap. But I continued to the Galleria with the express thought that I would stop at the shoe repair store on my way home and see if the cobbler could somehow prevent my shoe from tearing up more. On the drive to the Galleria, my tiny tear somehow became a humongous rip in my mind.

After a lovely lunch with my friend, I drove directly to the cobbler to fix this problem before it got out of hand. The cobbler suddenly became elevated to having a doctorate degree in 'Shoe Repair.' If anyone could fix my shoe, he could! I arrived at the shoe repair shop, parked my car in the lot, and began pondering whether I should go in or not. I finally decided that I was putting too much emphasis on my new pair of shoes. To make a long story short, I chose not to spend money to get a small tear fixed when these shoes only cost $39.00. I drove home without entering the hallowed doors of my idolized savior –THE COBBLER.

I realized then that I was placing undue importance on this material possession I called "my shoe." This trivial tear became a metaphor for sin, and the cobbler symbolized the Lord's willingness to mend our brokenness.

Just like a cobbler who wants to fix our shoes, God wants to fix us.

Some exciting things happen when you ask Jesus Christ to forgive your sins and accept him as your Lord and Savior. You become a valuable member of God's Kingdom and can be assured of eternity in Heaven. When Jesus died on the cross, he died for us. When we trust him, he gives us the most fantastic gift he could ever give—the gift of salvation. Even after that, we will all experience temptation, sin, and disobedience; even Jesus was tempted. It is hard to understand how both God and Satan want to control our lives. Therefore, we must choose every day to follow Christ. As we let the Holy Spirit work within us, we will begin to develop the fruit of the Spirit. The Bible says a Christian will be known by their fruits. Galatians 5:22-23 states, "But the fruit of the Spirit is love, joy, peace, patience, kindness, goodness, faithfulness, gentleness, and self-control; against such things there is no law."

Your local church can help you in developing a Christlike life. Churches are like families who show concern and love for each other. Your church, or potential church, might meet in a building, a home, a movie theater, or a warehouse. Wherever you decide to attend church is not as important as why you are meeting, and that is to pray, worship, witness, give, thank, and praise God. Churches often celebrate a new Christian's baptism and the Lord's Supper, which you should make every effort to participate in.

On our walk with Jesus, we will sin. We are human, but when we do, we would be wise to go to Jesus immediately to forgive those sins and deal with them before we sin more. We all sin, but do we continually turn to the Lord after one little sin? Sometimes, we do, but other times, we wait until our sins mount. The longer we wait to go to the expert, the bigger and bigger the problems and consequences of our sins get.

The Prodigal Son—Luke 15:11-32

The prodigal son went off with his inheritance. Excited about his new adventure, he squandered his wealth and became involved in ungodly behavior. He enjoyed himself until one day, he ate with the pigs. His sins accumulated, but finally, he decided he had it better at home, and he returned to his father. And the good news is his father accepted him. It would have been best if the 'prodigal son' never left home and sinned, but he did. Just as the prodigal son returned home seeking his father's forgiveness, we, too, can find peace in God's unconditional love and acceptance. Despite our failures, God continually extends his hand, inviting us to return to him.

Our situation and consequences usually worsen when we postpone or reject God. Our earthly desires may distract us, but God patiently pursues us until the days of pursuing are over.

Whether one has been involved in a crime, had an abortion, deceived a spouse, or other actions, God still loves us. He cares about us and will continue to put spiritual people, spiritual literature, spiritual songs, and more in our pathway as he convinces us to return to him.

Our heavenly Father sees the big and small tears (sins) in our lives, and he wants to fix them as soon as possible before they become tears with more dire consequences.

By deciding not to go to the cobbler, I didn't get the small tear in my shoe fixed. But it's just a shoe!!! Our lives are more important than shoes. God is there to heal all our lives including small and big tears. When we turn to him, and love him forever, we experience true freedom and well-being. It can mean the difference between Heaven and hell. Wherever you are in your spiritual walk, choose God. Don't wait. He loves and cares for all of us. Make God the Master Cobbler in your life. Today!

Be Unstoppable—Go the Distance with God,

For God so loved the world, that He gave His only begotten Son, that whoever believes in Him shall not perish, but have eternal life.
John 3:16

CHAPTER 6

EZEKIEL: WHEN GOD SAYS, "ENOUGH IS ENOUGH!"

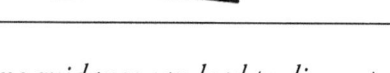

> *Ignoring divine guidance can lead to dire outcomes.*
> *[But] Ezekiel's message, though stern,*
> *is rooted in love and the hope of reconciliation.*
>
> BibleHub

E zekiel, an Old Testament prophet and priest, demonstrated remarkable courage by speaking out when directed by God, even in the face of ridicule. Despite the mockery, he fearlessly prophesied the impending judgment upon Jerusalem and Judah due to their rebellion and idolatry. His obedience to God's command, despite the potential consequences, is a testament to his unwavering faith.

Ezekiel, the Son of Man

I relate to Ezekiel in many respects. I want to write what God wants me to share with others whenever I write. I want to write and share when he speaks to me, just as Ezekiel did when he spoke. When Ezekiel spoke, he proclaimed God's message, which was disregarded by the people and caused his peers to laugh and disrespect him. Ezekiel's task was to foretell the future of Jerusalem and Judah to the people. He was to prophesize about the siege of Jerusalem, the desolation of Jerusalem, the idolatrous worship, the punishment for their wicked behavior, and their irreverent disrespect for the temple.

In Ezekiel 4-7, where these issues were the major topics of interest, Ezekiel is called the "son of man" at the beginning of each chapter. This title, 'son of man ', is significant as it emphasizes Ezekiel's humanity and his role as a prophet. He is the only prophet regularly called the "son of man" by God, a title that serves to differentiate him from the supernatural and bizarre visions he had—some of which occur in these chapters.

As we journey with Ezekiel, it's important to remember that he was a person, just like us. He was raised by religious parents, married in his twenties, and faced the same challenges of life we may have. What set him apart was his willingness to heed God's call, even when it led him to exile in Babylonia. He was an ordinary man, filled with the Holy Spirit to do an extraordinary job.

For twenty years, God called Ezekiel, and people criticized him and made fun of him. He even continued his call through the untimely death of his beloved wife. His calling to proclaim the fall, turmoil, and restoration of Judah, and especially Jerusalem, was solid. Ezekiel knew to be obedient was what God required of him. God shared this doom through action sermons, which consisted of Ezekiel acting out vivid physical depictions of God's impending judgment in front of the people. These action sermons were not just dramatic performances, but powerful tools used by God to convey his message. Ezekiel's obedience manifested in these action sermons. He understood that God's ultimate purpose was for God's people to acknowledge him as Lord. God used Ezekiel to confront sin, warn of judgment, and ultimately punish.

1. An Action Sermon: Build a Siege Wall

Now, you son of man, get yourself a brick, place it before you, and inscribe a city on it: Jerusalem. Then, lay siege against it, build a siege wall, raise up a ramp, pitch camps, and place battering rams against it all around. Then get yourself an iron plate and set it up as an iron wall between you and the city and set your face toward it so that it is under siege and besiege it. This is a sign to the house of Israel (Ezekiel 4:1-3).

2. An Action Sermon: Take a Sharp Sword

As for you, son of man, take a sharp sword; take and use it as a barber's razor on your head and beard. Then take scales for weighing and divide the hair. One third you shall burn in the fire at the center of the city, when the days of the siege are completed. Then you shall take one-third and strike it with the sword all around the city, and one-third you shall scatter it to the wind; and I will unsheathe a sword behind them (Ezekiel 5:1-2).

3. An Action Sermon: Face Toward the Mountains

And the words of the Lord came to me saying, "Son of man, set your face toward the mountains of Israel, and prophesy against them and say, 'Mountains of Israel, listen to the word of the Lord GOD!" Thus says the Lord God to the mountains, the hills, the ravines and the valleys: "Behold, I Myself am going to bring a sword on you, and I will destroy your high places."
Ezekiel 6:1-3

Then you will know that I am the Lord, when their slain is among their idols around their altars, on every high hill, on all the tops of the mountains, under every green tree and under every leafy oak— the places where they offered soothing aroma to all their idols (Ezekiel 6:13).

4. An Action Sermon: Prophesy That I am the LORD!

Moreover, the words of the Lord came to me saying, "And you, son of man, thus says the Lord GOD to the land of Israel, An end! The end is coming on the four corners of the land. Now the end is upon you, and I will send My anger against you; I will judge you according to your ways and bring all your abominations upon you. For My eye will have no pity on you, nor will I spare you, but I will bring your ways upon you, and your abominations will be among you; then you will know that I am the LORD!" (Ezekiel 7:1-4).

Let's Consider the Atmosphere.

At the time, a spiritual battle was going on between God and his people. The people were engaging in deliberate and continual rebellion and were about to reap the consequences. They were worshiping pagan cults. They were morally corrupt. Their leaders were not guiding the people. Their priests gave no wise counsel. Even their court officials led with despair.[1] God was not going to tolerate their sinful behavior anymore! God called Ezekiel and told him to prophecy to the people using signs, action sermons, and visions. He was asked to do strange things to describe the desolation that would happen in Jerusalem. God gave Ezekiel three specific prophecies regarding how the people's punishment would happen—one-third would die by plagues or famine, one-third would fall by the sword, and one-third would be scattered to every wind. Ezekiel denounced idolatry and told the people about upcoming famines and diseases. He was obedient, although up against calloused people who had no interest in hearing the words of God or prophecies of disaster, even though he reminded them that God would leave a remnant of His people.

Let's Consider the People.

The people were enjoying their sinful lives. They took pride in their gorgeous jewels. They worshipped their vile idols and enjoyed their wealth to the fullest. The people continued to enrich themselves with material possessions while using them for evil. But the Bible talks about disaster upon disaster about to be released upon them. The people could not believe God would punish or hurt them. We hear this today, too, when people say, "God is good, and would never do anything to hurt us." It is devastating when a Trojan Horse "pop-up" warning appears on your computer screen while looking at a website. When it happened to me, I immediately went to an authoritative source who could fix the problem—my husband.

But that is not what happens in the Book of Ezekiel; they did not turn to God, their authoritative source. The people of Judah were so involved in their pursuits that they ignored the prophecies, which instructed them to repent and turn to God. They were not prepared to hear God through his servant Ezekiel. Today, Godly ministers experience many people who sit and listen to this same message, but it goes in one ear and out the other.

Let's Consider the Leaders.

The leaders themselves were not accountable to God. Regardless, God made the people individually responsible for their actions, even though their leaders failed them.

Let's Consider God.

God's patience was all used up, and the penalty for their disobedience was coming no matter what. God was ready to unleash his anger and judge them for their conduct. God was sick and tired of the people's shameless sinning. He tells Ezekiel that he is about to cut off the food supply in Jerusalem and only give the people rationed water. He tells Ezekiel that the people will waste away because of their sins. In Ezekiel 5:10, parents were eating their children, and children were eating their parents. The results were a scattering to the wind. Nations would hate them. The wild beasts would be against them. And plagues and bloodshed were coming. Bones were going to be scattered, towns laid waste, and the high places of idolatry were going to be demolished. God would not spare the people or look at them with pity. God was going to withdraw from them. He was not going to have any more pity on them. A crisis was lurking around the corner!

Nevertheless, in His graciousness, God tells us why he is going to cripple the people. In Ezekiel 6:14b, God states that his desired result is, "They will know that I am the LORD."

In Ezekiel 5:11 NIV, God says, "I myself will shave you. I will not look on you with pity or spare you." Shaving in the Bible is associated with drastic measures. And drastic measures were coming. Pop singer Britney Spears shaved her head in February 2007 amid a personal meltdown. It was during a desperate time in her life, and just like Spears, God's people were about to become desperate!

What Happens When God Has Had Enough of Our Sins?

1. He warns us by confronting us with our sins. Sometimes, he speaks through our conscience, other times by other people, and sometimes through the Word of God. These three areas give us a chance to confront our sins and change. Occasionally, he warns us multiple times over an extended period.
2. We can choose whether to turn from our ways or not. Choosing to disobey is never a good idea.
3. If we do not turn away from our sins, he warns us that judgment is coming. It comes in God's timing, but it always comes—in this life or the afterlife.
4. God decides on the judgment. It is always God's prerogative to judge us for a defiant and stubborn spirit.
5. God punishes us. It is his choice when and how to punish us.

In *Tony Evans' Book of Illustrations*, he says,

> *If you go to the hospital for an operation, you want your doctor to use sterilized equipment and to be in a sterile environment because you do not want viruses and bacteria getting in the way of your health. Sin is a spiritual virus that has no place in the sterile environment of God's holiness.*

Ezekiel's call was to warn the Jews of the upcoming judgment in Jerusalem and Judah. They were not living in an environment honoring God's holiness and would soon be punished. However, Ezekiel was obedient; he obeyed God in the task of warning the people to leave their sinful lives. Many people of the land chose to continue in their sins. We are all called to be obedient no matter what side of the spectrum we are on—following the LORD or rebelling against Him.

Repentance is the only suitable option in a rebellious state. We are reestablished by looking at the source, Jesus Christ. If we are already living a holy and acceptable life, let's encourage others to seek restoration before something ruinous happens. In the case of the Jews in Judah, it was, unfortunately, death!

On January 24, 1994, in his State of the State Address, New York Governor Mario M. Cuomo made an analogy between baseball and violent crime. He said, "In baseball, it's three strikes, and you're out."[3]

Let's get the least number of strikes possible in our lives. Are we willing to be obedient like Ezekiel and endure being made fun of to be obedient to God? Let's not "strike out" in life. Let's not get to the point where God says, "Enough is enough!" to us. God's purpose is that we will know that He is the LORD" (Ezek. 6:14b). Ezekiel's obedience in proclaiming God's message serves as a model for all, highlighting the necessity of repentance and restoration.

Be Unstoppable—Go the Distance with God,

You shall not make for yourselves idols, nor shall you set up for yourselves an image or a sacred pillar, nor shall you place a figured stone in your land to bow down to it; for I am the LORD your God
(Leviticus 26:1).

CHAPTER 7

EXPLORING SPIRITUAL GIFTS

> *You may have never thought about it this way,*
> *but as a member of God's family,*
> *you are a gifted child.*
> *God has wrapped up a gift in you.*
>
> Adrian Rogers

B aking a delightful fudge cake demands precise ingredients. The necessary ingredients include shortening, unsweetened chocolate, water, sugar, vanilla, cake flour, salt, baking powder, baking soda, eggs, and buttermilk in the specific measurements. If one ingredient is present or mismeasured, the cake can usually retain some of its scrumptiousness. Similarly, blending the nature of God with an understanding of spiritual gifts enables Christ-followers to experience unity and love in serving Christ.

About the Apostle Paul

Paul, born as Saul in Tarsus, was a Jewish Roman citizen educated in Jerusalem who transformed from persecuting Christians to a zealous preacher after encountering Christ on the road to Damascus. When Christ appeared to him, it resulted in a salvation experience. Paul was baptized into the Christian faith and followed God's call to preach the gospel. He traveled from region to region, which are known as his three missionary journeys. These extensive journeys and letters to churches were crucial in defining spiritual gifts. His travels took him from city to city. and prison to prison. He wrote letters, also known as epistles, to the churches addressing issues such as division, sin, and more. Paul's teachings on spiritual gifts are mentioned in many "famous" Bible verses. It was through these letters or visits that Paul gave the people an understanding of spiritual gifts.

Understanding Spiritual Gifts

Ministry Tools Resource Center defines a spiritual gift as "a special divine empowerment bestowed on each believer by the Holy Spirit to accomplish a given ministry God's way according to His grace and discernment to be used within the context of the Body of Christ,. i.e., teaching."[1]

In his grace, God has given us different gifts for doing certain things well. So, if God has given you the ability to prophesy, speak out with as much faith as God has given you. If your gift is serving others, serve them well. If you are a teacher, teach well. If your gift is to encourage others, be encouraging. If it is giving, give generously. If God has given you leadership ability, take the responsibility seriously. And if you have a gift for showing kindness to others, do it gladly (Rom. 12:6-8 NLT).

There are different kinds of spiritual gifts, but the same Spirit is the source of them all. There are different kinds of service, but we serve the same Lord. God works in different ways, but it is the same God who does the work in all of us. A spiritual gift is given to each of us so we can help each other. To one person the Spirit gives the ability to give wise advice ; to another the same Spirit gives a message of special knowledge. The same Spirit gives great faith to another, and to someone else the one Spirit gives the gift of healing. He gives one person the power to perform miracles, and another the ability to prophesy. He gives someone else the ability to discern whether a message is from the Spirit of God or from another spirit. Still another person is given the ability to speak in unknown languages, while another is given the ability to interpret what is being said (1 Corinthians 12:4-10 NLT).

Here are some of the parts God has appointed for the church: first are apostles, second are prophets, third are teachers, then those who do miracles, those who have the gift of healing, those who can help others, those who have the gift of leadership, those who speak in unknown languages (1 Corinthians 12:28 NLT).

Distribution and Purpose of Spiritual Gifts

The Holy Spirit distributes spiritual gifts according to his will. In 1 Corinthians 12:11 and Ephesians 4:12-13, it says that the Spirit is distributed to each individual for the common good within the church. Our gifts are to be used for the common good—that is, the common good for the equipping of the saints for the work of ministry, and for the building up of the body of Christ (Eph. 4:12). People should use their gifts genuinely for unity within the body.

Two terms frequently used in connection with spiritual gifts or listings of the gifts are "charisma" and "*pneuma*." Regarding charisma, 1 Peter 4:10 says, "As each one has received a special gift, employ it in serving one another as good stewards of the manifold grace of God." Thus, charisma refers to the gift itself. While there are multiple definitions of pneuma, the *New Testament Greek Lexicon* defines it as the Holy Spirit — "the vital principle by which the body is animated and the rational spirit, the power by which the human being feels, thinks, decides; the soul."[2] It is important to remember that all spiritual gifts are intended to equip Christ-followers for service, edify the body of Christ, promote unity, and lead to maturity in faith.

For the equipping of the saints for the work of service, to the building up of the body of Christ, until we all attain the unity of the faith, and the knowledge of the Son of God, to a mature man, to the measure of the stature which belongs to the fulness of Christ (Ephesians 4:12-13).

How are Spiritual Gifts to be Used?

Gifts are used in love—not for personal edification or pride.

If I speak with the tongues of men and angels, but do not have love, I have become a noisy gong or a clanging cymbal. And if I have the gift of prophecy, and know all mysteries and all knowledge, and if I have all faith, so as to remove mountains, but do not have love, I am nothing (1 Corinthians 13: 1-2).

… But now faith, hope, love, abide these three, but the greatest of these is love (1 Corinthians 13:13).

Love

1 Corinthians 13 is commonly known as the love chapter; it makes its claim to fame in many wedding ceremonies. Separating it from 1 Corinthians 12:31 would be unfortunate since it sets the context that love is a pivotal point and the "greatest" attribute connecting with one's spiritual gifts.

This love chapter contains three major sections. First, Vv. 1-3 declares that if one speaks but does not have love, it sounds like a "clanging symbol," which refers to the famous bronze products made in Corinth. Second, Vv. 4-7 describes an agape love, the self-sacrificing love God desires from his children. Third, Vv. 8-13, Paul stresses love in relationship to spiritual gifts and concludes by stating in the last verse in the chapter—" But now abide faith, hope, love, these three; but the greatest of these is love."

American theologian and author Richard L. Pratt said, "If there is any similarity between the modern church and the ancient church, it lies in our failure to love. In fact, by most accounts, we are often worse than the Corinthians. At least the Corinthians had managed to remain united as a single church. They had not split their fellowship, even though they had abused it. Most Christians today tend to be self-centered. They do not place others first, and they certainly do not commit themselves to living the love of which Paul spoke."[3]

Categories of Spiritual Gifts and Definitions

Brandon Deibert defines the gifts of the Holy Spirit as "unique skills and abilities given by the Holy Spirit to faithful followers of Christ to serve God for the common benefit of his people, the church."[4] The Bible lists multiple spiritual gifts. The Apostle Paul states that we have different gifts according to the grace given to us. We are to use them proportionately to our faith (Rom. 12:6).

Gifts are categorized into public, personal, and paradigm gifts, each serving a unique function within the church and reflecting God's diverse giftings to individuals. Paradigm gifts usually refer to a transformation in a person's spiritual thinking.

Many scholars label gifts with various headings containing God-given abilities to help the Kingdom of God. While many gifts overlap, each Christ-follower possesses at least one gift, but many gain more as they mature in faith. Author Melissa Henderson, a trained layperson who provided Christ-centered care and support to hurt individuals, records a comprehensive list of spiritual gifts in her article "A Comprehensive Spiritual Gifts List to Discover Your Gifts and Calling," along with a brief explanation of what each gift represents. Only public, personal, and paradigm gifts are represented, even though the sign gifts should be considered and included in a future study of spiritual gifts. I, in turn, have bracketed examples of how these gifts might be used, although many more examples could be included, and the only limitations are one's imagination and the Holy Spirit's leadership.

Leadership: encouraging and helping others to build the kingdom of God.

[People, including pastors, sharing their faith and encouraging others to live their lives for Jesus]

Administration: helping with long-term goals and remaining on task.

[Organizing a mission trip]

Teaching: instructing in truths and doctrines of God's Word.

[Bible study teacher, mentor]

Knowledge: teaching and discipleship. The ability to learn, know, and explain God's Word.

[Bible study teacher, pastor, scholar, religion or seminary professor, writer]

Wisdom: the ability to discern works of the Holy Spirit and apply teaching and actions.

[Counselors, teachers, pastors, one-on-one friendships]

Prophecy: proclaiming the Word of God with boldness.

[Evangelist, preacher, and other spiritual leaders]

Discernment: being able to recognize the truth about a situation.

[Understanding beyond what others see as a danger in the church]

Exhortation: people with this gift are enthusiastic about the Lord and can motivate others.

[Encouraging someone to use their gifts and live up to their true calling for the Lord]

Shepherding: looking out for the spiritual welfare of others.

[Pastors and individuals in the church body who guide others and help them]

Faith: trusting God to fulfill His plan. People with this gift are encouragers.

[Communicator, writer, a creative person sharing Christ and his love to others]

Evangelism: the building up of the church so others will be led to Christ.

[Missionaries, sharing a testimony, Christian writers]

Apostleship: motivators, church planters, missionaries: people who look beyond the walls.

[Being a missionary or having involvement with people from other cultures]

Service/Helps: helping those in need of practical assistance.

[Serving at a church banquet, cutting the church lawn, babysitting for others]

Mercy: the person with this gift shows acts of compassion.

[Visiting the sick at their home, hospital, or wherever they are, writing notes]

Giving: People with this gift will give freely and with joy to further His kingdom.

[Usually, monetary giving but also includes giving of oneself giving]

Hospitality: Making people feel welcome, appreciated, and wanted.

[Hosting a Christian event in your home, letting someone stay with you if needed][5]

These examples may overlap. There are many different ways to use one's personality in coordination with one's gifts. The numerous ways one can use gifts can be incredibly vast. Sometimes, people confuse their talents with their gifts. They are often separate entities, but God frequently uses one's talents by combining the two. If you are gifted in teaching music, your piano talent helps utilize your gift. Evangelist Billy Graham says, "It appears that God can take a talent and transform it by the power of the Holy Spirit and use it as a spiritual gift. The difference between a spiritual gift and a natural talent is frequently a cause for speculation by many people. I am not sure we can always draw a sharp line between spiritual gifts and natural abilities—both of which come ultimately from God."[6]

Understanding the Role of the Holy Spirit

To understand the gifts of the Spirit, one must know how the Holy Spirit functions and who he is. The Holy Spirit is a person. When one speaks of the Holy Spirit, they are referring to the same Holy Spirit who led Jesus into His wilderness experience (Luke 4: 1, 13) and who fell upon Jesus at his baptism (Matt. 3:16, Mark 1:10, Luke 3:22, John 1:32). Drawing people to salvation and teaching about Jesus gives us confidence that one is a child of God. In John 14:16, Jesus says he will give his disciples another comforter to abide with them forever. That same comforter (the Spirit of Truth) abides with those who have accepted Jesus Christ as their Savior. In the *Holman Illustrated Bible Dictionary*, Chad Brand states that the Holy Spirit "grants spiritual gifts to the churches so that all persons within the body of Christ are spiritually gifted."[7] When people accept Christ through confessing their sins and accepting Jesus Christ in their lives, the Holy Spirit comes to reside in them, giving them the power and desire to use their spiritual gifts. It is through this process that one is filled with the Holy Spirit.

However, the gifts of the Spirit must not be separated from the giver of the gifts—God. This combination makes us understand that the Trinity (the three-in-one identity of God) participates in our spiritual giftedness. In "Spiritual Gifts for Biblical Church Development." Brian DeVries states, "All three Persons of the Trinity are actively involved in spiritually gifting each believer for ministry in the church." He continues to say that God the Father is the One who makes each gift effectual, and God the Son distributes gifts in the church by His Spirit. God the Spirit emboldens all Christ-followers with various abilities by working within and through them mightily. It is not in one's strength or courage that gifts are given and used but through the three-fold work of the Trinity.[8]

The Body of Christ (Church)

Dedicated Christians who possess special gifts use them to help people in the church grow together. This way, each member gets something valuable from each other, which, in turn, helps the whole community to become stronger and more mature (1 Cor. 12:7, Eph 4:11, 16). Some scholars, including DeVries, believe God always produces the fruit of the Spirit and gifts of the Spirit simultaneously. The fruit of the Spirit consists of love, joy, peace, patience, kindness, goodness, faithfulness, gentleness, and self-control (Gal. 5:22-23). Combining these two aspects of the Spirit makes for sweet unity and maturity in the body of Christ.

All Christ-followers, especially those in spiritual offices in the church and congregants, should use their gifts to strengthen the body of Christ. Pastors need humility and trust in the people in their church to allow them to use their giftedness. DeVries says, "church leaders are responsible for developing the spiritual giftedness of all members under their care so that these believers will be used by the Spirit to develop the church."

Many Christians leave one church to attend another where their gifts can be used. When Christ-followers' gifts are not appreciated or utilized in the body, the body suffers. Churches vary in programs, spirituality, and growth because gifts are underutilized, causing a lack of church care and unity. In many instances, this underutilization can cause pastor burnout by leaving all that others could do in the church staff's hands. DeVries states, "the Spirit has gifted each member of the body in different ways so that the holistic use of these gifts will function in unity to provide mutual care to all members."

Suppose a church member has the gift of teaching and is told every time he asks about it that there are no positions for them to teach. That member may go where there are positions—to another church or a ministry outside their church, or they could become frustrated and not recover from a lack of the church's attention to their giftedness and give up on the body. Both ministry staff and congregants must understand that the purpose of the gifts is primarily to build up the church. Hence, the pastoral staff and the congregants are responsible for building the ministry.

Distribution of Spiritual Gifts

God distributes spiritual gifts to Christians who can discern their gifts through various means, including spiritual self-assessment guided by biblical principles.

In the Old Testament, God's children would receive a direct revelation of God through the agency of God's Spirit. When this revelatory facet occurred, it became a central feature of the late Second Temple Jewish understanding of God's Spirit. In the New Testament, God's Spirit is seen in the ministry of Jesus Christ. Then, it proceeds when the Holy Spirit is sent to the disciples at Pentecost. While the Spirit helps in conversion, it is also this same Spirit that helps to discern our spiritual gifts. The Lord is the one who distributes gifts. Often, it takes some experimentation with various ministries to find the fit the Lord has called a person to do. Not knowing one's gift should not excuse a lack of ministry involvement. People can recognize their gifts by trying out assorted opportunities, receiving input from others, or taking spiritual gift inventory and survey tests, which can be found online, in churches, or in multiple books. Contrarily, DeVries does not like spiritual gift inventory assessments as much as he uses the Bible to discover spiritual gifts. He believes the Bible gives two testing criteria for finding one's spiritual gifts: The fruit of the Spirit listed in Galatians 5:22-23 and the spiritual qualities of godliness noted in 2 Peter 1. Either way, one should take responsibility and pursue one's spiritual gifts, leaving the results in the Holy Spirit's hand.

Conflicts and Clarifications

Confusion may arise regarding charismatic gifts, such as tongues, healing, and prophecy, leading to theological debates between cessationists and continuationists. While there are various ways to define *tongues*, tongues is usually referred to as the act of communicating in a language that one has not formally studied, often for the purpose of providing ministry to someone who understands that language. Some charismatic groups also consider tongues, laying on hands, fasting, faith, and prayer in this category. The question is whether God gave these sign gifts to people in the early church or whether they continue today.

Most cessationists believe that God can heal and do miracles, but they reject the idea that Christians can heal, prophesy, and speak in tongues. Cessationist Thomas R. Schreiner says, "As a cessationist, I believe God still heals and does miracles today, though I think such events are relatively rare. Still, I pray for the healing of the sick and believe God can do so miraculously. My argument is not that miracles and healings never occur. Instead, I claim that many believers today [do not] have the gifts of doing miracles and healing."[9]

A continuationist believes all sign gifts are valid and operable today. As one can see, sign gifts can cause confusion, misunderstanding, and divisiveness in a church. Respected historian C. Douglas Weaver believes, "*Baptists and the Holy Spirit* notes several recurring themes throughout the history of Baptist-continuationist interactions. One recurring theme is that some Baptists embrace miraculous gifts and begin to identify more with continuationism than their Baptist heritage."[10] Many Baptist-continuationist rivalries have occurred since the first wave of Pentecostals began speaking in tongues and prophesying in the early twentieth century.

The Book of Acts deals with the custom of speaking in and interpreting tongues in three places. When the disciples received baptism in the Spirit at Pentecost, they began to speak in tongues. In Acts 10, Simon was preaching. When the Spirit fell upon the assembly, the Gentiles spoke in tongues, showing the Jews that they had received the Holy Spirit. Lastly, when Paul encountered some disciples of John, they began to speak in other languages and to prophesy. Scholars use the word *glossolalia* when referring to tongues. In each of these instances, tongues are introduced to a different group of people: Jews, Samaritans (possibly), and Gentiles. Many believe that Paul believed that unless tongues are interpreted, it should not be used in public worship, because the purpose of spiritual gifts is to edify the body of Christ.[11] Conflicts also occur when discussing the Holy Spirit and its role in our lives, including holiness, gender, and racial egalitarianism, to name a few. It is difficult to separate issues from one another when speaking of the Holy Spirit, including how spiritual gifts are used.

Reasons for Personal Perspective

God's Holy Spirit has been functioning in lives for over six thousand years—through the Old Testament and New Testament and even today. The Holy Spirit guided Jesus' ministry and likewise guides us in our ministry. God's purpose is threefold.

- He promises to guide us into all truth.

- He wants to equip and guide us for his service, and

- He wants us to grow to become more Christ-like.

The following verses give insight into the mind of our triune God, the Father, Son, and Holy Spirit.

> When the Spirit of truth comes, he will guide you into all truth. He will not speak on his own but will tell you what he has heard. He will tell you about the future (John 16:13 NLT).

> And He gave some as apostles, and some as prophets, and some as evangelists, and some as pastors and teachers, for the equipping of the saints for the work of service, to the building up of the body of Christ (Ephesians 4:11 NASB).

> When God created human beings, he made them to be like himself (Genesis 5:1b NLT).

He does this because he knows us intimately.

> You made all the delicate, inner parts of my body and knit me together in my mother's womb. Thank you for making me so wonderfully complex! Your workmanship is marvelous—how well I know it. You watched me as I was being formed in utter seclusion,

as I was woven together in the dark of the womb. You saw me before I was born. Every day of my life was recorded in your book. Every moment was laid out before a single day had passed (Psalm 1:13-16 NLT).

Charles Stanley sums it up best when he says,

Time is a gift from God, and he has allotted each of us a measure in which to live and accomplish His purposes. We have only two options—to spend it temporally on our own interests or invest it eternally. Since time can never be retrieved or reversed, it's critical that we make the most of every opportunity the Lord provides.[12]

Just like the fudge cake mentioned earlier, where all the ingredients combine for the best results, we need all members of the body of Christ to employ their best selves. The same can occur when one uses their spiritual gifts in the supernatural power of Christ, within the body of Christ, in love and unity.

Be Unstoppable—Go the Distance with God,

Now, there are a variety of gifts, but the same Spirit. And there are varieties of ministries, and the same Lord.
1 Corinthians 12:4-5

CHAPTER 8

DISCOVERING AND UTILIZING SPIRITUAL GIFTS

*If you're operating in your giftedness,
you will receive some degree of affirmation and
your comfort level will be very, very high.*

Dr. John Bisagno

Have you ever participated in a spiritual gifts inventory survey? These surveys aim to pinpoint where you can best serve the body of Christ. I've taken quite a few of these surveys over the years, and I find myself consistently scoring high in certain areas and low in others. Through my survey results, I have understood that God has meticulously crafted and shaped me according to his will through the gifts he has bestowed on me. God has fashioned and knit me together just how he wants me to be. However, I have learned that God can still use me in areas where I don't feel comfortable, capable, or interested in.

The major spiritual gifts mentioned in the Bible that can be used effectively by Christ-followers within the church are leadership, administration, teaching, knowledge, prophecy, discernment, exhortation, shepherding, faith, evangelism, apostleship, service/helps, mercy, giving, and hospitality.

Sharing the truth about our gifting can be challenging. We don't want to sound proud or self-righteous if we possess certain gifts. In school, many of us wanted to work hard and excel in all our classwork, but spiritual gifts don't work that way. We want or wanted to score high in every subject. In a candid confession, I must admit that I consistently score low in the service/helps ministry gifts. Perhaps it is because I don't particularly like to cook. If you are ill, and you receive a restaurant gift card from me, instead of me preparing an elaborate meal, be happy or it could be that I live in a state of constant fatigue. I don't know. But I do know that I lean more toward teaching, administration, and discernment—even though I never like to mention the last area because it is misinterpreted so often. Nonetheless, despite my low areas, I acknowledge that God still calls me to serve and assist my friends, family, and the body of Christ. It is crucial to recognize that God will use us in any way and with any gifting he desires to. We are not required to operate only in our high gifting areas.

Periodically, we are challenged to step out of our comfort zone. I like animals, but I am not a huge animal lover. Yet one day, I felt strongly compelled to take a friend to the vet to comfort her as she experienced the gut-wrenching decision to euthanize her dog. It was certainly out of my comfort zone, but God used me. The result was I was blessed being with her during this sad time in her life. By stepping out of my comfort zone, I received an unexpected blessing, And you can too.

When God leads you or me on a mission outside our gifts, think of it as the Lord stretching us through the Holy Spirit. When God sets us apart for a mission, he can use any gift or personality trait to fulfill his purposes. The Lord will walk beside us, empowering us to fulfill his goal. I find it exciting and adventurous to see the new and sometimes bizarre ways God uses me, like when I once shared the gospel with a Buddhist, only to be told he could not accept the Lord because their relatives were on the mantle (in a jar) watching! Let's approach our life with the attitude that we are ready to be used by the Lord in whatever area he wants to use us.

Sometimes, we are on the receiving end of gracious acts of service or help. Sometimes we are not. I have experienced both and benefited from both. I was once in a position where I was ostracized without a natural or tangible explanation of why. I went through speculation, hurt feelings, anger, and loneliness. I was particularly hurt because the criticism came from fellow Christ-followers. It was a tough time, and the recollection stays with me. Even today, thirty years later, I think about it. At the time, I remember wishing someone (a human being besides my husband) was walking this road with me. However, God allowed me to walk through this experience alone—along with my hurt feelings and emotions, with only God to talk to. None of us like suffering alone. But that experience has made me more sensitive to the sufferings and ill-treatment of others. It has given me more "Discernment Smarts" to recognize someone who is inwardly suffering or needs help. That's how the Lord works.

We all need encouragement at times in our lives. As I mentioned, serving is tough for me; I need reminders on how to do it. As I share some tips on how we can help others, think of the people you know. You may need help from others right now, or it may be time for you to help someone else.

How to Serve and Help Others

Offering practical help, being present, showing kindness and patience, and offering encouragement are meaningful ways to serve others. If God prompts us to help someone, let's do it enthusiastically and see where it leads. Never underestimate the significance of even the most minor acts of service to the Lord. They truly matter.

Reflecting on my past service to the Lord, one memory stands out vividly. My husband and I were members of a church getting ready for the first service in their new church building. The day before our "grand opening," the congregation helped in making the church ready. My task was to clean the interior windows of the church and remove sawdust off the windowsills. No, there were no cleaners hired! We were indeed a community of Christ-followers serving and fellowshipping together. Why does this seemingly minor task resonate as a noteworthy contribution to God's Kingdom now? My task wasn't a glorious teaching assignment or organizing the church for Vacation Bible school. Maybe because God was preparing me for "greater" things, or perhaps he was emphasizing that sometimes the little, humble 'behind-the-scene' service is as crucial as prominent visual positions. As time has passed, I see how serving God in obedience is substantial to him, regardless of the assignment.

When we faithfully serve God in the small things, he will give us more, reveal our spiritual gifts, smile upon us and allow us to mature. So whether you offer a smile to a lonely soul, change a diaper in the nursery, or send an encouragement card to someone, remember you are the feet of Christ. He is working through you in the seemingly little things. Once you discover your spiritual gift(s), be practical and present, be kind and patient, and be an encouragement to others.

1. Be Practical

Ask yourself what you can do to help others. Can you bring a meal? Can you take their child to soccer practice? Can you make some calls? Usually, people don't want to be an imposition on others but use your judgment and try to put yourself in their shoes to see what you can do or offer. I have found that rather than saying, "Call me if you need anything," it is better to say, "I'm stopping by the grocery store, and I can pick up some groceries for you. What do you need?"

2. Be There.

A person may need someone to listen to them. It is incredible how we can help by just listening. We don't even have to respond. I think Job's friends would have been a lot better off in the "Service/Helps Department" if they had just listened to Job instead of feeling they had to point out his failures, faults, and inconsistencies.

3. Be Kind and Patient.

When my husband and I lived for a short while in The Netherlands, my husband broke his ribs in 12 places) – OUCH! There is a reason I am not a nurse. Just being in the hospital made me nauseous a few times. The smells, sounds, and sights in the hospital were not my cup of tea, and a few gags occurred in my system! While John was recuperating, I had to put his socks on his feet. I had to pick up everything he dropped. I had to help him put his arm in his shirt and jacket. But I didn't mind because I love him! You may encounter similar events like this. If so, give the needy recipient your time, love, kindness, and patience. Healing takes time, whether healing is in the area of physical, emotional, or spiritual realm.

4. Be an Encouragement.

Encouragement takes many forms It can be a timely note or a phone call. It can give hope or security. Ask the Lord how you can encourage those he brings in your path. He will show you. To use an old cliché, "You may be the only Jesus someone sees." Think about how Jesus would encourage those in need, then, as Nike says, "Just do it." God may not call you to help in every situation you encounter. But, if God is giving you the 'holy hunch' to be involved in a person's life, take the role with enthusiasm and thankfulness! And see where God leads it. While we may not always use our top-level gifts in every situation, let's yield to God's leading and praise him for his work. As follower of Christ, it is important to honor and worship him. We should give him all the praise and adoration that we have within us. Hearts and souls dedicated to living for God allows him to have his way in our lives every day, from every breath we take to every moment we are awake.

Be Unstoppable—Go the Distance with God,

As each one has received a special gift, employ it in serving one another as good stewards of the manifold grace of God. Whoever speaks, is to do so as one who is speaking the utterances of God; whoever serves is to do so as one who is serving by the strength which God supplies; so that in all things God may be glorified through Jesus Christ, to whom belongs the glory and dominion forever and ever. Amen.
1 Peter 4:10-11

CHAPTER 9

THE POWER OF DISCERNMENT

> *God never gives us discernment in order that we may criticize,*
> *but that we may intercede.*
>
> Oswald Chambers

M ost likely, we all know people with that special discernment into what is happening within our culture, in people's lives, and inside the church. Not only can they understand spiritual happenings, but they are usually gifted in expressing their thoughts so those enlightened by the Holy Spirit can fully grasp God. Recently, I have been reading several books by A.W. Tozer (1897-1963). Tozer was a self-taught theologian, pastor, and writer whose influential words still linger in the hearts of his readers even after his death. Out of his more than 40 books, *The Knowledge of the Holy*, *The Pursuit of God*, and *God's Pursuit of Man*, Tozer seems to grasp a discerning and surrendered spirit on the deeper life Christ-followers should be experiencing. It is that life where, after salvation, we grow, depend, and surrender (or strive wholeheartedly) to live our lives in the presence of God.[1]

Sons of Issachar

The men previously mentioned and others like them remind me of the sons of Issachar. 1 Chronicles 12:32 says, "Men who understood the times, with knowledge of what Israel should do." King Saul was now dead, and David was crowned King of Israel. During this period, great wisdom and discernment were needed to understand what was happening and what to do during this transition. Being very analytical and perceptive, the sons of Issachar were aware of what was occurring and what should be done; their discernment far exceeded that of the average person. They skillfully knew how to express their sentiments so others could take hold of them and grasp the gravity of the situation.

Don't you love it when you are in a meeting, and someone knows how to resolve the real issues? I experienced this first-hand as a jury foreman in a very intense five-week trial some years ago. We were on the third day of deliberations, with the jury split 6-6 on a verdict. I was perplexed about how to proceed with my eleven jury partners when one of the men in the group stood up, went to a drawing board, and mapped out the entire plan and overview of what we needed to do to resolve our divisiveness. What a relief! The Sons of Issachar operated in the same way. Their awareness of their culture was uncanny.

Because of that, I want to share some of the dynamic quotations I encountered when reading my marathon of Tozer's books recently. Hopefully, these will resonate a powerful drawing and passion for you to live a holy and surrendered life to God the Father, Jesus the Son, and the Holy Spirit.

Due to time and space, I will share quotes from six of my most recently read books by Tozer:

The Knowledge of the Holy

> Wisdom, among other things, is the ability to devise perfect ends and to achieve those ends by the most perfect means. It sees the end from the beginning, so there can be no need to guess or conjecture. Wisdom sees everything in focus, each in proper relation to all, and is thus able to work toward predestined goals with flawless precision.[2]

The Pursuit of God

> When we lift our inward eyes to gaze upon God we are sure to meet friendly eyes gazing back at us, for it is written that the eyes of the Lord run throughout all the earth … When the eyes of the soul looking out meet the eyes of God looking in heaven has begun right here on earth.[3]

God's Pursuit of Man

When the Spirit illuminates the heart, then a part of the man sees which never saw before; a part of him knows which never knew before, and that with the kind of knowing which the most acute thinker cannot imitate. He knows now in a deep and authoritative way, and what he knows needs no reasonable proof. His experience of knowing is above reason, immediate, perfectly convincing and inwardly satisfying.[4]

Delighting in God

I have discovered that the frustrating aspect of preaching and teaching is that the preacher and teacher cannot do the work of change for people. It must be a work of the Holy Spirit within the heart of the believer.[5]

The Crucified Life

The biggest thing in the world is not whether you live to be 100 years old; the biggest thing in the world is whether you can hear God speaking to you now. That is what counts.[6]

A Cloud by Day, A Fire by Night: Finding and Following God's Will for You

When we allow God's Word to go beyond our ears and into our hearts, it stimulates us to do what which God is calling us to do.[7]

As a follower of Christ, it is believed that every individual possesses a certain amount of discernment to face the trials and obstacles in their lives. However, for those blessed with the gift of discernment, it can sometimes be challenging to own it, mainly because of misunderstandings of others and the fear that their discernment could result in pride. There is also the feeling that they may be misreading the Lord. Nonetheless, when used rightly, the gift of discernment can be a beautiful tool that the Lord uses in the lives of others and themselves. If you possess the gift of discernment, it is recommended to thank God for this gift and humbly ask the Lord for guidance to understand how and when to use it.

Be Unstoppable—Go the Distance with God,

And it is my prayer that your love may abound more and more, with knowledge and all discernment, so that you may approve what is excellent, and so be pure and blameless for the day of Christ.
Philippians 1:9-10

CHAPTER 10

DISCOVERING GOD'S CALL

God has a record of not calling the equipped,
but rather equipping the called.

A.W. Tozer

After our youngest child was in 2nd Grade, I worked for eighteen years and then decided to "retire" and dedicate more time to serving God. One day, I earnestly prayed, asked, "Lord, how can he use me? I told him, "I don't play the piano, and I'm not keen on the gym." The Lord prompted me to go into my closet. At first, I resisted; the thought of praying in my messy bedroom closet didn't appeal to me. But the nudge persisted, and I reluctantly got up from my chair, walked into my closet, stood upright and said, "Okay God, now what?" He instructed me to gaze upwards at the top shelf where my journals were. There I noticed over forty years worth of prayer journals I had written. God's voice, although not audible, but in spirit, said, "Patti, you have gained enough experience; it's time to write prayer journals yourself. I have prepared you over the years, surrounded you with books, and nurtured your love for writing. Now is your moment to share and inspire others. This is your destiny for this season of life." God was affirming my next assignment through my past. In that moment, God reassured me. I immediately began compiling my first prayer journal, opening a new chapter in my life dedicated to writing.

Many people worldwide wonder, "Lord, how can you use me?" Once we truly understand that Jesus is the way, the truth, and the life, we can confidently ask God about his will for our lives. Through our willingness to perform small acts of service, he reveals more ways for us to serve Him. I had no idea that for forty years the Lord was preparing me for a new season.

Four Aspects to Help us Discover God's Call in Our Lives Bible reading.

1. Preparation

Early on in my Christian walk, I wanted to equip myself for ministry and seek God's guidance on my path. A series of books on spiritual maturity established a solid foundation for my maturation, which I will mention later. I wanted to deepen my commitment to whatever God had planned for me. Throughout this process, I often questioned how God could possibly use someone like me—someone who had struggled with writing in college. Writing essays and participating in college classes created deep anxiety in me. Yet, I knew deep down that God cared for me and was preparing me for something. My faith grew through Christian literature and my discipleship experiences at two key churches—in Ft. Worth and Houston. I accepted Christ on the second floor of the student union building at Baylor University, I was baptized at University Baptist Church in Fort Worth, which marked a pivotal moment in my faith, which continued to flourish even more at First Baptist Church in Houston. God was preparing me, and he will prepare you.

Practice

To understand where God wants to use us, it is a good idea to try exploring different areas of service. Listen to feedback from others about your strengths, take a spiritual gifts inventory, and read books on Christian areas that interest you. Pray earnestly for guidance on how you fit into the body of Christ, both locally and globally. Then, put what you learn into practice by reflecting on what you learn as you discern your place of service.

During my own period of discernment, I immersed myself in the Bible. I wanted to learn how God could use me. I began small acts of service, like writing encouraging notes, organizing Bible study materials, and compiling short studies. Reading solid Christian literature deepened my reliance on the Holy Spirit through prayer, reaffirming my understanding that God loved me and had a unique spiritual plan for my life—and he has one for you, too. The beauty of this journey was recognizing that my writing was an act of obedience to the Lord. Because of this, I haven't been concerned about if my books sell or not, because it is up to him to use them as he sees fit. Obedience always triumphs our fleshly desires.

Bible Reading and Studying

God primarily communicates with us through his Word. Reading and studying the Bible helps us understand what is right and wrong, what is honorable and dishonorable, and what he wants us to do. Continuous engagement with Scripture opens up a life filled with salvation, hope, trust, and direction.

Prayer

While I've read numerous books on prayer, nothing compares to taking quiet time each day to worship and praise God. He loves us uniquely and desires our full attention. In prayer, we can reflect, meditate, confess our shortcomings, and share our burdens. It's easy to think that only pastors or ministry leaders are called to serve God, but God invites everyone to seek his kingdom and engage in a close, personal relationship through prayer. God loves us and yearns for us to communicate with him, not solely to request things, but just to chat about what is on our mind. Section 2 addresses the power and importance of prayer in more detail.

Get Ready to be Used by God

We each have a journey, and God has a specific purpose for us. Don't let fear, laziness, or perfectionism hinder you from seeking his will. While my passion for reading and sharing his principles through writing has become a tool for God to use, every person can find their unique assignment by staying open and obedient to his guidance.

Be Unstoppable—Go the Distance with God,

Have I not commanded you? Be strong and courageous! Do not tremble or be dismayed, for the LORD your God is with you wherever you go.
Joshua 1:9

CHAPTER 11

AMOS: THE LIFE OF AN ORDINARY MAN

All of God's people are ordinary people who have been made extraordinary by the purpose he has given them.

Oswald Chambers

M any men and women feel ordinary! Being ordinary is synonymous with being average. Being ordinary means one might attend an average school, live in an average neighborhood, or be uneducated. One of the worst sentiments one might feel about being ordinary is presuming there is no purpose or call in life. In today's culture, we are impressed with wealth, beauty, popularity, accomplishment, and fame. But let's look at Amos — an ordinary man with a passion for God who was called to proclaim God's message of judgment to Israel and other nations due to their sin and disobedience.[1]

Amos

Amos, an Old Testament minor prophet, was considered a seemingly ordinary man with an extraordinary calling from God.

In Amos 7:14-15 NLT, he replies,

> I'm not a professional prophet. I was never trained to be one. I'm just a shepherd, and I take care of trees. But the LORD called me away from my flock and told me, Go prophesy to my people in Israel.

Amos might have even been a seasonal worker because he lived in Tekoa, a town 16 miles from the Dead Sea, where sycamore trees are not cultivated due to the altitude and climate. Thus this implies that he might have had to leave Tekoa for certain months of the year to care for and grow the sycamore fig trees. Many commentaries believe Amos did not have formal training, but he became learned in the ways of God. During Amos' lifetime, Israel was filled with pride, beauty, elegance, and riches. As Amos went about living "the ordinary life" God gave him, he was called by his heavenly Father for a particular task. He lived during the reign of Jeroboam II around 786 BC to 746 BC. Amos recognized his calling from God during this time to proclaim the message the Lord gave him. He did not arrive on the scene to tickle anybody's ears. Amos arrived able, prepared, and willing to work passionately on the assignment God gave him. In the Book of Amos, you will find that Amos speaks little of himself; he is there to pronounce the judgment God sent him to do. Speaking God's words throughout Amos, Amos became known for his repetitive saying, "Thus says the LORD" before many of his proclamations. He spoke God's word throughout Amos.

As I read the Book of Amos, I became aware of some of the characteristics Amos possessed before and during his announcing Israel's destruction.

Key Characteristics that Defined Amos:

- He sought the Lord.

- He had a deep-rooted faith.

- God was preparing him.

- He walked with God.

- He accepted his lot in life.

- He was wise in the ways of God.

- He was close enough to God to know what the Lord said.

- He spoke what the Lord said.

- He was confident in what he said.

- He was not afraid of bringing bad news to others.

- He was not fearful of talking to others outside of his class.

- He sought good and not evil.

God Can Use You

Besides Amos, the Lord used other "ordinary" men throughout history: David, Eliab, Gideon, and the apostles. Even Jesus was a simple man God called the most critical influence in all civilizations. God can use anyone willing to heed his call.

Someday, God may ask you to step out of your comfort zone. We carry around barriers in our lives. We don't take the steps needed to be used by God. God will use those already steeped in Scripture and those willing to walk in his ways. He will choose and seek us as we prepare to expand our influence with him. With Amos, he was selected for a particular assignment at a specific time. Maybe he returned to tending sheep and sycamore trees after finishing this assignment. We don't know as there is no record. But we understand he was available and willing when God wanted to use him. In our lives, we should remember that God can do whatever he wants to, and he will equip anyone willing to carry out his plans. You may not be an educated person; you may not have been born into an elite family, but God can use you.

The Apostle Paul says,

> Brothers, think of what you were when you were called. Not many of you were wise by human standards; not many were influential; not many were of noble birth. But God chose the foolish things of the world to shame the wise; God chose the weak things of the world to shame the strong. God chose the lowly things of this world and the despised things — and the things that are not — to nullify the things that are, so that no one may boast before him (1 Corinthians 1:26-29 NIV).

God gives us the strength to do what he calls us to do. God desires to use us to the fullest. He knows if we are unprepared, and he wants to prepare us. He knows if we are imperfect, but he sees our potential to pursue his purposes. We may have a dream or a vision but cannot achieve it. Don't give up. Water and prune your vision and wait for God's appointed time. But, while waiting, follow his leads, as small or insignificant as they might seem, as this is part of his preparation for you. Trust that his Spirit is working and perfecting you until he calls you as Amos did. Then, when he shows you that he is ready, you will be prepared to act.

How to Prepare for Ministry

When engaging in any kind of assignment/ministry, secular or spiritual, it is essential to remember specific ideas. These ideas include

- Seeking the Lord,

- Developing a deep-rooted faith,

- Allowing God to prepare you,

- Walking with God,

- Accepting your lot in life,

- Being wise,

- Speaking what is honorable,

- Being confident in God's words and whispers,

- Developing a fearless spirit in speaking for God,

- Understanding that God can use you with anyone regardless of social class, intellect, race, or religion, and

- Seeking good, not evil.

Seeking the Lord is paramount in any ministry. This means making time to pray, worship, and read the Bible. Developing a deep-rooted faith is also essential, which involves trusting in God's plan and firmly believing in his promises. Furthermore, allowing God to prepare you is crucial, ensuring you are equipped for the tasks ahead. Walking with God means you are constantly communicating with him and always looking to follow his lead. Accepting your lot in life involves being content with where you are and the circumstances you find yourself in. Being wise is also important, as it enables you to make sound decisions and offer guidance to others.

Developing a deep closeness to God through Bible study and prayer is critical, as this helps you to understand God's will and his character. Speaking of what is Godly means that you are always mindful of your words and their impact on others. Confidence in God's words and whispers involves unwavering faith in his guidance and direction. Developing a fearless spirit in speaking for God means you are not afraid to share his message, even in the face of opposition or adversity. Understanding that God can use you with anyone, regardless of social class, intellect, race, or religion, is also important, as it reflects God's love for all people. Finally, seeking good, not evil, is crucial, as it ensures that one's actions always align with God's will and purpose. Did you notice that any of these preparations mirror Amos' characteristics?

Testimony

Looking back at my life, I can see how God had been preparing me for my secular and current ministry of teaching and writing. When I was around seven or eight years old, I loved the science projects where I had to find leaves, label them, and glue them on cardboard. I call that gathering information and "presenting it." As a senior in high school, I had an English assignment, where we had to find poems and quotations, put them together in a booklet form, and find pictures from newspapers or magazines related to the poems or quotes. I still have that high school assignment, and I laugh at my lack of Biblical knowledge then. A commonly known Bible verse from Psalm 46:10 says, "Be Still and know that I am God (NIV)," I used that verse along with a picture noting that I said the source was "Unknown."

In many areas, I gathered information, and presented it, and loved doing so. However, being so shy I enjoyed presenting my collections on paper, not verbally. I honestly consider myself best at being a compiler, not a writer.

Thus, for years, I imagined I was an awful writer. But God gave me little assignments, such as, writing "Table Talks" for Wednesday night church dinners, making educational bulletin boards, and volunteering as a church librarian. Writing is not easy for me. I labor long hours to fulfill God's call and assignments. But, gradually, with practice and the Holy Spirit's prompting, I am feeling more confident. This reluctancy to move forward was tough to overcome as I ruminated upon my first college English essay, which resulted in a big fat red F.

One time, at our family's church, I was "assigned" to research an apartment complex where the church wanted to start a ministry. It was an impressive assignment, at least to me. I used my detective skills, took notes on the bumper stickers in the parking lot, noticed the ages of the children in the complex, spoke to the apartment manager, and, of course, put together a booklet with the results to present to the church. I love researching—any kind of research.

In your life, see what you have enjoyed, give your talents to the Lord, and ask him to show you how he can use you even in the smallest of things. All God's assignments are profitable, so as we go from one to the next, keep preparing yourself for the next.

It's hard to believe that the Lord allowed our home to flood during the winter freeze of 2021. This unexpected event led my husband and I to relocate to a completely different locale on the outskirts of Houston, yet we were in awe of his direction and guidance throughout the process. Within just three months of moving, I began teaching a Bible study at the Weston Lakes Club facilities. Reflecting on the many places we could have chosen to live, I am convinced that, in his graciousness, God knew exactly where I needed to be. I honestly believe that this is why our downstairs was completely demolished, left standing only with its wooden structure, before renovations could begin.

We may find ourselves questioning whether God ever changes the course of life we believe he has set for us. The truth is that God has the power to do whatever he deems necessary to fulfill his purpose in our lives. A change in our circumstances or actions doesn't necessarily indicate a change in his intentions, especially since he already knows our ultimate destination. While our path may change along the way, the goal remains steadfast. God grants us the freedom to choose, but as his beloved sons and daughters, he will guide us toward the place he has prepared for us. Though our journey may shift, his ultimate purpose for us never wavers. God may adjust the steps we take, but the final outcome, which serves his glory, is certain.

For I, the LORD, do not change (Malachi 3:6).

Jesus Christ is the same yesterday and today and forever (Hebrews 13:8).

I have witnessed the Lord's guidance in my life, leading me step by step along a journey that often felt orchestrated. As a Catholic girl, I found myself at Baylor University—entirely unaware that it was a Baptist institution until a few weeks before classes began during orientation. Every decision made has contributed to my spiritual growth and maturity in faith. Perhaps this is why I embrace change so readily; I have experienced firsthand how God works through transitions in my life. My journey took me from London, Pittsburgh, Houston, Waco, Fort Worth, Houston again, St. Louis, Houston again, Lagos, Nigeria, to Weston Lakes. In each move, God shaped me in unexpected ways. Moving has become the way the Lord leads me from one season to another. Therefore, I am not afraid of relocating because I anticipate the Lord placing me exactly where he can use me or teach me what I need to learn.

In Waco, I took a significant step in my spiritual journey by accepting the Lord. My faith deepened further in Fort Worth, where I was baptized, marking a pivotal moment in my life. After moving from Fort Worth to Houston, I met my husband during a Wednesday night church service. We married, started a family, and those early years at home with my little ones became the most cherished time of my life. Later, I found joy in a fulfilling career as a high school librarian. My librarian role not only nurtured my passion for education but also honed my speaking skills, enabling me to teach more effectively. Throughout this journey, the call to ministry has always lingered in my heart. I recognize that the Lord has a unique plan for my life, one that can unfold in ways I can only begin to understand. Some events, I willingly concede, remain part of God's beautiful mysteries.

Do you see how this works? God is a God of order, preparing us one step at a time. And he does it repeatedly until he graciously shows us our path. This will happen to you, too, when you obey his direction. I am not saying I never failed along the way, but when we fail, we need to pick ourselves up and start over again, following him and seeing where he will lead. If God can work with me, he can work with you!

God Can Use the Most Unlikely People

God can use the most unlikely people to do a job for him. In *God Uses Ordinary People*, Mark Hiehle tells the following story of a man God used to meet a woman's needs and how the recipient viewed it.

I once heard of a woman who had locked her keys in her car at a mall. Not having the funds to call a locksmith, she prayed and asked God to help her. Shortly after, a rough-looking man approached her and asked if she needed help. She told him that her keys were locked in her car, and in no time, the man used a wire and lifted the lock. The woman thanked him and said he was an angel and an answer to prayer. The man said, "Oh, I am not an angel, ma'am. I just got out of prison." The woman looked to heaven and said, "Oh Lord, You are so good! You sent me an expert."[2]

I love it!

The Lord consistently calls his children to do his work. We have the choice whether to answer him or not. Our problem is that the world around us allows us to question whether we have enough desire, time, money, and intellect to follow through in his calling. We need to listen to the Lord, seek out his will, follow his leading, and let him supply all we need to accomplish his purposes through us. Let's seek out our reasons for not moving forward. Is it because we don't feel spiritual enough? Then, work on that through prayer and Bible study. Is it because you need money to start the ministry God is calling you to? Start with what you have and allow God to find what you need to move on. It is not our strength that gets God's work done, but our willingness and trust in him to accomplish the call and ministries he puts on our hearts.

As the former governor of Arkansas, Mike Huckabee, said, "It's when ordinary people rise above the expectations and seize the opportunity that milestones truly are reached."[3]

We do this by not depending on our abilities and intellect; but on God as our source to achieve mighty things for him—even though we might be "ordinary," like Amos.

What does God have in store for you in this season of your life?

Pray, read, listen, and then act.

Be Unstoppable—Go the Distance with God,

He who is faithful in a very little thing is faithful also in much; and he who is unrighteous in a very little thing is unrighteous also in much.
Luke 16:10

CHAPTER 12

LESSONS FROM
THE GOOD SAMARITAN

If we are going to have any influence on the people who are outside of Christ, it will only be because we are good stewards of the love of Christ within us.

A.W. Tozer

The parable of the Good Samaritan, found in Luke 10:30, addresses a question posed by a lawyer regarding eternal life. In "How to Read the Bible for All It's Worth" by Gordon Fee and Douglas Stuart, parables are defined as "simple stories for those on the outside to whom the 'real meaning,' the 'mysteries,' were hidden; these [belonging] only to the church and could be uncovered by means of allegory."[1]

While the story begins in Luke 10:30, it's essential to understand why Jesus chose to share this particular parable. The inquiry from the lawyer and Jesus' subsequent response set the stage for the lesson. An expert in religious law stood up to test Jesus, asking,

> "Teacher, what should I do to inherit eternal life?" Jesus replied, "What does the law of Moses say? How do you read it?" The man answered, "'You must love the LORD your God with all your heart, all your soul, all your strength, and all your mind.' And 'Love your neighbor as yourself.'" Jesus affirmed him, stating, "Right! Do this and you will live!" (Luke 10:25-28 NLT),

The story features eight characters: the lawyer, Jesus, a Jewish Priest, a Jewish Levite, a man traveling from Jerusalem to Jericho, a Good

Samaritan, robbers, and an innkeeper. The narrative unfolds with robbers attacking a traveler on his journey from Jerusalem to Jericho, leaving him half-dead along the road. A Levite, seeing the injured man, chooses to pass by on the other side, as does a Jewish priest. These two figures, expected to exhibit kindness based on their societal roles, intentionally avoid offering help to someone in dire need. In contrast, a Samaritan traveling on the same road sees the beaten man and is moved with compassion. He bandages the man's wounds, applies oil and wine, places him on his animal, takes him to an inn, and cares for him. The next day, the Samaritan pays the innkeeper, instructing him to look after the injured man and stating he will repay any expenses upon his return. Finally, Jesus poses a question to the lawyer: "Which of these three do you think proved to be a neighbor to the man who fell into the robbers' hands?" The lawyer correctly deduces, "the one who showed mercy toward him." Jesus replies, "Go and do the same" (Lk. 10:30-37). While we do not know the lawyer's response to this command, it prompts us to reflect on how we might react in a similar situation. This theme of compassion resonates with my own experience.

God's Test

In Spring 2021, my husband John and I spent eighty-seven days in a hotel while our home underwent extensive renovations. On one of those days, as we were leaving the hotel, we witnessed a police officer assisting a woman in a wheelchair. We presumed she was an abuse victim and that the officer was helping her find a safe place. Later that evening, we returned to find her sitting alone in her wheelchair, exposed to the cold rain near the hotel entrance, unable to seek shelter under the canopy. My husband felt compelled by the Holy Spirit to approach and help her. After introducing ourselves, we learned about her complex mental health issues. While we spoke with her, the same police officer returned and shared that she had been evicted from another hotel due to nonpayment. John asked the hotel clerk if we could bring her to our room to help her get dried off. After calling her mother, we found that she was unwilling to help her daughter, due to her ongoing struggles with mental illness and drug abuse. The woman exhibited signs of withdrawal, which the officer identified as possibly related to methamphetamine use. I took her to our bathroom to clean up and change into some of my dry clothes. Despite the officer's efforts, he couldn't place her in a women's shelter. Fortunately, John was able to find her a safe place to stay for the night, and together with the officer, they took her to the motel and ensured her accommodation was paid for. Some may wonder whether we witnessed to her. In truth, her immediate needs were physical rather than spiritual, although we assured her multiple times that we would be praying for her. We never saw her again, and I hope her family eventually came to her aid.[2]

Afterthoughts

Reflecting on this experience reinforces the significance of compassion, sharing burdens, and loving one another as commanded in the Bible. Ultimately, the police officer remarked that he had never witnessed such an act of kindness before, affirming that what transpired that night was indeed a God-thing. What remains vivid in my memory is the image of my husband wheeling this lady out of our hotel room. From behind, I saw her wearing my favorite silver pants and green-and-black tunic—a symbol of the love and kindness that can emerge during moments of need.

Lingering in my mind is, "But by the grace of God, this could be me."

Be Unstoppable—Go the Distance with God,

But the Lord said to Samuel, "Do not look at his appearance or at the height of his stature, because I have rejected him; For God sees not as man sees, for a man looks at the outward appearance, but the Lord looks at the heart."
1 Samuel 16:7

SECTION 2

The Power of Prayer and Biblical Characters

CHAPTER 13

THE POWER AND IMPORTANCE OF PRAYER

> *Prayer is the most natural outpouring of the soul,*
> *the unhindered turning to God for communion and direction.*
>
> E.M. Bounds

After college, when I moved to Fort Worth, with no job or money. I knew only one person, Judy—my new roommate. We were both flat broke and quickly realized that our apartment had no kitchen glassware.

In our desperation, we prayed, and God answered our prayer in the most unexpected way as he often does for us. To attract more customers, McDonald's ran a promotion where people could visit a restaurant, sing the Big Mac jingle and receive a free McDonald's glass without needing to purchase anything. Judy and I, having no singing ability, decided to venture out one Friday night. We hit three McDonald's locations and belted out the jingle.

♫ Two all-beef-patties, special sauce, lettuce, cheese, pickles, onions, on a sesame seed bun.

To our delight, we returned home with six free drinking glasses! While our method may seem unusual, it's a reminder that sometimes God answers prayers in unexpected or even fun, unimaginable ways.

Prayer serves as a divine tool that God provides for us to deepen our intimacy with him. He offers this opportunity to every believer because each person matters to him. Prayer isn't only about seeking rewards; its primary purpose is to communicate with the Lord—to truly know him and understand his will. Through prayer, we align our desires, requests, and lifestyles with God's plan. It is a time of praise and worship, confession, gratitude, and heartfelt communication with him. Biblical examples of prayer reveal that God is attentive and responsive. He is not a distant deity that we need to persuade to take an interest in our lives.

What is Prayer?

As I state in my book *Answer Me: Developing a Heart for Prayer*

> *Believers are called to pray. God can do whatever he wants, but he delights in working through our prayers. Sometimes, we hesitate to pray because we do not believe that there will be results.*[1]

Praying is not about seeking goosebumps or high emotions, although that might result. It means being "in the zone," where we communicate openly and honestly with God about what weighs on our hearts. Spending time in God's presence and meditating on his Word will help us pray and discern his will.

The Holy Spirit's Role in Prayer

God's Holy Spirit searches our hearts to convict, correct, and encourage us by makings us aware of our dependence on Jesus Christ and revealing areas where we need to confess and move on. If we don't know how to pray, the Holy Spirit provides divine assistance and guidance. When reading God's Word, the Spirit helps us grasp his ways. When we pray, the Holy Spirit aids us in praying according to God's will because he understands God's mind.

How Does God Answer Our Prayers?

God's responses are often be categorized as a *yes, no, wait, not now,* or *slowdown.* It's important to recognize that even a "no" is an answer. When his answers don't align with our wishes, it may be due to our asking contrary to his will or because he has something else in store for us. We might not be ready yet to receive what we seek, or God might be using our wait to strengthen our faith, prepare us for the answer, or mature us in the Christian life. Regardless, we must persevere in prayer.

Why is Waiting So Hard?

Waiting is hard because we tend to want what we desire right now. We resist waiting for anything or anyone, including God. Often, waiting feels like suffering, but it's crucial what we do during our waiting periods. Everything unfolds according to God's will or allowance. Since he engages in every aspect of life, who better to answer our prayers than the One who sees the complete picture? Miracles or divine interventions come from God. He can do more than we can ask or imagine—nothing is impossible for our all-powerful God. The Bible serves as our instruction manual for a godly life, and absorbing God's Word is essential for praying according to his will and living a life that honors him. While God will not grant desires that contradict his words, he always remains faithful to his promises. Just as God made a way for my roommate and I to get free drinking glasses, I hope you will trust him to guide you as you submit to his will. As one of my former pastors joyfully exclaimed when God surprised him by answering one of his prayers, "Lord, you've got to be kidding me!" I long to be joyfully astonished by the mighty and unexpected ways God may answer my prayers. He knows what is best for both me—and for you.

Be Unstoppable—Go the Distance with God,

Rejoice always; pray without ceasing; in everything give thanks; for this is God's will for you in Christ Jesus.
1 Thessalonians 6:16-18

CHAPTER 14

INTERCESSORY PRAYER

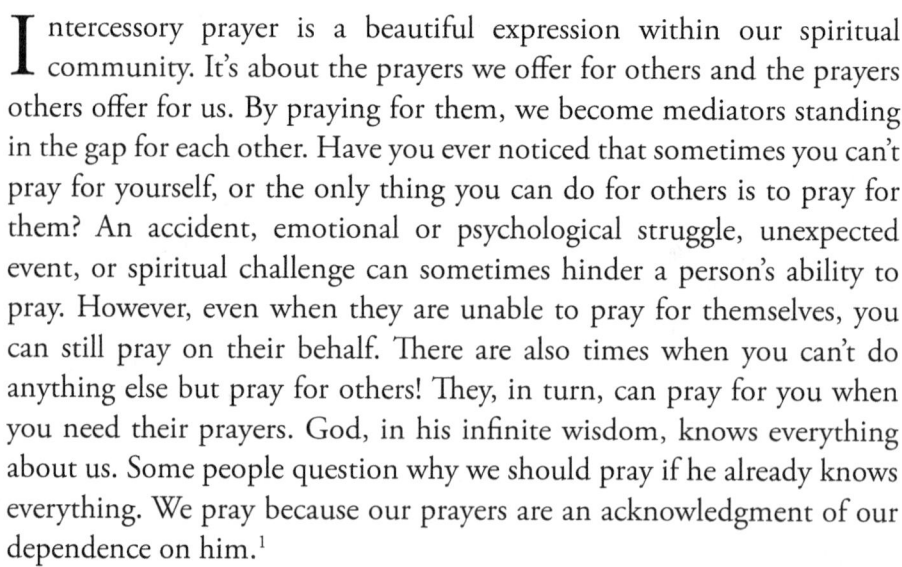

> *God brings you to places, among people, and into certain conditions*
> *to accomplish a definite purpose through the intercession of the Spirit in you.*
> *Your part in intercessory prayer is not to agonize over how to intercede,*
> *but to use the everyday circumstances and people God puts around you*
> *by His providence to bring them before His throne,*
> *and to allow the Spirit in you the opportunity to intercede for them.*
> *In this way God is going to touch the whole world with His saints.*
>
> Oswald Chambers

Intercessory prayer is a beautiful expression within our spiritual community. It's about the prayers we offer for others and the prayers others offer for us. By praying for them, we become mediators standing in the gap for each other. Have you ever noticed that sometimes you can't pray for yourself, or the only thing you can do for others is to pray for them? An accident, emotional or psychological struggle, unexpected event, or spiritual challenge can sometimes hinder a person's ability to pray. However, even when they are unable to pray for themselves, you can still pray on their behalf. There are also times when you can't do anything else but pray for others! They, in turn, can pray for you when you need their prayers. God, in his infinite wisdom, knows everything about us. Some people question why we should pray if he already knows everything. We pray because our prayers are an acknowledgment of our dependence on him.[1]

Testimonies

As parents, we often turn to prayer when it comes to the well-being of our children. One such instance occurred when our four-year-old daughter Jennifer misplaced her purse at the local library. We prayed fervently, and soon after praying, the library called to tell us her purse was found. Jennifer's heart was calmed, especially after a quick trip to the library to pick up her purse. Similarly, when our eleven-year-old son John Jr. sustained a serious back injury while practicing dirt bike stunts, we prayed for his recovery, and miraculously, he was healed. Another incident happened when our sixteen-year-old son Jimmy collided with a cement wall while playing basketball. Still, thanks to the power of prayer, he survived, even though we were unaware of his sub-dural hematoma until much later. These are just a few examples of how prayer has answered our family calls for help in times of need.

On October 29, 2014, while living in Lagos, Nigeria, our driver was stuck in bumper-to-bumper Lagos traffic. I was sitting in the back seat of the car when an elderly-appearing man knocked on the back seat car window where I was sitting. His wrinkles proved he had had experienced a heart-breaking life. His dry, swollen hand went up to his dry, cracked, parched lips, begging for something to drink. I had half a can of soda in the car. but due to company security policy due to kidnappings and armed robberies, which were ongoing in Nigerian cities, we were restricted from opening our windows or doors to anyone. This poor emancipated man stood there for what seemed like an extremely long time, and all I could do was turn my head away and pray. While I wished I could quench his thirst, I couldn't. There are really times when you can't do anything but pray. This was one of them.

As mentioned before, I have been prayer journaling since 1973. It is very humbling to look back over my prayer requests. One day, I looked through some of my prayer journals, and saw that early in my Christian walk, most of my prayers were about me and then about me some more, but as I matured in the faith, I noticed my prayers became more oriented to other people. I still pray about my concerns and life, but they are a lot less about me and more about others now.

My husband and I have often received intercessory prayer, where others have been praying for us. It could be our friends, family members, co-workers, or even people we do not know simply lifting up prayers on our behalf in the name of Jesus. It is as simple as that. During the times we needed prayer, we can honestly say we felt the prayers of others reaching heaven and coming on us to help in our situations. Often, the Holy Spirit, a key figure in the Christian faith, gave us the knowledge to know who was praying for us, without them ever telling us who they were. Those uplifting prayers on our behalf covered us with peace, security, healing, and comfort.

Biblical Examples of Intercessory Prayer

The Bible contains many examples of intercessory prayers. First, in the Book of Ezra, the scribe and scholar named Ezra, discovers an apathy developing among the Jews returning from Babylon to Jerusalem. The officials told Ezra about the Israelites and Levites not separating themselves from the Babylonian people and about their wicked acts and direct violations of God's will which included intermarrying with foreign women.

Ezra responded,

> When I heard this, I tore my cloak and my shirt, pulled hair from my head and beard, and sat down utterly shocked. Then all who trembled at the words of the God of Israel came and sat with me because of this outrage committed by the returned exiles. And I sat there utterly appalled until the time of the evening sacrifice (Ezra 9:3-4 NLT).

He then said,

> "O my God, I am utterly ashamed; I blush to lift up my face to you. For our sins are piled higher than our heads, and our guilt has reached to the heavens. From the days of our ancestors until now, we have been steeped in sin. That is why we and our kings and our priests have been at the mercy of the pagan kings of the land. We have been killed, captured, robbed, and disgraced, just as we are today" (Ezra 9:6-7 NLT).

While Ezra prayed and made this confession, weeping and lying face down on the ground in front of the Temple of God, a huge crowd of people from Israel—men, women, and children—gathered and wept bitterly with him (Ezr. 10:1 NLT). We can feel the dire pain that Ezra felt toward those returning Jews. He was interceding on their behalf. Have you ever interceded for someone with that much passion before?

Second, another person who boldly came to God's throne in prayer is the Apostle Paul. Paul prayed for those who believed in Christ.

> *And it is my prayer that your love may abound more and more, with knowledge and all discernment, so that you may approve what is excellent, and so be pure and blameless for the day of Christ, filled with the fruit of righteousness that comes through Jesus Christ, to the glory and praise of God (Philippians 1:9-11 ESV).*

Third, Jesus was the ultimate intercessor of all time. He prayed for Peter that his faith would not fail. He prayed for those following Christ and his disciples. He prayed for those who crucified him. Many times, Jesus prayed with deep cries and tears for those around him. In Luke 22:32, Jesus says, "But I have prayed for you, Simon, that your faith may not fail. And when you have turned back, strengthen your brothers" (Lk. 22:32 NIV). And as Jesus prayed, "so should we."

Who Should We Pray For?

There are so many people and so many needs that require prayers. I have found most directions to pray for someone come from the following list:

- Seeing a need,
- Feeling a holy hunch that someone/some issue needs prayer,
- Hearing about a need and it being brought to my attention and
- Discerning a possible prayer need.

Intercessory prayer is powerful. It's like putting yourself in someone else's shoes, feeling their pain, and praying from God's perspective. This week let's look around for those whom God brings to us to pray for. Many faces today need our prayers. Seek that face in the crowd and pray diligently and boldly in the name of Jesus Christ.

One day, I stopped at a drugstore to purchase some computer paper. However, I checked out the candy row to see if they had a bag of *Tootsie Pops*. I had searched two other affiliated stores previously to no avail. Lo and behold, I discovered this particular store had my favorite "low-calorie" candy—three points per pop, for those who know what I mean! It happens to all of us. We go into a store with good intents to purchase only one or two items and come out with much more. I added some colorful *Post-it Page Markers* to my other two items. As I left the drug store, I hit a red light under Houston's Katy Freeway. There I saw a young man. His legs were so skinny, obviously diseased. All I had to give him was a *Tootsie Pop*. I cannot say I was extremely generous by giving him the entire bag, but I wanted to give him something sweet to eat. I wrestled opening the bag; finally, I had to use my teeth to open the bag. Not cool, but I was afraid the light was going to turn green. Once the bag was open, I reached in and pulled out one orange and one red Tootsie Pops, but then I stopped. The Lord said, "Give him your best." God knew that orange and red were my least favorite flavors, but chocolate and purple were my favs. So, I quickly reached for the bag, pulled out a chocolate and purple *Tootsie Pop*, opened my window, and handed them to him. It might not seem like a big sacrifice, but when you understand the last two bags of *Tootsie Pops* I bought had no purples or chocolates in them, you can understand my "sacrifice" a little better.

When this gentleman saw them, he gave me a big old grin through his crooked yellow teeth. He looked me straight in the eye, and said, "Thank you." To me, it was a smile from God. Yes, it was a small gesture on my part, but it started both his and my day out right, and both of us ended up with a little sweetness. Literally! As I drove off, I realized God had given me a person to pray for. That is intercessory prayer. I hope you find instances in your life like this! Freely you received, freely give (Matt. 10:8b).

Be Unstoppable—Go the Distance with God,

First of all, then, I urge that entreaties and prayers, petitions, and thanksgivings, be made on behalf of all men.
1 Timothy 2:1

CHAPTER 15

IT: ISAIAH AND
THE POWER OF PRAYER

---

*Isaiah was so attuned to God, because of the great crisis he had just endured,
that the call of God penetrated his soul.
The majority of us cannot hear anything but ourselves.
And we cannot hear anything God says.
But to be brought to the place
where we can hear the call of God is to be profoundly changed.*

Oswald Chambers

In this chapter, the recurrent theme revolves around "It." However, let's clarify that when I mention "It," I am not referring to Information Technology or the abbreviation of *Italy*. Instead, I'm delving into the Middle English usage of the word, serving as a noun or pronoun representing a challenge, decision, or problem—one that you may be grappling with presently or have encountered in the past. Examples of "It" range from navigating your child's alternative lifestyle, coping with your spouse's infidelity, or discerning false teachers or doctrine at your church. For the sake of this discourse, all referrals to "It" will apply to any trepidation that prompted Christ-followers to call upon the Lord, just like the Prophet Isaiah did. As you start this chapter, think about a difficulty or concern you have had in the past or present. Substitute that incident for your "It."

Background

The Book of Isaiah is prophetic, dating back to around 700-680 BC,—more than seven hundred years before Jesus was born. This prophetic text serves as an instruction guide for past, present, and future generations. Isaiah came from a privileged family that provided him with a stellar education. His forty-year ministry began in Judah, in the Southern Kingdom of the nation of Israel. The nation of Israel consisted of two kingdoms—the Northern Kingdom, known as Israel, and the Southern Kingdom, known as Judah. Isaiah's call to the ministry came through an intense revelation he received when worshiping the Lord. As a result of this vision, his life was transformed into a heartfelt full-time service to God, much like most pastors who are called into the ministry today have experienced. Isaiah yearned for the nation of Israel—both Northern and Southern Kingdoms—to return to their God. Furthermore, he knew God needed someone to proclaim this essential pronouncement to the people. He heard and accepted the call to be that person.

Isaiah ministered during the kingship of Uzziah, Jotham, Johoahaz I, and Hezekiah. During their reigns, political mayhem faced the Jewish people. Assyria conquered the Northern Kingdom, and the restoration of Israel consumed Isaiah's heavy ministry load.

American pastor and writer Warren Wiersbe states, "Isaiah was a man who loved his nation. The phrase 'my people' is used at least twenty-six times in his book. He was a patriot with a true love for his country, pleading with Judah to return to God and warning kings when their foreign policy was contrary to God's will . . . He was also a man who hated sin and sham religions. [He knew] Jehovah was holy, but the nation was sinful, and Isaiah called the people to repent."[1] Conceivably, Isaiah's calling in the day and time he was living caused his "It"—his despair! In many instances, our "It" may be—just like Isaiah's—a burden we do not know how to manage or a challenge we are facing. As we capture the essence of our "It," let's unearth and follow the subsequent biblical principles to help us unruffle our difficulties in pursuing God's will for our lives.

When Facing Your "It," Pray

Recently, when pondering my "It," I prayed this prayer.

Help me, my heavenly Father! I think about "It" daily. I have been thinking about it not only for days, weeks, and month but for years. I do not understand why or how I am supposed to think about it. I want to discern your will even if it is not your will. Please make your desires my desires and your thoughts my thoughts. I do not care how you speak to me about it. Just speak. Please resolve any hindrances to me being totally aligned to your will. You may be using it as a springboard to refine my character. There is so much unknown about it. Help me, Lord!

Many of our prayers, such as mine, are never made known to the "general public" or even to those closest to us. Sometimes, we cry out to God, and only God and ourselves know the depths of our concerns. And that's okay! Our lives should be structured so that prayer comes first to our minds when seeking solutions to our problem, our "It." Prayer is to be our first line of defense. Unfortunately, sometimes, we get hung up when faced with how to pray and how to follow God's commands in the Bible. Our distress, our challenge—our "It"—drags on, repeats itself, and sometimes returns after we think we have overcome it. When our "It" consumes us and tries to destroy our close relationship with the Lord, we can pray for a miraculous sign and ask God for his answers and confirmation.

King Ahaz had a problem. He did not want to do business with God. When Judah's water supply from the Euphrates River reached its limit and threatened to flood, Ahaz should have broken his alliance with the Assyrians and called for the nation of Israel to pray, but he didn't. He continued in his unbelief and continued to trust in Assyria for help, not God. In Isaiah 7:11, God speaks to Ahaz, saying, "Ask for a confirming sign from the LORD your God. You can even ask for something miraculous" (Isaiah 7:13). While Ahaz refused a sign from God, we do not have to. When we face "It," we can ask our heavenly Father to confirm his will and ask him for a miraculous answer. When the nation of Israel was invaded by the Assyrians, it was a shame Ahaz didn't depend upon God and prayer.

When Facing Your "It," Seek the Truth

Now, let's fast-forward to Isaiah 29.

As followers of Jesus, we may initially be confused about our "It," and we may err, and stumble, and question God. Nevertheless, it is always in our best interest to remember that we can know God's truth if we "ask, seek, and knock," when "It" raises its ugly head. Jesus said, "Ask, and it will be given to you; seek, and you will find; knock, and it will be opened to you" (Matt. 7:7). King Ahaz's problems were twofold. He did not want to listen to Isaiah's prophetic voice and do business with God. His lack of proper leadership trickled down, making the Israelites and others living in the area apathetic toward God's things. Isaiah tried to present God's light to the people of Israel, but they kept rejecting it—even disdaining his words. They did not care to understand God's prophecies spoken through Isaiah, just like many people today cannot comprehend the light of Christ or the things of God. People globally may "understand" the Bible from an intellectual or historical viewpoint, but not from a spiritual heart-and-soul vantage point.

God saw a nation disregarding their spiritual inheritance, but he reminded them that one day, they would know the truth. The city of Jerusalem in the Southern Kingdom had watched the Northern Kingdom fall to the Assyrians, but this judgment did not bring them to repentance, and Judah eventually fell to Babylon in 586 BC. We must keep praying and reading the Bible until God, in his compassionate and gracious manner, shows us the correct answer, method, or path to walk. The psalmist says, "Your word is a lamp to my feet and a light to my path" (Ps. 119:105 NKJV).

When Seeking Your "It," Understand God's Intentions

As we seek his answers and clarifications on our "It," we must navigate through the Bible until we can affirm God's intentions. God's intentions regarding us are numerous; even though they may be hidden from us until the right time.

God has a unique plan for each of our lives and he desires to see us live in his will and purpose. He has given us his Word as a guide to help us understand his intentions and how we can best fulfill his plan.

According to Mark 1:15 and Acts 16:31, God wants us to have a saving faith in him through repentance and acceptance of his Son, Jesus Christ. He desires that we become more like Christ and conform to the Lord's ways. Moreover, God wants to deliver us from the evil one, as stated in Matthew 6:13. Romans 8:28 assures us that he wants to give us the best possible future. Proverbs 3:5-6 reminds us that he wants to lead us and direct our paths. Isaiah 41:10 assures us that God wants to strengthen and protect us as we navigate this life. Lastly, by following his will and guidance, we can experience a life of fulfillment, joy, and peace.

God's intention, through his Prophet Isaiah, was to protect both kingdoms—the Northern Kingdom of Israel and the Southern Kingdom of Judah. In Isaiah 30, Judah, the Southern Kingdom, is admonished not to turn to Egypt for protection from Assyria. Following his call, Isaiah exhorts the people to trust God again.

> *And though the Lord give you the bread of adversity [your it] and the water of affliction, yet your Teacher will not hide himself anymore, but your eyes shall see your Teacher. And your ears shall hear a word behind you, saying, 'This is the way, walk in it, when you turn to the right or when you turn to the left* (Isaiah 30:20-21 ESV).

At this point, the Israelites should have expected God was going to hide from them. His intention was to deliver them from evil as it is for us as well by cleansing sin, leading them into righteousness, but the people laughed, scoffed at Isaiah's prophecies, and continued turning their backs on God.

When Seeking Your "It," Trust God

Trusting God to show you how you must handle your "It," is imperative. While the people in the Northern Kingdom did not listen to Isaiah and proceeded hurriedly into the arms and captivity of the Assyrians, we should not be in such a hurry, jumping ahead of God with our impatience. We should follow Proverbs 3:5, which states. "Trust in the LORD with all your heart and do not rely on your own understanding." Foremost, knowing our salvation is secure, and knowing we are in the right relationship with God through the cleansing of our sins and our acceptance of Jesus Christ, we allow the Holy Spirit and the words of God to infiltrate our being. We all make mistakes, but the key is learning and from them and moving forward. By embracing our imperfections, we can inspire others to do the same. God's thoughts can seep into our mind supernaturally. He enlightens us through his Word, gives us clarity in our thought, and forgives us when needed. We must apply these truths to help us to show his light to others.

When Facing Your "It," Be Patient

We are impatient people. Wanting to know and understand everything God does only proves that position. Having deep confidence that he will show us what we need to know, is of utmost importance. Certain things will remain a mystery either forever or until a later time. Once we recognize that, we understand that his answer to our concerns will be clarified. The way he chooses to answer is his answer to us. As I was pondering, praying, and reading the Word, seeking advice about my current "It," I read the following verse:

> *The light of the moon will be as the light of the sun, and the light of the sun will be seven times brighter, like the light of seven days, on the day the LORD binds up the fracture of His people and heals the bruise He has inflicted (Isaiah 30:26).*

While Isaiah is speaking here of end times, God's Word spoke supernaturally to me in the latter part of the verse. His Spirit whispered to me saying,

> *I am binding up your wound and it will result in your healing. Though your dream has been shattered, the severe wound is healed. While the purpose of your "It" is still unknown to you, trust that it was put there by me to grow you and to make you more like my son Jesus Christ.*

Yes, God speaks to us personally through his Word. It has happened time after time with me.

When Facing Your "It," You Must Accept His Answer

Impatience often defines us. Wanting to know and understand everything God does proves this. However, he will reveal what we need to know, which is important. However, some things will remain a mystery, either forever or for later, and recognizing this helps us understand that his answers or no answers are always true guidance. Even though my dream was shattered, whether for good or just for now, I must trust that this "It" was meant for my growth to become more like his son, Jesus. When facing your "It," you must accept his answer. In our daily walk with the Lord, he may bless us by answering our prayers, bringing us great joy. Yet sometimes he may guide us toward what is best for our future. While waiting for God's response may take years, the Lord will be working on our character, improving our service, or preparing us for our next season.

Wrap Up

Throughout history, God honors the promise he gave to Abraham. He promised to make Abraham a father of a great people. In turn for their obedience, God would guide them and give them the land of Israel. In the latter days, many Israelites will turn to the Lord and completely fulfill the prophecies of Isaiah. Until that time, let us believe that Isaiah's call to turn to God and live righteous and holy lives for his glory applies also to us today—Today!

Going back to your "It," why not pray, seek his truth, grasp his intentions, trust him, believe in him, and accept his answer? And if you don't get an answer, keep praying. Never give up unless you get that definitive no.

Be Unstoppable—Go the Distance with God,

Search me, O God, and know my heart; try me and know my anxious thoughts; And see if there be any hurtful way in me. And lead me in the everlasting way. Psalm 139:23-24

CHAPTER 16

TEN TIPS FOR
A RICHER PRAYER LIFE

Don't forget to pray today
because God did not forget to wake you up this morning.

Oswald Chambers

In Matthew 26:41, Jesus urges us to engage in the powerful yet challenging act of prayer: "Keep watching and praying that you may not enter into temptation; the spirit is willing, but the flesh is weak." Many people fall short despite having the privilege of communicating with God through prayer. But why do we struggle with it? Sometimes, we resist the desire to pray, or we feel uncertain about how to pray. Satan will do everything he can to hinder us from praying through apathy, distractions, laziness, or sin. In our flesh, we lack the strength to pray as we ought to. However, God's Holy Spirit empowers us to pray and enhances our prayer life. While prayer is a unique act between us and God, don't limit God. The following guidelines will help you understand how to pray:

Principle 1: Embrace the Scriptural Mandate for Prayer

God specifically commands us to pray. The principle of "calling on God" shows up multiple times in Scripture, like in Jeremiah 33:3, Psalm 50:15, and Romans 10:13. The Bible clearly instructs us to pray, and the Lord responds to our prayers, revealing great and hidden things that are unknown.

Principle 2: Adopt a Comprehensive Approach When Praying

Prayer involves praise, worship, thanksgiving, confession, and petition. Believers from both the Old Testament and New Testament prayed. Prayer unleashes the Holy Spirit and ignites change within us. God's people and the church thrive through prayer.

Principle 3: Recognize the Sacred Duty of Prayer

Christ-followers must pray. God can do whatever he chooses, but he delights in working through our prayers. Praying requires discipline. It is our duty to pray for ourselves and the needs of others. Sometimes, we hesitate to pray because we doubt the outcomes.

Principle 4: Petition God with Confidence

God encourages us to ask for what we need. The Bible highlights numerous subjects we can pray about for ourselves or others, such as good health, God's will, wisdom, and strength. Matthew 7:11 states, "If you then, being evil, know how to give good gifts to your children, how much more will your Father who is in heaven give what is good to those who ask Him!"

Principle 5: Exercise Boldness in Prayer

Be bold—avoid general or half-hearted requests to God. God encourages us to approach him with boldness. Ask the LORD for a verse that speaks directly to you. Claim God's promises in prayer.

Principle 6: Engage with Scripture in Prayer

Many people discover the power of praying Scriptures as a way to communicate with God, thus boosting their confidence in prayer. To "pray the Scriptures," try substituting names, pronouns, places, and circumstances into the Word of God.

Principle 7: Seek Unity in Prayer

Sometimes, we pray without seeing results. When answers seem absent, consider asking others to join you in prayer. Jesus promises to be present when two or more gather in his name. When we unite in prayer, God's power multiplies as our prayers uplift and intertwine through the Holy Spirit.

Principle 8: Combine Prayer with Scriptural Study

Spending time in Bible study and prayer sharpens our spirits to his leading. It's easy to succumb to today's culture of liberalism, but when God's words dwell within us, we are less likely to stray. We must "Study to show thyself approved unto God, a workman that needeth not to be ashamed, rightly dividing the word of truth" (2 Tim. 2:15 KJV).

Principle 9: Trust in His Divine Providence

Fate does not govern the universe. God controls every occurrence within it. Everything happens because he allows it. Since God oversees all events in the world, he can answer our prayers as he sees the big picture unfolding in our lives.

Principle 10: Submit to God's Will in Prayer

While no set procedure exists for knowing God's will, his will never contradicts the Bible. His will can be revealed through biblical guidance, prayer, the counsel of mature believers, faith, insights from the Holy Spirit, and sometimes miraculous interventions.

Be Unstoppable—Go the Distance with God,

For through Him we both have our access in One Spirit to the Father. Ephesians 2:18

CHAPTER 17

PRAYING FOR YOUR CHILDREN

> *A God-centered home*
> *[is] where each member has the right to respond to God's love*
> *in Christ and to be taught how to live from a spiritual perspective.*
>
> Billy Graham

In October 1985, my journey led me to Cypress Christian School in Cypress, Texas, where our daughter Jennifer attended a once-a-week Mother's Day Out program. There, I picked up a sheet of paper that changed my life and, more importantly, my children's lives. At the time, I had a one-year-old daughter and was pregnant with our first son. The mimeographed page, which I found lying on a table, became my guide for how to pray for my children. These guidelines have been written in my Bibles, copied for friends, stored in my computer, and, more importantly, prayed over—multiple times! Now that our children are all adults in their late 30s and 40s, I still use this list to pray for them, their spouses, and our grandchildren.

How to Pray for Your Children

1. That they will know Christ as Savior early in life.

> *O God, You are my God; I shall seek You earnestly; My soul thirsts for You, my flesh yearns for You, In a dry and weary land where there is no water.*
> *Psalm 63:1*

... and that from childhood you have known the sacred writings which are able to give you the wisdom that leads to salvation through faith which is in Christ Jesus.
2 Timothy 3:15

2. That they will have a hatred for sin.

Let those who love the LORD hate evil, for he guards the lives of his faithful ones and delivers them from the hand of the wicked.
Psalm 97:10

3. That they will be caught when guilty.

It is good for me that I was afflicted, That I may learn Your statutes.
Psalm 119:71

4. They will be protected from the evil one in each area of their lives: spiritual, emotional, and physical.

I do not ask You to take them out of the world, to keep them from the evil one.
John 17:15

5. They will have a responsible attitude in all their interpersonal relationships.

Then Daniel began distinguishing himself among the commissioners and satraps because he possessed an extraordinary spirit, and the king planned to appoint him over the entire kingdom.
Daniel 6:3

6. That they will respect those in authority over them.

Every person is to be in subjection to the governing authorities. For there is no authority except from God, and those which exist are established by God.
Romans 13:1

7. That they will desire the right kinds of friends and be protected from the wrong friends.

> *My son, if sinners entice you,*
> *Do not consent.*
> *If they say, Come with us,*
> *Let us lie in wait for blood,*
> *Let us ambush the innocent without cause;*
> *Proverbs 1:10-11*

8. That they will be kept from the wrong mate and saved for the right one.

> *Do not be mismatched with unbelievers; for what do righteousness and lawlessness share together, or what does light have in common with darkness? Or what harmony does Christ have with Belial, or what does a believer share with an unbeliever? Or what agreement does the temple of God have with idols? For we are the temple of the living God; just as God said,*
>
> *"I will dwell among them and walk among them;*
> *And I will be their God, and they shall be My people.*
> *Therefore, come out from their midst and be separate," says the Lord.*
> *"And do not touch what is unclean;*
> *And I will welcome you."*
> *2 Corinthians 6:14-17*

9. That they, as well as those they marry, will be kept pure until marriage.

> *Flee sexual immorality. Every other sin that a person commits is outside the body, but the sexually immoral person sins against his own body. Or do you not know that your body is a temple of the Holy Spirit within you, whom you have from God, and that you are not your own? For you have been bought for a price: therefore glorify God in your body.*
> *1 Corinthians 6:18-20*

10. That they will learn to totally submit to God and actively resist Satan in all circumstances.

> *Submit therefore to God. Resist the devil and he will flee from you.*
> *James 4:7*

11. That they will be single-hearted – willing to be sold out to Jesus.

> *… rejoicing in hope, persevering in tribulation, devoted to prayer,*
> *Romans 12:12*

12. That they will be hedged in so they cannot find their way to the wrong people or wrong places and that the bad people cannot find their way to them.[1]

> *Therefore, behold, I will hedge up her way with thorns,*
> *And I will build a wall against her so that she cannot find her paths.*
> *Hosea 2:6*

While I don't know your particular situation or how old your children are, these guidelines may be the one thing that steers you to pray for your newborn, preschooler, elementary-age child, pre-teen, teenager, and adult children. When addressing the Lord over the years, some of the preceding principles have been more critical than others. For example, when my children were young, I would pray Number 1 mightily. When they were teenagers, I would pray for Number 12 continually. Praying Number 3 is scary now that they are all adults, but hopefully, by praying this when they were they were younger, there is little chance of them being in a precarious situation, like jail. But if there is, I know where and to whom to turn. So here is the deal—praying God's Word and protecting our children is essential in training them and fostering a healthy and God-centered life. When we become parents, we are in it for the long haul, so no matter what the age of your children, never stop praying for those whom God has given you care over, whether they are your children, your stepchildren, your godchildren, or any child God has entrusted into your care. And remember, praying for your children does not stop once they become adults. Parenting and praying is a lifetime commitment. And, if you haven't been praying for your children, it is not too late. I implore you to start cultivating a godly character in your children and their children through your prayers.

Our Hamster and Dog

I began teaching our son John Jr. how to pray when he was six. I would tell him it was best to close his eyes to stop being distracted and talk to God. I would tell him to speak to God about what he wants and what he would like him to do and then listen to the voice of God in his head. Vacation Bible School was on the horizon when I taught him how to pray. Unfortunately, it was the same time we lost our hamster named Pizza. We honestly thought the dog ate him. But after three weeks of hoping Pizza would show up, he did. He had lost his hair, was dehydrated, and looked like he was on his last leg. Continuing with the story, on the day of or the day before, I asked our son John what he felt the Lord was telling him since I was still in my prayer-teaching mode. He did not hesitate. He told me God told him not to go to Vacation Bible School (VBS) and stay home with Pizza. Talk about a mom's dilemma. If I made him go to Bible study, he wouldn't understand why he couldn't obey what the Lord told him. If I let him stay home while the other two children went, would I be depriving him of learning more about God? Although many disagreed with my decision, I took the other two kids to VBS while John Jr. and I ate breakfast, had fun, and enjoyed our alone time. Sometimes, we would peek in on Pizza. Although John Jr. didn't require much discipline as he grew up, I still found myself praying for him often. I remember when he was a preschooler, struggling with a deep fear of dogs. I also prayed when he was just six years old and began to seek the Lord in his life. Then there was a time in sixth grade when he broke his back, a moment that weighed heavily on my heart, but through prayer and a wonderful doctor, he recovered!

From the beginning, I prayed for all our children to find godly and loving spouses, even before they were born. I'm grateful that God has answered those prayers and enriched their lives in wonderful ways. As your children transition into adulthood, continue to pray for their needs, families, and interests. In the journey of parenthood, it is essential to maintain a sense of calm amid various choices. Introducing children to the beauty of prayer can serve as a guiding light during tough decisions, especially when our actions may not be immediately understood. Remember, parenting doesn't end when they turn eighteen; our love and prayers continue to support our adult children through all of life's twists and turns.

Our youngest son, Jimmy, always the adventurous type, chose to pursue his education beyond high school at Babson College, a prestigious business school founded in 1919 in Wellesley, Massachusetts, near Boston rather than stay in the comfort of being close by in Texas. So, it wasn't surprising when he developed an interest in collecting antique books written by Roger W. Babson, the founder of his college. As most parents would be, we were grateful he did not want to start a collection of weird things like banana peels, toenail clippings, or super-soakers! So, books were an excellent choice since I could find and give these rare books for birthday and Christmas gifts—if I could find them. I am glad Jimmy no longer collects baseball cards, sneakers, or sunglasses! Books are good. And rare books are even better! While it gives a mom something to look forward to on special occasions, I know he appreciates that mom loves and cares about what is important to him.

Love and care for your children now—no matter what age they are!

Be Unstoppable—Go the Distance with God,

With all prayer and petition pray at all times in the Spirit, and with this in view, be on the alert with all perseverance and petition for all the saints, and pray on my behalf, that utterance may be given to me in the opening of my mouth, to make known with boldness the mystery of the gospel, for which I am an ambassador in chains; that in proclaiming it I may speak boldly, as I ought to speak.
Ephesians 6:18-20

CHAPTER 18

HABAKKUK: A MODEL OF PRAYER AND WORSHIP

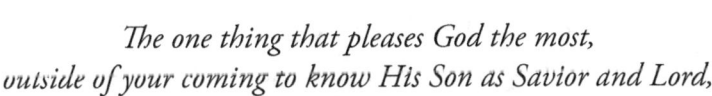

> *The one thing that pleases God the most,*
> *outside of your coming to know His Son as Savior and Lord,*
> *is to hear your voice speaking to Him in prayer and worship.*
>
> Charles Stanley

As a new Christ-follower, one of the first Bible witticisms I ever heard was about Habakkuk, a great prophet in the Old Testament.

Q: What Bible character stood on his watch?

A: Habakkuk, because he said, "I will stand upon my watch, and set me upon the tower, and will watch to see what he will say unto me, and what I shall answer when I am reproved" (Hab. 2:1).

I'm unsure why I thought that anecdote was so funny or whether I felt the ancient prophet really stood on a wristwatch. However, it caused me to read the Book of Habakkuk. And I learned a valuable lesson about how God works when we come to him with heartful prayers during times of stress and anxiety.

Habakkuk is like many of us. We ask, "How can a holy God stand by and watch evil continue?" God assures Habakkuk that he controls everything and knows what he is doing. All the time, while possessing a complaining spirit, Habakkuk continues to dialogue with his Lord God. As their communication continues, we eventually see that their discussion finally leads Habakkuk to a faith in God's plan that, in his timing, he will deliver his people

About Habakkuk

The author of the book is the Prophet Habakkuk. Written between 615 and 605 BC, the prophecies declared during this time came to fruition in the following decade. In *Books of the Bible: At a Glance*, a summary of the book's three chapters states, "Habakkuk cried out to God during a very dark time in Israel. [He] likely prophesied in the first five years of King Jehoiakim's reign…The Assyrians had control of the Northern Kingdom (Kingdom of Israel) after a brutal invasion more than a hundred years earlier. Habakkuk preached from the Southern Kingdom (Kingdom of Judah), which was still intact but less than [fifty] years away from its invasion by Babylon that destroyed the Temple."[1]

Besides my favorite verse of Habakkuk 2:1, other vital and Spirit-led verses walk us through the Book of Habakkuk. Henceforth, the following discusses major points from Habakkuk 1-3.

Habakkuk and God's Dialogue—Chapters 1-3

In Chapters 1 and 2, Habakkuk questions God when he sees injustice and violent behavior unpunished. Moreover, he could not understand why evil Chaldeans were being used to punish Judah. Habakkuk's complaining to the Lord and God's reassurance to wait for an answer led him into Chapter 2, where God is revealed as a righteous God with a purpose for doing what he was doing. The book's final chapter consists of a faithful prayer by Habakkuk that contains a compelling argument that, with faith, God can work in any situation or circumstance. The dialogue captures a heartfelt exchange: Habakkuk asks how long he must call for help without getting a response, while God assures him of his divine plan. Habakkuk's prayer in Chapter 3 beautifully encapsulates his journey from questioning to trust, highlighting a transformation through faith, concluding with expressions of joy and strength in the Lord.

What Truths Can We Learn from Habakkuk?

The Book of Habakkuk provides relevant insights into God's character and how we can respond to tricky situations in our lives. Through the Prophet Habakkuk's conversations with God, valuable truths penetrate even today. See Habakkuk 1:2-3, 5, 13; 2:1, 3, 4-20; 3:18-19.

In Habakkuk, we learn that communicating with God is beneficial, and we are encouraged to talk to him about anything. We are reminded that God answers us when we pray within his will and to have faith while waiting on him. The book also teaches us to accept that God will punish sin in his timing, and we must continue to rejoice during periods of hardship and suffering. Additionally, we can trust in God to protect us from calamity and to rest in the LORD while awaiting his answers. When we become frustrated, we can turn to prayer and praise, knowing that God is still working out all things for our good, even when he is silent. Habakkuk urges us to be strong when encountering challenging circumstances and to recognize God's work even amid dire circumstances. By studying the Book of Habakkuk, we learn to trust in God's faithfulness, even when we don't understand his ways, and to rejoice in him. These truths from Habakkuk's conversations with God are timeless and applicable today.

Be Unstoppable—Go the Distance with God,

But the wisdom from above is first pure, then peace-loving, gentle, reasonable, full of mercy and good fruits, impartial, free of hypocrisy. And the fruit of righteousness is sown in peace by those who make peace.
James 3:17-18

CHAPTER 19

HANNAH: A BIBLICAL CHARACTER OF PRAYER AND WORSHIP

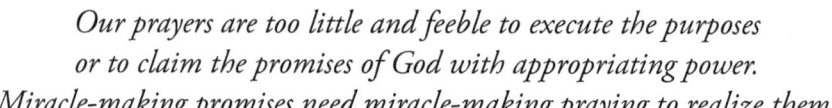

> *Our prayers are too little and feeble to execute the purposes*
> *or to claim the promises of God with appropriating power.*
> *Miracle-making promises need miracle-making praying to realize them.*
>
> E.M. Bounds

Hannah's Distress and Dedication

In the first two chapters of 1 Samuel, we encounter a touching story expressing Hannah's unwavering commitment to God. Elkanah, her husband, was married to two women—Peninnah and Hannah. While Peninnah had children, Hannah was barren. Each year, during the pilgrimage to the temple to worship and sacrifice, Hannah would weep because Peninnah would provoke her due to her having no children. Being oppressed in spirit for one year, Hannah prayed fervently and wept bitterly and made a vow that if the Lord gave her a son, she would let the priest Eli have the child for service. At first, Eli mocked her and accused her of being intoxicated. Despite his initial skepticism, he saw that she was afflicted and not drunk; he said, "Go in peace; and may the God of Israel grant your petition that you have asked of Him" (1 Sam. 1:17). In due time, Hannah conceived and gave birth to a son whom she and

Elkanah named Samuel. Hannah said, "For this boy, I prayed, and the LORD has given me my petition which I asked of him. So, I have also dedicated him to the LORD; as long as he lives he is dedicated to the LORD" (1 Sam. 1:27-28). After weaning him, they brought the boy to Eli to serve in the house of the Lord.

Hannah's Worshipful Response

Hannah started by worshiping the LORD in the temple, but we see it more profoundly after she dedicated Samuel to serve. In her beautiful *Song of Thanksgiving and Worship,* we read:

> *My heart exults in the LORD,*
> *My horn is exalted in the LORD,*
> *My mouth speaks boldly against my enemies,*
> *Because I rejoice in Thy salvation.*
> *There is no one holy like the LORD,*
> *Indeed, there is no one besides Thee,*
> *Nor is there any rock like our God.*
> *1 Samuel 2:1-2*

In *Real Worship: Playground, Battleground, or Holy Ground,* Warren Wiersbe states that while Hannah's worship journey differed from that of other biblical figures, like Abraham, Jacob, Isaiah, or Mary of Bethany, Hannah drew inspiration and elements from each of them in her worship of the Lord. For example, Hannah conversed with God (like Abraham), she made a vow (like Jacob), she heard Eli speak (like Isaiah listened to the angels), and she gave her best to the LORD—Samuel (like Mary of Bethany gave perfume).[1] Furthermore, she trusted in the promise of God when Eli told her to go in peace and that her petition would be granted.

There are multiple reasons we know she worshiped God. First, she approached the LORD with an honest and sincere heart. Second, she had a focused purpose in communicating her desire to God. Third, she waited for God with a humble attitude; we see that by Hannah's initial deep cries in the house of God that worship filled her heart even before her prayer of thanksgiving. Fourth, Hannah centered her life on God and his power by pouring her entire being into the LORD. Hannah's ultimate blessing included transforming from a barren woman to a child-bearing mother. After she conceived and weaned Samuel, her worship prayer included: a holy heart, a mouth speaking boldly against enemies, a rejoicing in her salvation, and an acknowledgment that there is no one besides God.

Our Shared Journey

In today's context, Christians can emulate Hannah's worshipful attitude, especially in times of trauma, distress, and uncertainty. Christ-followers are encouraged to be patient enough to wait on him and maintain confidence in God's provision. Being impatient can diminish confidence in the Holy Spirit leading in one's life. Like Hannah, we can pour our hearts before God, trusting in his sovereignty and wisdom. We might not go to the temple to worship, but we can attend church. We might not be experiencing barrenness, but we are experiencing something. We might not get our prayers answered as Hannah did, but as mentioned earlier, God knows the big picture of our lives, and we can trust whatever he is doing.

Be Unstoppable—Go the Distance with God,

Come, let us worship and bow down, let us kneel before the LORD our Maker. Psalm 95:6

CHAPTER 20

TRANSFORMATION TIPS FOR TEACHING AND PREACHING

> *What good is truth if it has no transforming element in my life?*
>
> A.W. Tozer

Despite my background as an elementary school teacher and Bible instructor, I find delving into preaching books more captivating than teaching books. I have read preaching books since 1975 when I was first introduced to them while hanging around seminary students. They seem much more interesting to me than reading books on teaching.

While my focus has always leaned toward Christian theology over Christian education, I found preaching books improved my teaching methods more. When I read, I often change the words *preach* and *preacher* to *teach* and *teacher*. Additionally, I change the word "sermon" to either "class" or "lesson" and replace "sermon" with "lesson" or "class".

Visiting My College Campus

Even today, I enjoy perusing college books on multiple topics. Absorbing knowledge (even if I don't remember anything) from multiple degree plans captivates my attention, even if momentarily—but, as far as I am concerned, the math shelves could be roped off indefinitely.

One day I visited the Baylor University bookstore as a graduate. I noticed all the textbooks were roped off in preparation for the fall semester to begin. I asked one of the student employees if I could jump the rope to examine the selection of the theology books. Fortunately, this student said, "Sure! Just go around this way," and pointed me in the right direction. Without delay, I looked at all the theology books ready to be bought by the eager religion and seminary students on campus. Through scanning, skimming, and sometimes speedreading, I ran across a book titled *On Preaching: Personal & Pastoral Insights for the Preparation & Practice of Preaching* by H.B. Charles, Jr.[1] After flipping through the pages, scanning the chapter titles, and reading the book's back cover, I decided this book might be another book for my library collection—one that would help me become a better Bible *teacher*. The book was informative, easy to read, and reignited my teaching passion.

The three "Table of Contents" chapter titles are

1. Preparation for Preaching
2. The Practice of Preaching
3. Points of Wisdom for Preaching

While the original chapter titles focused on preaching, I mentally adapted them to align with the subject of teaching.

1. How To Prepare for a Teaching Assignment
2. What does The Practice of Teaching Entail
3. Tidbits of Wisdom for Teaching

Even if you have been *preaching* or *teaching* for a long time, this book is an excellent resource for beginning and seasoned *preachers* and beginning or seasoned Bible *teachers*. You never know when God will present a preaching or teaching journey to you, and you don't have to be in so called "ministry" to partake in this God-given responsibility and joy

Teaching Tips

Charles clearly states the tremendous responsibility of preparing to be all God intends you to be for the work he has called you to do. However, there are some tips for those involved in *teaching* classes within a church environment—like Sunday School, Discipleship Training, Men's or Women's Bible study classes, and unique *teaching* times. There are also ways one does not usually think of when talking about the gift of teaching—like being an elder, clarifying religious issues to a visitor or member, evangelizing, teaching an everyday skill, and more.

In *On Preaching*, Charles states, "There are those who draw a hard distinction between *preaching* and *teaching*. But this dichotomy cannot be backed up by Scripture. In the same verse that Paul charges Timothy to *preach* the Word, he bids him do so with "complete patience and *teaching*: Preaching and *teaching* go together.

To preach the Word requires *teaching* the Word, although some differences abound. In the following insights, all the italicized words have changed from the word *preaching* or *teaching*, or a derivative, from the original statements pulled out from this book. Charles' profundity expresses thoughts about *teaching* and *preaching* much more eloquently than I can.

Quotations From *on Preaching* from H.B. Charles

- Time management is one of the most crucial areas of stewardship in a *teacher's* life.

- Do whatever you have to do to be ready to *teach* the Word of God and the testimony of Jesus Christ!

- Your *teaching* is the most effective way you can impact your class.

- Pray that the Lord would open your eyes to see wonderful things in the Word.

- Saturate every part of your study with prayer. Pray that Christ would oversee your study. Trust the Holy Spirit to lead you to the truth. Seek the mind of God in the text. Repent as the text confronts you with sin in your life. Pray for wisdom as you read. Ask for clarity as you write.

- Work as if it all depends on you, but pray as if it all depends on God.

- Think of yourself empty. Read yourself full. Write yourself clear. And pray yourself hot. Then go to your class and be yourself. But don't *teach* yourself—teach Jesus to the glory of God!

- [PRAY] Father, please give me the physical strength and spiritual energy to speak your Word with faithfulness, clarity, authority, passion, wisdom, humiliation, and liberty.

- Clarity is essential for faithful *teaching*.

- The *teacher's* ultimate authority is found in the Word of God.

- What the Word of God says is infinitely more important than our testimonials.

- The *teaching* moment is not about you. We must decrease that Christ may increase.

- Our job is to *teach* in such a way that brings the hearer before the living God. Then we are to get out of the way! But our sinful flesh will constantly seek to be in the spotlight.

- Prayer helps to keep our egos in check. It helps us to *teach* with a humility that makes much of Christ and little of ourselves.

- Every class we *teach* should be saturated with the Word of God.

- We should *teach* with the conviction that the Bible is given to us for our transformation, not just information.

- Go to God in prayer and ask Him to guide you for what you should *teach*. Ask for clear direction. Seek God diligently. Trust the promise that God will generously give wisdom to those who ask for it in faith.

- *Teaching* is hard work. It is not for the slothful.

- We all have weaknesses in our *teaching*. We all have growing to do. We all have blind spots that cannot be seen without trusted people being honest with us. But those blind spots are there, whether we identify them or not. We should actively seek them out and strive to address them.

- Keep the main thing the main thing in your classes, and do not let subdivisions of your outline lead you away from the main idea.

- The class will never be interested in a lesson that doesn't seem to be interesting to *the teacher*.

- The effective *teacher* must also work to clarify meaning, make ideas stick, and call the listener to action.

- Be flexible. The [one] who guides the preparation of your study governs the presentation of it. And he has the right to edit your presentation as you *teach it!* Your job is to *teach* the message the Lord gives you and he leads you, not to say everything you wrote in your lesson preparation.

- Take every *teaching* assignment seriously. Pray and prepare diligently and give the Lord all you've got.

- Desire to be the best *teacher* you can be for God. Don't compete with other *teachers*.

- *Teaching* is not about the *teacher*. It is about the royal message that we *teach*.

- No Christian should ever be found boasting in himself, especially a *teacher* of Jesus Christ.

- People should learn more about Christ from your lessons than they learn about you.

- Do your own homework. [Never plagiarize another's work. If you quote others or take from their writings or sermons, give credit where credit is due.]

- [Remember] God uses weak people, not gospel superstars. We are weak and fragile clay pots at the Master's disposal to convey the treasure of the message of Jesus Christ.

- Do your best to present yourself to God as one approved, a worker who has no need to be ashamed, rightly handling the [w]ord of truth.[2]

Be Unstoppable—Go the Distance with God,

When Jesus had finished giving instructions to His twelve disciples, He departed from there to teach and preach in their cities.
Matthew 11:1

CHAPTER 21

REVOLUTIONIZING LIFE THROUGH PRAYER AND BIBLE STUDY

We look upon prayer simply as a means of getting things for ourselves, but the biblical purpose of prayer is that we may get to know God Himself.

Oswald Chambers

E ngaging in prayer and Bible study can profoundly revolutionize one's personal life, offering the comfort and security we all seek.

Prayer

In the charming children's story, *The Relatives Came*, by Cynthia Rylant, a child's extended clan gathered one afternoon to enjoy each other's company amid laughter, love, and family festivities. What better summer day could any child have, other than relishing the comfort and security of aunts, uncles, and cousins?[1]

Similarly, during a summer vacation in 1962, my scattered relatives converged in Connecticut, where my grandmother and aunt lived. My relatives came from everywhere—California, New Mexico, Pennsylvania, and Vermont for a similar "kinfolk" reunion. As an eight-year-old child, dressed in my blue-flowered tunic and shorts, I stood in my aunt and uncle's backyard mesmerized by the hustle and bustle of summer activities. The adults ran in and out of the house, preparing for the long-awaited family summertime barbeque. My relatives were laughing, smiling, and just plain old, happy to be together. The picnic and card tables were covered with red and white checkered tablecloths. The tea was poured, the aroma from the barbequed hot dogs and hamburgers permeated the backyard. From my vantage point, I could see the bright blue sky surrounded by the tall New England trees. I remember my mind vividly centered on God. I wanted to test God's power by praying for rain, and a request granted that day reaffirmed God's response to a sincere, childlike prayer. I wanted to know if I could pray for rain even though no sign of rain was evident anywhere, knowing that rain would ruin our family celebration. I prayed for rain. And rain it did, just as Psalm 77:17 says, "the clouds poured out water." As we readied ourselves to eat, tiny rain droplets slowly landed on my head. Before long, more significant, heavier drops began streaming down from the sky. My aunt made the final call, waving us all into the house. "Hey kids and everyone, we are moving everything inside! Grab something and get inside NOW!" I never told my relatives that I was the cause of the rain that day, but God chose that incident to show me that he can move mountains and change the minute events in our lives through honest, sincere, childlike prayer.

Do I believe God answered my prayer? Yes, most certainly! I asked, and God answered. I am not saying he always answers so quickly or affirmatively, but he did that day. Why? Because in the big scheme of my life, maybe God needed me to experience His "realness" and "power."

We pray prayers like

> *"God, give me strength and healing in my sickness."*
> *"Lord, I don't understand why my son/daughter has turned against you."*
> *"I don't know when to retire. I am seeking your timing as I move into the next stage of my life."*

Day after day, these types of prayers reach God's throne. God hears them all and takes notes of all of them, even Cornelius' prayer. "Cornelius, God has heard your prayer and remembered your gifts to the poor" (Acts 10:31). God hears our prayers and remembers all our deeds. He is ready to answer our requests, but we must do our part—that, is to pray and seek out his wisdom and direction by familiarizing ourselves with his Word, the Bible.

Bible Study

The Barna Group, a market research firm specializing in studying Americans' religious beliefs and behavior, has carefully and strategically tracked the role of faith in America, developing one of the nation's most comprehensive databases of spiritual indicators. Since 2011, Barna and the American Bible Society have collaborated to assess the State of the Bible, compiling one of the most extensive databases regarding public perceptions and engagement with the Bible. They define Bible users as people who engage (read, listen to, or pray) with the Bible at least three to four times a year outside a church or church event. In their 2023 report, Barna revealed a notable decline in Bible engagement, with only 39% of Americans maintaining a 2-3 engagement per year. On the other hand, individuals who do not regularly engage with the Bible still recognize its importance as a value in our society. While the frequency of Bible engagement appears to be decreasing, there remains a large acknowledgment of its significance of personal and the well-being in the American society.[2]

While the frequency of Bible engagement appears to be decreasing, a large acknowledgment of its significance for one's personal and well-being in the American society abounds.

Prayer and Bible reading are inseparable; they go together. Prayer involves communicating with God, and the Bible is God communicating with us. Embracing the Word of God and expanding our biblical knowledge is the key to learning the beautiful truths of our God. Early in my Christian walk, I learned to value the Bible. Unfortunately, some believers don't pray or read the Bible at all or in a limited capacity. While their reasons may vary, many believe the following:

- Why pray and read the Bible when God will do whatever he wants to anyway?

- Nothing will happen when I pray.

- I don't have the time or the discipline to pray or read the Bible.

- I tried praying before, and nothing happened.

- The Bible isn't relevant to me.

My response to that is:

- Prayer and Bible reading make us become more like Jesus.

- God will comfort us through prayer and his Word when we need it.

- Prayer and reading the Bible teach us how to model ourselves after Jesus.

- We need to find, know, and understand God's will for our lives. The Holy Spirit, prayer and the God's words help us discern his will.

- Prayer and Bible study make us aware of evil while helping us to recognize our sins and the necessity of forgiveness.

- Prayer and embracing God's Word help us to submit to God and resist Satan.

- Prayer and Bible reading protect us from evil.

Prayer and Bible study complement each other like egg yolks and egg whites—one offering spiritual nourishment and the other physical nourishment. Spiritual nourishment provides comfort, security, and confidence in God's overarching plan for our lives. As we seek his guidance through prayer and immerse ourselves in his Word, we align ourselves with his will, finding strength, solace, and protection.

If you have never read the entire Bible, I encourage you to do so.

Discovering who God is, uncovering more about yourself, and receiving inspiration and insights will supply you with an understanding that only the Holy Spirit can give. You will be joyfully surprised in what you learn—many call those God's "Aha" moments, experienced by many legendary Bible personas. But they can happen to us as well in determining our life's work, our purpose, and our character.

Be Unstoppable—Go the Distance with God,

Be anxious for nothing, but in everything by prayer and supplication with thanksgiving let your requests be made to God, And the peace of God, which surpasses all comprehension, shall guard your hearts and minds in Christ Jesus. Philippians 4:6-7

CHAPTER 22

CONTINUING TO SERVE GOD WHILE AGING

Aging does not have to mean reducing our service to the Lord. As I recently filled out my health history at my new cardiologist's office, I reminded myself I have gray hair and crepey skin, and my weight loss program is not cutting it most weeks. Richard Stefanacci defines aging in the *Merck Manual* as "a gradual, continuous process of natural change that begins in early adulthood."[1] He believes becoming old is answered by looking at our chronological, biological, and psychological age. But nothing is mentioned about our spiritual age, which is a significant matter. Let's consider why some Christ-followers discontinue working for the Lord as they age, and the importance of renewing a relationship with the Lord until one's body or cognition completely disappears.

Reasons our Service Diminishes with Age

Multiple factors influence why aging folks cease working heartily, grow weary, or drop out of church altogether. Some are physical limitations, such as driving restrictions or a change in living location. In other cases, medical reasons, such as eyesight, hearing, and mobility issues affect one's ability to attend, let alone serve. However, some offer frivolous "reasons" for spiritual inactivity. They may believe the pastor isn't "feeding" them anymore or feel worthless or left out at church. Others lose focus and fall away from the one true path, instead enjoying a sinful lifestyle or becoming distracted by golfing, lake houses, and stock investments. These circumstances and interferences can make serving the Lord challenging. This is understandable. Fortunately, many still can experience a godly presence where they are.

Hope and Renewal

If you fit into the category of one who has lost the joy of your salvation but wants to experience God again, there is hope. In *Experiencing the Presence of God,* Tozer states, "Almost all who preach or write on the subject of faith have much the same things to say concerning it. They tell us that it is believing a promise, that it is taking God at his word, that it is reckoning the Bible to be true and stepping out upon it."[2] God promises peace through trials, and his comfort stays. Praise God if you have faithfully served him your entire Christian life and continue to do so by serving, studying the Bible, meditating and seeking him. But if you have been a "pew sitter" for most of your Christian life, or one who has strayed or drifted from the Lord, understand there is no age limit where you can't seek God again.

Death is inevitable. One never knows when that final day will come upon us. A few years ago, on the day a new season was to start in my life, I fell headfirst down 13 wooden stairs. A trip to the emergency room confirmed a concussion. I had read enough to know many such falls are fatal. Deep in my spirit during my recovery period, the Lord revealed the experience was to show me he was not finished with me yet. I needed that word to keep going and not waste my life on triviality. God is not through with you, either. You may have messed up. However, the Lord wants you to kindle anew your life, and it can be done. He will come along and pick you up right where you are. And he can and wants to do it today. It is not too late. Your age is irrelevant to God. He wants you to return to the fold.

How to Start a Relationship with the Lord

All ages, young and seasoned, should want their life to be pleasing in his sight. Surrendering as entirely as you can to the Lord, deciding to live righteously, repenting, and confessing sins, start the journey to beginning or renewing a relationship with the Lord.

Below, I am outlining the contents of the bookmark titled "How to Experience New Life in Christ." This bookmark features guidelines designed for individuals of all ages, providing practical tips on how to grow in their faith and finish their spiritual journey well with the Lord. As someone who is enthusiastic about bookmarks, I find these statements absolutely true!

How to Experience New Life in Christ

1. Everyone is a sinner and is separated from God (Rom. 3:23).
2. God loved us all so much that He gave His Son to die for our sins (Rom. 5:8).
3. Death means separation forever from God. Eternal life comes by trusting Jesus Christ (Rom. 6:23).
4. In order to begin your new life to Christ (be saved), you must believe that Jesus died for your sins and declare that you accept Him as Savior (Rom. 10:9).
5. This is God's promise to you if you accept Jesus. He will accept you (Rom.10:13).[3]

If you want to accept Jesus into your life, that's a really important choice! You can do it by saying a special prayer. Start by asking God to forgive all the things you've done wrong and let him know that you believe Jesus died for you. Tell him you want to welcome Jesus as your Lord and Savior. Remember, it's not just about saying the words; it's about starting an amazing journey with God that can change your life!

For All Believers, Young and Seasoned

- Avoid things that seek to take God's place in your heart. Pursue God in all areas of your life.

- Ask God to give you a hunger for his Word. Read your Bible, seek his will, and pray daily.

- Allow the Lord to speak to you through Scripture and his Holy Spirit. Thank the Lord for a second, third or fourth chance for allowing his presence in your life.

Here am I. Send Me.

The Prophet Isaiah told the Lord: "Here am I. Send me" (Isa. 6:8). The Lord used Isaiah powerfully, pleading for repentance and a restored life for the people of Judah. If God could use Isaiah during a time of profound sinning among the people, he also can use you. As a growing, restored, or new believer, you may be surprised at the circumstances God places in your life. Ask God to show you them and then act upon his direction. In my life, I have seen how one act of obedience leads me to the next experience or training I need from him, and the process snowballs year after year. As I did, you will gradually notice the fruits of the Spirit emerging in your life (Gal. 5:22-23).

Paul wrote:

> *Brothers and sisters, I do not regard myself as having taken hold of it yet; but one thing I do: forgetting what lies behind and reaching forward to what lies ahead, I press on toward the goal for the prize of the upward call of God in Christ Jesus (Philippians 3:14-15).*

As for me, I will continue using my age-renewing crepe-corrector body lotion, because the tube says it will visibly improve my skin, but that is for the external "me." But I am more concerned with the internal, and I pray you will be, too.[4]

Be Unstoppable—Go the Distance with God,

But if anyone does not provide for his own, and especially for those of his household, he has denied the faith and is worse than an unbeliever.
1 Timothy 5:8

SECTION 3

Navigating the
Path of Christian Living and
Biblical Characters

CHAPTER 23

SOLOMON'S WISDOM

> *Wisdom knows the difference between insight and judgmentalism.*
> *Wisdom discerns the intent of the heart.*
> *Wisdom knows when to speak strongly and when to speak redemptively.*
>
> John Bisango

The *Elementary Bible Truths Handbook* defines *wisdom* as "the ability to use one's knowledge and experience to make good judgments."[1] While this is a good general definition, it does not differentiate between secular wisdom and godly wisdom. The late Pastor Adrian Rogers bridged this gap by saying, "Wisdom is seeing life from God's point of view. When you pray and have the Spirit of God and the Word of God in you, you will begin to have wisdom. Knowledge comes by looking around, but wisdom comes by looking up. God will lead you and give you wisdom. When a person is walking in the Spirit, he can say, "I have the mind of Christ. [I'm] not afraid to trust what the Spirit says. That is not natural; it is supernatural."[2]

Solomon's Wisdom and Saga

1 Kings 3:16-28 puts godly wisdom in the forefront. King Solomon is tasked to solve a dispute between two women. This story unfurls a gripping tail at the apex of divine wisdom. It has all the drama, including two bickering prostitutes, a "she said, she said" scenario, no witnesses, and two babies—one dead and one alive. With the clash of personalities,

ambiguous testimony, and a life-and-death decision, its plot could easily fit on a daytime drama set.

Guiding Light: The Search for Wisdom

Solomon was King David's son from his wife Bathsheba. His upbringing in a highly wealthy household allowed him to have just about every privilege a child raised by a godly king could expect—fine food, a good education, religious training, little conflict, and more.

Solomon's life was most likely free of conflict until it was time for him to ascend to the throne of Israel. His brother Adonijah tried to force a coup, doing all he could to get the kingship for himself that David already promised to Solomon. Fortunately, he did overthrow Adonijah's attempt to rule Israel and became king.

Solomon knew he needed God's wisdom to enlarge the kingdom and construct the temple his father David had already prepared for him to erect. Solomon loved God, and as a young ruler, he wanted the wisdom to rule this vast kingdom fittingly. Knowing he needed to dedicate himself totally to the Lord, he sought wisdom and guidance. In a dream at Gibeon, not far from Jerusalem, he offered multiple sacrifices to the Lord. Then, God came to him in a dream and asked Solomon to ask him for anything he desired.

God said, "Ask what you wish Me to give you." Solomon responded.

You have shown great lovingkindness to Your servant David, my father, according as he walked before You in truth and righteousness and uprightness of heart toward You; and You have reserved for him this great lovingkindness, that You have given him a son to sit on his throne, as it is this day. Now, O Lord my God, You have made Your servant king in place of my father David, yet I am but a little child; I do not know how to go out or come in. Your servant is in the midst of Your people which You have chosen, a great people who are too many to be numbered or counted (1 Kings 3:5b-8).

Then in 1 Kings 3:9, Solomon specifically asked God for his wisdom.

So give Your servant an understanding heart to judge Your people to discern between good and evil. For who is able to judge this great people of Yours? (1 Kings 3:9).

Solomon wanted to administer justice and judgment using true godly discernment. It was customary in those days for ordinary people to have access to the king, and he took his job seriously. Shortly after asking for wisdom, Solomon was introduced to two prostitutes, both seeking to resolve a dispute between them and a living baby.

One Life to Live: Solomon Judges Wisely

Two women, temple prostitutes, gave birth to sons around the same time. One night one of the woman's babies died because she laid on him. The distraught woman took the other woman's son and laid him in her bosom and laid her dead son in the other woman's bosom. When the other woman rose to nurse her baby, there was a dead baby lying with her. She knew that was not her son. The women argued about whose baby the live baby belonged to. Not being able to resolve the issue, the two women came to King Solomon, because he was good and wise for justice. These two temple prostitutes, or should I say, these two distraught mothers, stood before King Solomon, waiting for his judgment as to which woman should be allowed to keep the live baby. Solomon told his men to bring him a sword and divide the child in half and give half to each of the women. One of the women said, "No!" She knew the living son was hers, but she said to give him to the other woman so he would live. The other woman said to divide the baby, so neither of them would have the baby. Solomon then knew which was the mother of the child, and he said to give the baby to the woman who does not want the child divided. Solomon was wise, but he never intended to follow through on dividing the baby. He was looking to see which woman had the most compassion toward the child to find the birth mother. And he did!

> And the king said, "Divide the living child in two, and give half to the one and half to the other; the first woman whose child was the living one spoke to the king, for she was deeply stirred over her son and said, 'Oh, my Lord, give her the living child, and by no means kill him." But the other said, "He shall be neither mine nor yours; divide him!'" Then the king answered and said, "Give the first woman the living child, and by no means kill him. She is his mother. When all Israel heard of the judgment which the king had

handed down they feared the king; for they saw that the wisdom of God was in him to administer justice" (1 Kings 3:25-28).

Most mothers can recognize their children, especially after days of loving and caring for them. However, the disagreement over the newborn's "ownership" continued to the top court. King Solomon was not privy to DNA testing and listened to both women's sides. He gathered facts and information. Although Solomon had many responsibilities, as kings do, such as peacemaker, builder, worshiper, administrator, and scholar, this was his opportunity to be a discerner, noted Wiersbe.[4] Solomon was looking for the birth mother. Most Bibles and commentaries refer to the first woman mentioned in the story as the natural mother and the second woman mentioned as the untruthful mother. Both mothers were distressed—one because she knew she might lose her baby, and the other one because she lost her baby, and her maternal instincts were so strong that she was willing to lie and deceive to have any baby.

God works out the most magnificent things and coordinates situations in his timing to serve for the glory of God. In this case, God took two prostitutes: they lived in the same house, allowed them to get pregnant at the same time, and had them deliver their babies three days apart—as a catalyst for the people of Israel to see his wisdom. This incident was the primary conversation piece in Israel for weeks and maybe months. Solomon's wisdom displayed that he deserved his reputation as a genuinely wise king.

We live in a time different from the 900s BC. Today, we encounter obstacles just like the people did in Solomon's day. Many times, we need wise people to arbitrate our difficulties and problems. Right now, we might be like the first woman in this story desperately needing advice or the second woman who lied and deceived, or we might even be like Solomon—the one to whom people come for leadership or arbitration. Following King Solomon's example, let us do what he did and commit to following God's wisdom.

Sixteen Steps the Bible Provides as We Seek God's Wisdom

The Bible provides us with various steps we should follow as we seek wisdom.

1. Ask for wisdom. Solomon asked for God's wisdom. (1 Kings 3:9; James 1:5).
2. Fear the Lord (Job 28:28) and love him. (Psalm 107:43).
3. Gain knowledge (Colossians 3:16) by reading and becoming knowledgeable in the Word - both the Old and New Testament. (2 Timothy 3:15).
4. Apply the Word (Ephesians 2:10) by being peaceful and considerate. (James 3:17).
5. Hold our tongue. (Proverbs 10:19).
6. Offer good counsel. (Psalm 37:30).
7. Listen to advice. (Proverbs 15:31).
8. Control our temper. (Proverbs 19:11).
9. Turn away from evil. (Proverbs 3:7).
10. Reduce distractions in our lives, such as idols like materialism, education, self-centeredness, social media, and jealousy. (Exodus 20:3).
11. Be humble. (not proud) (Proverbs 11:2).
12. Do not boast. (James 4:16).
13. Pray for discernment. (Proverbs 17:24).
14. Pray and meditate in his presence. (Joshua 1:8).
15. Repent as needed. (Acts 3:19).
16. Win souls. (Proverbs 11:30). By following these steps, we can journey towards wisdom and draw closer to the Lord.

Just like with the story of the two temple prostitutes, we see bad behaviors today. In Lance Benzel's February 2020 article, Juliette Parker, a former Colorado Springs mayoral candidate, posed as a "friendly" baby photographer to steal Elysia Miller's newborn child. Meeting Miller on Facebook's newborn baby site, they connected. Parker met under the guise of taking free baby pictures to build up her portfolio and administered GHB—the date rape drug—to Miller to steal her newborn baby. Fortunately, Miller, after feeling drowsy, called 911, and the plot was averted.[5]

While we live in a world with moral quandaries and ethical problems, the timeless wisdom of Soloman's early leadership can illuminate our paths. It may be difficult after we have been lied to, deceived, humiliated, criticized, or disregarded, but God has a purpose for each and every one of us. Living fully dedicated to the Lord is costly, but wisdom is supreme. Therefore, get wisdom! Though it costs all you have, get his wisdom and understanding. Then, we are on the path to divine insights and illuminations and becoming unstoppable in our love and service to our God.

Be Unstoppable—Go the Distance with God,

For the Lord gives wisdom: From his mouth come knowledge and understanding.
Proverbs 2:6

CHAPTER 24

CHOOSING GOD'S PATH

> *If you love to walk in God's company,*
> *you must abide in your place and calling.*
>
> William Gurnall

God has a path for believers in Jesus Christ. The Bible calls it the path of life. Do you feel you are on the right path in life? Do you want to follow the Lord closely? Or are you slipping slowly down the wrong path? As a child, I used to grab ten to fifteen Little Golden Books at a time and read one after another. One that always attracted me was *Scuffy the Tugboat* by Gertrude Crampton.[1] Scuffy was an adventurous little tugboat who believed he was meant for bigger things. He leaves his home, the man with the polka-dot tie, and the little boy who cared for him, and sets off to explore the world. After his daring and treacherous adventure down a brook and then a raging river, Scuffy realizes home is where he'd rather be. Twice during his adventure, Scuffy said, "This is the life for me." The first time, he was leaving his prior sensible life to seek adventure. The second time was when he realized he already had been right where he needed to be all along—at home, safe in the arms of the man and boy who loved him. God wants us to understand that we can know our path. Hopefully, it is the one he has set apart for us, but we must choose it. And it doesn't always mean staying where you are.

Decision: Make a Choice for Righteousness or Unrighteousness

In Psalms 16, King David declares he wants refuge in the Lord. In his communion with the Lord, he writes. "You make known to me the path of life; in your presence there is fullness of joy: at your right hand are pleasures forevermore (Ps. 16:11 ESV)." God wants us to be on the path of righteousness. In the *Tyndale Old Testament Commentary* on Psalms 1–72, Derek Kidner defines a person on the right path of life as one whose affections are centered on God. This person finds satisfaction in God's ways and does not pursue other gods. God's protection and instruction bless him.[2] Life involves important decisions. We can choose to accept Jesus Christ as our Lord and Savior or decide not to. Additionally, we can choose whether or not to follow God's ways and principles. The first step is to make sure our hearts are aligned with God by confessing our sins and accepting the gift of life that Jesus offers. Once we do this, we can be confident that our future holds eternal life. However, even after making this commitment, we will still face spiritual struggles, but the Lord will be by our side through them. Just like David, we can trust that the Lord will guide us on the right path in life. The righteous want to walk in victory, but sometimes we find ourselves desiring things God has proclaimed unsuitable for us. We have that struggle between the spirit (righteousness) and our flesh (unrighteousness), so we must seriously ponder what foundational path we are on and where we want to be. Notwithstanding, people cannot experience God's true purpose when they travel the destructive path. We may find ourselves in a continuous cycle of repeatedly sinning and confessing. To break that cycle, we must deny ourselves, take up Jesus' cross and follow him.

And he [Jesus] was saying to them all,

> *If anyone wishes to come after me, he must deny himself, and take up his cross daily and follow me (Luke 9:23).*

> *In the way of righteousness is life, and in its pathway, there is no death … (Proverbs 10:28).*

> *If we confess our sins, he is faithful and just and will forgive us our sins and purify us from all unrighteousness (1 John 1:9).*

Reroute and Redirect

A navigation system is an instrument that determines a vehicle's position and route to a particular place. The navigation system tells the driver to turn left or right at a specific junction. It is a valuable tool with many benefits, such as helping people reach their destination, guiding drivers through congested areas, tracking packages, locating vehicles and more. It is similar to the way God directs us in our lives. He shows us which way to turn, signals us on which way to proceed, helps us reach the destination and call of our lives, and guides us continually through the rough times in our lives. He will reroute and direct our thoughts or actions if we genuinely want to follow his path. Our navigation system must take its orders from the Lord. He will reroute and redirect our thoughts and actions if we genuinely want to follow his path.

This is "The Life for Me"

Scuffy's journey seemed promising at the outset, presenting a facade of adventure and opportunity. Yet, beneath that appealing exterior, it revealed a path fraught with challenges that compromised his true well-being. What appeared to be a beautiful journey led him away from the fulfillment he sought, illustrating the profound lesson that not all that glitters truly serves our highest good. While Scuffy enjoyed some of life's simple pleasures, he kept traveling along the river, he was jammed with logs and became scared of the river moving faster and faster. As the floodwaters rose, the tugboat sought security and protection of its home harbor.

God can do the same for us as we travel our life's paths; He gives us security and protection. Just like the man with the polka-dot tie who scooped Scuffy out of the water after his journey away and brought him home, God will do the same for us when we choose him, live for him, decide to follow righteousness, and allow him to reroute us when we stumble.[3]

Be Unstoppable—Go the Distance with God,

The path of the godly leads to life. So why fear death?
Proverbs 12:28 LB

CHAPTER 25

CROSSING THE JORDAN: EMBRACING CHANGE

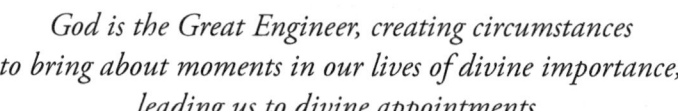

> *God is the Great Engineer, creating circumstances*
> *to bring about moments in our lives of divine importance,*
> *leading us to divine appointments.*
>
> Oswald Chambers

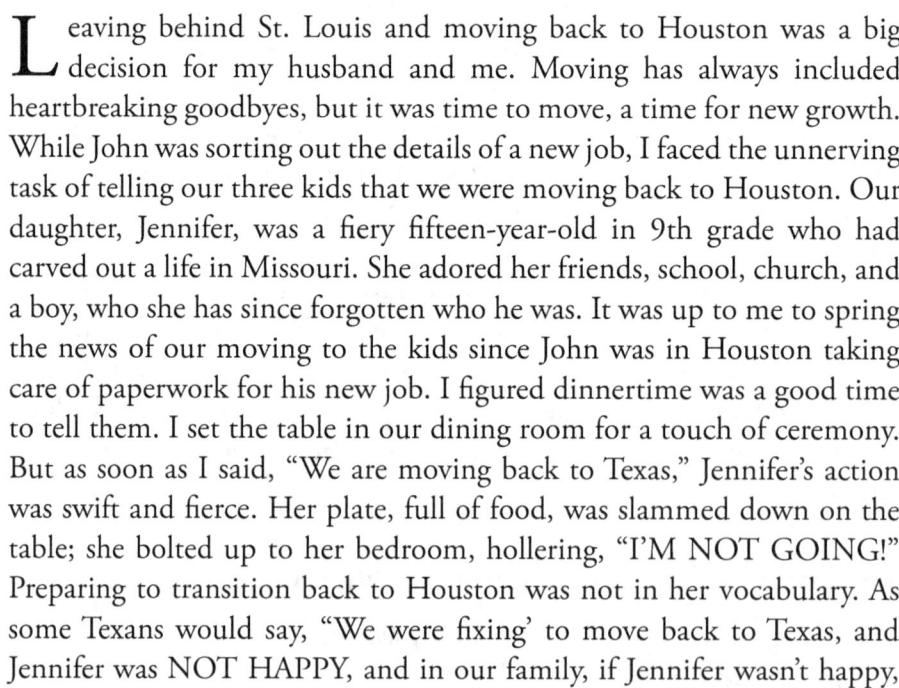

Leaving behind St. Louis and moving back to Houston was a big decision for my husband and me. Moving has always included heartbreaking goodbyes, but it was time to move, a time for new growth. While John was sorting out the details of a new job, I faced the unnerving task of telling our three kids that we were moving back to Houston. Our daughter, Jennifer, was a fiery fifteen-year-old in 9th grade who had carved out a life in Missouri. She adored her friends, school, church, and a boy, who she has since forgotten who he was. It was up to me to spring the news of our moving to the kids since John was in Houston taking care of paperwork for his new job. I figured dinnertime was a good time to tell them. I set the table in our dining room for a touch of ceremony. But as soon as I said, "We are moving back to Texas," Jennifer's action was swift and fierce. Her plate, full of food, was slammed down on the table; she bolted up to her bedroom, hollering, "I'M NOT GOING!" Preparing to transition back to Houston was not in her vocabulary. As some Texans would say, "We were fixing' to move back to Texas, and Jennifer was NOT HAPPY, and in our family, if Jennifer wasn't happy, no one was happy." I experienced the same thing when my parents moved from Pittsburgh, Pennsylvania, to Houston, Texas when I was in high school. And a boy was involved in my picture, too. I hurt and empathized with her, but this was to be her path, as it was mine.

Life is one big transition with many other transitions in between. There will be expected, unexpected, and even traumatic transitions. We transition from 1st to 2nd grade, and from high school to college. We encounter changes when a tree falls on our house, in car accidents, and in the death of friends and loved ones. Transitions and change are part of life. However, we can successfully transition from Point A to Point B by following the same principles the Israelites used to cross the Jordan River to reach the Promised Land. Moses and the Israelites originally crossed the Red Sea, but because of their unbelief and disobedience, they never made it to the Promised Land. Now Joshua was about to cross the Jordan with a new breed of Israelites who took God by his word. And unlike their predecessors, they embraced faith over fear. Let's explore the principles relevant to them and to us today!

Principle 1: Trust in Wise Leadership

The Israelites anchored themselves to Joshua, a leader chosen by God himself. Unlike Absalom, who heeded unwise counsel, Joshua followed divine counsel. In 2 Samuel, Absalom willingly listened to advice from Ahithophel, David's former advisor. He advised Absalom to defeat King David, God's ANOINTED, to gain kingship. In the end, Absalom died a grueling death while fleeing from King David's army. Do we sometimes depend on wrong, unwise, ungodly leaders to give advice on our transitions? In the Book of Joshua, the people did not get inferior advice like Ahithophel did. Joshua led with trustworthy leadership skills and a previous proven style as Moses' aid. Joshua was a leader worthy of being followed. A leader knows the way and can help others reach their goals. God was with Joshua and told him to be strong and courageous. God said that not only once but thrice in Chapters 1: 6, 9, and 18.

If you need heart surgery, you will not go to a foot doctor and ask him to perform your surgery, would you? No, you would seek out the best cardiologist you could find—one with experience, good tools, good education, and proven results showing they know what they are doing.

And what does that mean to us? It implies that we must trust the best of the best whenever we anticipate a new season. God first, but then we must trust the Bible and the godly people Jesus puts in our path. We should not trust in false leaders, questionable books, X, Alexa, artificial intelligence tools, or any religious online podcast without discerning the Spirit within them.

God tells Joshua,

> *No man can stand before you all the days of your life. Just as I have been with Moses, I will be with you; I will not fail you or forsake you. Be strong and courageous for you shall give this people possession of the land which I swore to their fathers to give them (Joshua 1:5-6),*

Along with following wise advice, we must also meditate and pray.

Principle 2: Find Strength in Faith and Reflection

Moses had already commissioned Joshua to lead the new generation of Israelites to the Promised Land. But before crossing the Jordan, Joshua immersed himself in meditation and prayer, drawing strength from the Scriptures.

In the Book of Joshua, God told Joshua to meditate.

> *This book of the law shall not depart from your mouth, but you shall meditate on it day and night, so that you may be careful to do according to all that is written in it; For then you will make your way prosperous, and then you will have success (Joshua 1:8).*

Meditation, in the biblical sense. involves reflecting deeply on God's Word, allowing it to shape our thoughts, desires, and actions. This practice sanctifies the mind and draws us closer to Christ. To meditate means to ponder. The LORD told Joshua to meditate on the Law— meaning the Scriptures at that time— day and night. To meditate, we need to think, be quiet before the Lord, and have the desire to think things through, especially when transitioning from one place to another.

Christian meditation should not be confused with secular meditation. Christian meditation involves a quietness before the Lord, allowing the Holy Spirit to touch our hearts and give us an understanding of himself.

This meditation involves God filling us with himself, while secular meditation involves emptying ourselves. The problem is we do not know what will fill us, but with godly meditation, we can expect and anticipate an entangling of our spirit with God's holiness.

This principle is illustrated in Psalm 1:2 where King David tells us that God delights in us when we meditate day and night on his instructions. Joshua knew that whatever lay ahead for him, hearing God's Word and meditating on it would be valuable. Before the actual crossing of the Jordan, Joshua tells the people to "Consecrate themselves for tomorrow the LORD will do amazing things..." He was setting the people apart, to be holy, through meditation, prayer, and the Scriptures. The Bible has answers in how to do that for us—ALWAYS!

> *But his delight is in the Law of the Lord, And on His Law he meditates day and night*
> *(Psalm 1:2).*

> *Tremble, and do not sin; Meditate in your heart upon your bed, and be still (Psalm 4:4),*

> *Do not be anxious about anything, but in everything by prayer and pleading with thanksgiving let your requests be made known to God (Philippians 4:6.).*

A well-known pastor told the story about how every Thursday is his trash day. He brings the trash to his curb in plenty of time for them to pick it up. But he noticed he had never had a trashman come to his front door and ring the doorbell, asking where his trash was if he forgot to put it out. The moral of this story is we must bring our concerns to Christ. He doesn't say to wait and do nothing. We need to take the step of taking our decisions and upcoming transition decisions to him.[1]

As for us, we must act and confess our sins, anxiety, and concerns to the Lord. We must follow solid teaching, leaders and meditate on the holy Word of God. Then, and only then, will we be prepared for the changes in our lives. We pray and meditate because it calms our nerves. Some trials are complex, and difficulties are expected, but when we live a life empowered by God, we find strength in our faith.

Principle 3: Prepare for the Journey

Preparation is the cornerstone of successful transitions. As we face moves, changes, and transitions, we must remember that God already knows everything about us.

In Psalm 139:1-3 King David mentions that God has searched him and knows and is acquainted with all his thoughts and ways. He even knows when we sit down and stand up. However, even though he knows everything about us, he lets us make choices—just like he gives us the choice of accepting Jesus Christ. Joshua instructed the Israelites to prepare themselves before the crossing; we, too, must prepare ourselves for the road ahead. In the first chapter of Joshua, he tells the Israelites to prepare for something big—to prepare before crossing the Jordan.

> *Joshua commanded the officers of the people, saying pass through the midst of the camp and command the people, saying, prepare provisions for yourself, for within three days you are to cross this Jordan, to go in to possess the land which the Lord your God is giving you to possess it (Joshua 1:10-11).*

The Israelites were notified to prepare provisions before crossing Jordan. They were allotted three days to prepare themselves and organize their provisions, most likely food, to be ready for consumption upon crossing the river. Preparing beforehand helps us to gain confidence in our choices and decisions. If we face a catastrophic situation, like an untimely death in the family, being prepared spiritually and psychologically gives us a head-start on continuing. It is hard, but readiness ensures we face change with confidence.

Most transitions call for us to adjust and adapt to something. They can be difficult if you don't prepare. Preparation time is never wasted. Being prepared is one of the best ways to guarantee that all will work out. If you don't plan to make a good resume, you might not get the job you want. If you don't prepare to enter the next season in life, you might not have the money you need for the years to come. British pastor Charles Spurgeon has said, "Prepare. Be in journeying order."[2]

Let me tell you a little secret. We all care about money in one way or another! We need money for our vast living expenses, but it should not become an idol in our lives. As I read my Bible to discern whether to "retire" or not, it took me until about halfway through the Bible before I could honestly say I was willing to give up my five-more years of salary and how much those extra five years would have added to my retirement money. But once the Lord and I resolved that issue, I began to hear him more clearly in my prayer and meditation time. He showed me that money was not what was important in his eyes but obedience. I ended up leaving my job at the end of the school year. Six months later, my husband said, "Patti, there is a job in Nigeria I would like to apply for, what do you think?" Many people say, "Lord, I will do anything for you, but don't send me to Africa." But off we went to Lagos, Nigeria. It was there I experienced a different culture and met some lovely Nigerian women. Nigeria was where I needed to be for the Lord to teach me some things I could not have learned in the United States. Only through praying, planning to leave my job, and obeying God was I able to experience one of the best moves of my life. It was part of my journey.

The moral of these two stories is: Don't attempt to undertake your ministry or life change without adequate preparations. Don't let unpreparedness cause you to miss an opportunity. The choice is yours. As transitions come closer, there is a time when we must make decisions on how to move forward. And they may come unexpectedly. And guess what? Now, if a truly seeking believer tells me that God is leading them to do something or leading them to leave their locale, I encourage them to follow God's leading. If he could lead me to Africa and I learned more about him there, he can lead you to your next season in life too.

Principle 4: Take Courageous Action

As Nike advocates, we sometimes need to "just do it." Trusting in God's provision, we forge ahead, knowing victory awaits on the other side.

In Joshua 3:17, the Israelites set out. They had to take the first step. They followed instructions, came to the Jordan, and lodged there before crossing. They were standing at the edge of the river, which was rapidly moving. Due to snow melting from the surrounding mountains, rushing waves abounded more than at any other time of the year. The Israelites saw a turbulent river but were ready to act in faith. They did not know what was going on with the water down in the city of Adam. They only knew the river waters had stopped. They were to start to cross the Jordan and change their life. They remembered their parents telling them how the Red Sea opened for Moses to allow them to leave Egypt. God is a God of the supernatural. Victory was coming to the Israelites.

Standing on the summit of Mt. Nebo in Jordan in 2023, I felt an overwhelming sense of awe wash over me. As I gazed out at the faint outline of the Jordan River, I couldn't help but reflect on the profound moments that unfolded there—the Israelites' act of obedience and their preparations to step into the Promised Land. It was an incredibly surreal experience, one that deepened my faith. I realized that when God calls me to take a leap of faith, I must be ready to obey and trust Him completely. Even when I don't understand his plans, I have to believe that he always knows what is best for me.

Nike, the company, was originally called Blue Ribbon Sports, but in 1971, they changed their name to Nike after the Greek God of Victory. While I wouldn't say I like that the company was named after a Greek God, but I do like the word VICTORY because that happened to the Israelites when they crossed the Jordan. They experienced victory, just like when we accept Jesus Christ through the forgiveness of our sins, and when we accept him as our Savior, we also experience victory.[3]

Crossing the Jordan was a turning point on the way to freedom—for them and us.

In *Joshua: An Introduction and Commentary*, Old Testament scholar Richard Hess calls crossing the Jordan a rite of passage. Whenever there is a rite of passage, we see change, transformation, and transition to something new. There comes a point when we have to decide whether to stay where we are or decide to move on. Once the Israelites crossed the Jordan, they were ready and empowered to conquer the Promised Land.[4]

The Israelites followed Godly leadership—So should we. They meditated, prayed, and allowed the Scriptures to keep them sane; So should we. They prepared for their transition. So should we, and they did something. So should we.

In Charles Stanley's devotional "The Power of Life," he describes what a journey entails.

Life is like an untraveled trail with complex twists and turns. There are detours that lead us to sin or muddled thinking, but God is the perfect, full-service guide. No one can go wrong by keeping to the pathways he selects. The Lord watches over your steps because he desires to see your purpose fulfilled and His plan come to fruition.[5]

Most life transitions create memories that last a lifetime. Our transition experiences can be shared with friends and family, which makes them unique teaching tools for our sons, daughters, or grandchildren. Always be open if God leads you to move and change locations—maybe God will use you in a mighty way in a new locale or teach you something you absolutely need to learn or resolve in your life, as he did in mine.

Jennifer's initial resistance to returning to the Houston area eventually melted into gratitude. Looking back, she sees how moving to Houston shaped her life. She attended Texas Tech University, met her husband there, and now enjoys a loving marriage, and family. Sometimes, the most unexpected transitions lead to the greatest blessings. Don't let fear hold you back from a blessing. Experiencing God's favor is an exciting and uplifting feeling.

Even though we might think a transition is out of the question, remember lessons from the Jordan River's experiences: welcome the journey, trust in divine guidance, and step forward with courage. Your step of faith promises new beginnings and undiscovered joy. And it can happen at any age!

Every move I have ever made has proved to be another step directed by God. While I may not always see it at the time, looking back, I can always see God's hand in it.

Be Unstoppable—Go the Distance with God,

Prepare plans by consultation and make war by wise guidance.
Proverbs 20:18

CHAPTER 26

EMBARKING
ON THE JOURNEY OF PRIDE

---

*A proud man is always looking down on things and people:
and, of course, as long as you are looking down,
you cannot see something that is above you.*

C.S. Lewis

B ob's pride swelled as he ascended to the coveted position of Vice President at work. The promotion went to his head, and for weeks, he bragged to everyone that he was now a VP. His bragging abruptly stopped when his wife, so embarrassed by his behavior, said, "Listen Bob, It's not that big a deal. These days, everyone's a vice president. Why they even have a Vice President of Peas down at the supermarket!" Somewhat deflated, Bob rang the local supermarket to find out if this was true. "Can I speak to the Vice President of Peas please?" he asked, to which the reply came: "Of fresh or frozen?"[1]

Adrian Rogers in "The Problem of Pride" says "the world defines pride as a feeling that you respect yourself and deserve to be respected by other people and a feeling that you are more important or better than other people." From a spiritual viewpoint, Rogers said, "Pride is a declaration of independence." It is like saying, "God, I am self-sufficient. I have everything I need. Your services are no longer required."[2] The Lord clarifies what the Lord hates.

These six things the Lord hates, yes, seven, are an abomination to Him: A proud look, A lying tongue, Hands that shed innocent blood, A heart that devises wicked plans, Feet that are swift in running to evil, A false witness who speaks lies. And one who sows discord among brethren (Proverbs 6:16-19).

Pride exists in the heart of man, and it almost always heralds destruction. King Uzziah's tale serves as a distressing warning. Uzziah, an Old Testament King of Judah, became king when he was only sixteen. He started his fifty-two-year reign seeking the Lord and was mentored by the Old Testament Prophet Zechariah. Uzziah was a very good man and a great leader. However, he changed as he became successful in his political and military endeavors. He grew very proud and thought very highly of himself. As he prospered, his pride began to develop, and he became furious when confronted by Azariah and eighty other courageous priests of the Lord about his burning incense to the Lord. Proud people do not like being confronted and told what they should or shouldn't be doing. While he was still angry at the priests, God allowed him to fall to leprosy. He was not remembered as the great king he was, but his legacy was tarnished by leprosy, which overshadowed his prior achievements, an apt example of pride coming before the fall. Yet not all pride is reprehensible. At the end of his life, he was known more for his arrogance and pride than the man he first was. His "destruction" is manifested in 2 Chronicles 26:22-23 when it says,

"Now the rest of the acts of Uzziah, from first to last, the Prophet Isaiah the son of Amoz wrote. So Uzziah rested with his fathers, and they buried him with his fathers in the field of burial which belonged to the kings, for they said, 'He is a leper.'"

If you are proud of your child's accomplishments or are pleased with re-staining an old dresser, that is pride in the good sense. The Apostle Paul was proud of the Corinthians' spiritual progress. However, ungodly pride seeps into our lives. It can disrupt our relationships and actions, creating barriers to reconciliation between family and other individuals. Pride also overlaps with other relationship fields—even our relationship with God.

Paul said, I am acting with great boldness toward you; I have great pride in you; I am filled with comfort. In all our affliction, I am overflowing with joy (2 Corinthians 7:4).

Recognizing the signs of pride allows us to introspect and grow. A person may possess various degrees of being a proud person. The same holds when we discuss humility in the next chapter.

Signs of Pride

In their relationship with the Lord, they believe in their intellect regarding spiritual issues, find it hard to share their spiritual needs, glory in themselves, neglect God because they feel they are good enough or know enough already, cannot confront their sins because they would rather deal with vague generalities, possess an aura of self-righteousness, believe they do not need to repent, and try to hide their sins and faults.

In their relationships with others, they blame others, but not themselves, boast in their achievements and accomplishments, lead by demanding, focus on the failures and bad points of others, have to prove that they are always right and you are wrong, have a difficult time asking for forgiveness, look down on people and things, seek adoration and praise from others, and want to be served by others.

In their actions and thoughts, they blame others, but rarely themselves A proud person might believe a company or ministry should be privileged to employ them, defend themselves by being argumentative when criticized, experience difficulty saying they are sorry, have little concern about their reputation or how others perceive them, brag with confidence in their knowledge, and display a self-righteous attitude.

While a proud person finds it hard even to pray, let us pray for our brothers and sisters in Christ and for those who are putting off accepting the Lord due to pride so they will be filled with the hope, joy, and peace that can be received when we are close to Jesus. Pray the Holy Spirit will soften their hearts to hear the Word of God and desire his presence in their lives. As Christ-followers, we must humbly seek divine intervention and pray for a heart transformation. Our desire should be to turn from our pride toward humility so we can emerge more humble and wiser.

Be Unstoppable—Go the Distance with God,

A man's pride will bring him low, but a humble spirit will obtain honor. Proverbs 29:23

CHAPTER 27

CULTIVATING HUMILITY

> *A humble person is not one who thinks little of himself,*
> *hangs his head and says, "I'm nothing."*
> *Rather, he is one who depends wholly on the Lord*
> *for everything, in every circumstance.*
>
> David Wilkerson

S cheduled to speak at a large Presbyterian church in Melbourne, Australia, missionary Hudson Taylor anticipated the moderator of the service to introduce him in eloquent and glowing terms. The moderator told the large congregation all Taylor had accomplished in China and presented him as "our illustrious guest." Taylor stood quietly for a moment and then opened his message by saying. "Dear friends, I am the little servant of an illustrious Master."[1]

What humility! Humility is not a fashionable word to throw around. You don't hear many people talking about it; it is rarely spoken about from the pulpit, and if one says they are humble, it usually means they are not.

When I wrote about pride in the last chapter, I knew I was obligated to tackle the tricky topic of humility next. On a personal level, I desire to be humble, but I fear true humility is way beyond my reach. I feel more comfortable writing about topics I have some degree of knowledge about. Humility can't be bought or achieved by intellectual means. It can only be obtained as we grow closer and closer to the Lord Jesus Christ. So, because the Bible addresses humility, I will attempt to give some perspective.

Spurgeon forcefully defines humility. He exclaims,

> *Humility is to feel that we have no power of ourselves, but that it all cometh from God. Humility is to lean on our beloved, to believe that he has trodden the winepress alone, to lie on his bosom and slumber sweetly there, to exalt him, and think less than nothing of ourselves. It is in fact, to annihilate self, and to exalt the Lord Jesus Christ as all in all.²*

As believers, we are called to be humble people. The Bible says,

> *If my people who are called by my name humble themselves and pray and seek my face and turn from their wicked ways, then I will hear from heaven and will forgive their sin and heal their land (2 Chronicles 7:14 ESV).*

To become humble, we must be willing for the Lord to peel pride from our character and be God-centered like the Lord Jesus. However, we each have areas in our lives that usually hinder our quest for humility. We typically do not like sharing this personal information with others lest they glean something about our character that we don't want them to see—at least, that is how it is with me. As you read the following few paragraphs, think about some of the triggers that prevent you from becoming Christlike, for instance, jealousy regarding a friend's fabulous vacation, pride because your child received a higher SAT score than their peers, or coveting a co-worker's larger, custom home.

Signs of Humility

A humble person exhibits a profound relationship with the Lord by demonstrating several key qualities. They never boast of their humility or compare themselves to others; instead, they measure their lives against the example of Christ. They yearn for daily encounters with God and find joy in recognizing his presence in all aspects of life. This person strives to follow Christ's example as closely as possible, listens to God's guidance, and longs for the touch of the Holy Spirit. Furthermore, they embody the 'Fruit of the Spirit' as described in Galatians 5:22-23, which includes love, joy, peace, patience, kindness, goodness, faithfulness, gentleness, and self-control. Their recognition of the need for continual repentance and their ability to wait patiently upon God highlight their deep reliance on God.

In their interactions with others, humble individuals celebrate the achievements of those around them and take genuine joy in serving and loving others. They prioritize giving credit where it is due and are quick to overlook the failures of others, focusing instead on encouragement and praise for their peers. This selfless approach allows them to rejoice in others' successes while refraining from seeking recognition for themselves.

A humble person takes personal responsibility for their actions and feels deep remorse over their sins. They are quick to ask for forgiveness and readily say "I'm sorry," demonstrating a commitment to authenticity and reconciliation. Generosity, wisdom, and gratitude are hallmarks of their character, as they consistently project sincerity in their actions and words. They understand that there is so much to learn in the spiritual realm, exercise control over their speech, and approach their achievements with modesty, recognizing that humility in their hearts guides their thoughts and actions.

Jesus – A Biblical Example of Humility

The Bible has many examples of humble people: Samuel, Esther, David, and Daniel. But the Bible's most unassuming person must be the Lord Jesus Christ. He washed the feet of his disciples (John 13:12-17). He gave his heavenly Father all glory and honor (John 5:19,30,41). But, the most significant act of humility anyone could give is that he submitted to God so thoroughly that he took the form of a servant, humbled himself, and became obedient to the point of dying on the cross for our sins. His love for God and us was that strong.

It is one thing to talk about how to recognize a humble person, but we need to get to the point where we pursue or desire to pursue that kind of life ourselves with our hearts and souls.

But how?

How to Pursue a Life of Humility

Pursuing a life of humility, which God expects of us, involves our willingness and desire to rid ourselves of pride and be humble like Jesus

Christ. As we pray for humility, we must put our faith in God's ability to humble us. When we study his Word, we are much more able to depend on the power and guidance of the Holy Spirit. This power leads us to follow his leading more carefully and creates a more disciplined life for us—free from sin.

Humility does not appear overnight. It is a trait that takes time to develop. We need time to grow into a person permeated with wisdom and grace. We will be tested to see if we will follow him in many circumstances. We need time to be taught what is right and wrong. We need time for the Word of God to blend into our life and character. But, as we experience more of God, we will find following him much more effortless as days pass. With his grace, God's strength will permeate us. As we fall more in love with God, Jesus, the Holy Spirit, the Bible, and our time communicating with him, we will grow in humility. We might not even notice it, but others will. Look for opportunities to practice humility. Pray for those opportunities. Stop tooting your own horn and let God have his way with us because he is our "Illustrious Master."

Be Unstoppable—Go the Distance with God,

Do nothing from selfish or empty conceit, but with humility consider one another as more important than yourselves; do not merely look out for your own personal interests, but also for the interests of others.
Philippians 2:4-5

CHAPTER 28

NURTURING KINDNESS: EMBRACING THE SPIRIT'S FRUIT

To some people I will be the only expression of Christ's love that they will ever experience.

A.W. Tozer

What is Kindness?

Kindness is love in action—many struggle to treat others with kindness and genuine care in our fast-paced lives. However, as Christ-followers, we can look to the New Testament for guidance, where Jesus exemplifies a worthy path to follow. When Christ's love and His Holy Spirit reside within us, kindness influences our thoughts and actions. We benefit from kindness; it cultivates positive relationships, minimizes conflict, and aids us in creating a nurturing community.

Kind Words

One of my friends wrote:

You found me hiding pains and helped my healing. I am the vibrant woman I am today because you stopped where I was stuck; you became the step I needed to climb up and out. I am eternally grateful for your loving kindness.

I cherish comments like this—not to gain any accolades, but these encouragements confirm that I am following Christ, and he is using me. They boost my confidence to do better and to strive to be more kind and loving. I appreciate those who refrain from telling me my bad characteristics unless told with kind and caring words that only the Holy Spirit can put in their hearts. Ask yourselves if you are benevolent, cordial, courteous, gentle, hospitable, patient, tender, loyal, empathetic, polite, understanding, considerate, and thoughtful? These quality traits display kindness in a person's heart.

Moses' father-in-law, Jethro, knew how to show grace and kindness when leading Moses to a better life when all his pastoral duties overloaded him. Jethro said,

> *The thing you are doing is not good. You will surely wear out, both yourself and these people who are with you, for the task is too heavy for you; you cannot do it alone* (Exodus 18:*17-18*).

Then, he began to counsel and teach him how to handle disputes by having difficult decisions brought to him and having minor decisions dealt with by the judges. Now, that's kindness in action!

> *But I say, walk by the Spirit, and you will not carry out the desire of the flesh. For the flesh sets its desire against the Spirit, and the Spirit against the flesh; for these are in opposition to one another, so that you may not do the things that you please. But if you are led by the Spirit, you are not under the Law. Now the deeds of the flesh are evident, which are: immorality, impurity, sensuality, idolatry, sorcery, enmities, strife, jealousy, outbursts of anger, disputes, dissensions, factions, envying, drunkenness, carousing, and things like these, of which I forewarn you, just as I have forewarned you, that those who practice such things will not inherit the kingdom of God. But the fruit of the Spirit is love, joy, peace, patience,* **kindness***, goodness, faithfulness, gentleness, self-control; against such things, there is no law. Now those who belong to Christ Jesus have crucified the flesh with its passions and desires. If we live by the Spirit, let us also walk by the Spirit. Let us not become boastful, challenging one another, envying one another* (Galatians 5:*16-26*).

Kindness from Christ-followers

Praise God! Reflecting on my life, I realize how blessed I am to have encountered kind-hearted individuals who have shown me compassion in different ways. It's incredible how simple acts of kindness can have a lasting impact on someone's life. I remember vividly the college professor who showed me understanding when I shared extreme difficulty in understanding anything in my New Testament class in college. He actually told me I needed a Bible for the class, which I did not know. Thanks, John Davidson! It was a challenging time for me, but his kindness gave me hope and helped me to keep going. I also appreciate the friend who consoled me during a stressful time. His words of comfort and support helped me to heal and move on. Then, the ladies who brought meals to me after my children were born. Their kindness made the transition to motherhood smoother, and it was such a relief to have one less thing to worry about. I'm also grateful for the elderly churchmen who mentored my husband and me as young adults through their examples and invitations to have lunch with them. They showed us what it means to live a life of faith and service, and their guidance has stayed with us to this day. Thanks, Roger Vann. Finally, the friend who rejoiced with me when I showed her our new home while she lived in an extraordinarily small apartment with her husband and four young children. Her happiness for me was genuine and sincere, and it reminded me of how much the Lord has provided for us. Overall, I'm grateful for all the kindness I have received in my life, and I'm reminded of how we can all make a difference in someone's life through simple acts of kindness. The Lord has truly blessed me, and I'm thankful for everything he has provided for me.

Showing Family Kindness

Regarding our three children, demonstrating kindness to them was an invaluable trait to instill in them as they navigated life's journey. We affectionately refer to our son, John, as our extra loving boy. He eagerly showed up at our bed after his siblings drifted off to sleep to get some extra love. Maybe it was a middle-child syndrome, but we didn't care. We offered John cherished extra hugs without hesitation. Embrace moments like these.

It is important to cherish the sweet things our children say, like when our young John wanted to know when it would be "Boy Day" after noticing there was a Mother's Day and Father's Day. I recorded these precious moments in each of my children's baby books, creating a timeless keepsake that reminds us of the innocence of their childhood. Remember to treat your kids with kindness, so they will grow to be kind. The Bible urges us to be kind to one another. It is a fruit of the Spirit.

Marital Kindness

Kindness is the trait I look for, or it finds me in my relationships with others. (Okay, I value honesty too!) My initial attraction to my husband was his kindness. I knew he was kind by the way he treated me and by the little niceties he showered on me. The trait that you look for, or looked for, in a spouse may be different. You may be enamored by a person with a peaceful spirit, a loving personality, a joyful person, a patient person, a faithful person, a gentle person, or a person with deep self-control. Marriage is sometimes exceedingly difficult, but being kind to your spouse can keep the spark alive.

Tips for a Happy Marriage. Not Exhaustive.

- SHOW KINDNESS.
- Always speak positively about your spouse.
- Assist each other to be the best person they can be.
- Be supportive of their interests.
- Be your spouse's biggest cheerleader.
- Bring happiness to your spouse by not expecting something in return.
- Communicate often.
- Encourage your spouse to grow in their spiritual life.
- Forgive each other.
- Help each other, spiritually, physically, emotionally, and psychologically.

- Overcome obstacles together.
- Show thoughtfulness about what they care about.
- Speak verbal compliments to each other.
- Strengthen your intimacy.
- SHOW KINDNESS.

Ministerial Kindness

My husband and I have been members in wonderful, but not perfect churches throughout our married life. Each church was one of a kind in providing whatever we as a family needed to grow spiritually during the various seasons of our lives. When I look back at most of the people I have known in ministry, the enduring memory of kindness resonates in my mind. I often witnessed a pastor's kindness directly or saw them shower kindness on others. While not exhaustive, I will mention some of the kindnesses I have received from pastors:

1. The pastor who preached the gospel when I turned from my sin and believed in my Lord Jesus Christ. Thanks, William Lawson!
2. The pastor who counseled me and baptized me. Thanks, James Harris!
3. The pastor who gave me the best marriage advice ever: to marry someone you love! Thanks, John Bisango!
4. The pastor who filled in to marry us when our intended wedding pastor had to cancel two days before the wedding. Thanks, James Riley!
5. The interim pastor, who loved our six-year-old daughter, led her to Christ, and baptized her that very same day. Thanks, Bob Harris!
6. And the pastor I saw sweeping and cleaning up the kitchen after our daughter's wedding shower at his church. Thanks, Jerry Howe.

God's Kindness

Romans 2:4 says, God's kindness is meant to lead us to repentance. Being kind not only benefits others but ourselves as well, and Proverbs 21:21 tells us that if we are kind, we will find life, righteousness, and honor. As servants of God, we should follow his example and be kind to everyone, avoiding quarrels, as mentioned in 2 Timothy 2:24. Additionally, the Bible tells us to remember people kindly, as stated in 1 Thessalonians 3:6. Ultimately, we should be kind to one another as God in Christ forgave us, as stated in Ephesians 4:32. By doing so, we can reflect God's kindness and love to those around us, leading to a better and more peaceful world.

> *The Lord's bond-servant must not be quarrelsome, but be kind to all, skillful in teaching, patient when wronged (2 Timothy 2:24).*

> *But now that Timothy has come to us from you, and has brought us good news of your faith and love, and that you always think kindly of us, longing to see us just as we also long to see you (1 Thessalonians 3:6).*

> *Be kind to one another, compassionate, forgiving each other, just as God in Christ also has forgiven you (Ephesians 4:32).*

As Christ-followers, we face many different situations and personalities. Sometimes, we don't feel like being kind. Fatigue, restlessness, hunger, or sin may cause our focus to shift away quickly from God and his attributes. Faced with our sometimes-unkind attitudes, we should repent daily and pray that our lives will reflect the love of God in all we do—including being kind. Being kind involves loving others, being patient, and seeking God's wisdom in everything we say. And, when we fail, let's confess our harsh and callous hearts to God and start over—even if it means addressing and apologizing to those we have hurt. God loves us and desires us to love him back in all we do.

Testimony

Starting my day with a list of things to accomplish is standard. One day my list consisted of a doctor's appointment at 9:00 AM, picking up my new eyeglasses and meeting my retired teacher friends for lunch. Miraculously, my 9:00 AM appointment was over at 9:15 AM, if you can believe that. So, I had two hours to kill before I could pick up my glasses. I couldn't go home because our home was 45 minutes away in the opposite direction. Therefore, I pulled into a grocery store parking lot, sat in my car, and read for an hour. I was taking a graduate class at the time, and I was reading about how much illustrations add when preparing a message—little did I know an illustration opportunity was about to be bestowed on me. After reading, I found myself sitting in the parking lot; I decided to go and sit in front of my optometrist's office until they opened an hour later. But God had different plans. As I was leaving the grocery store parking lot, I saw a restaurant and decided to grab a takeout cup of coffee. While waiting for my coffee to be brewed, I noticed an elderly lady propped up beside her table with her walking cane nearby. She was sitting alone. When my coffee was ready, I felt the holy nudge to talk to her, so I walked up to her table and said, "Are you alone? Would you like some company?" She graciously said, "Yes, of course." Her name was Joanne. We had a wonderful time chatting. I heard about this lady's life, and she heard about mine. A lot of talking happened in thirty minutes. She was a widow. Her husband passed away about fifteen years ago, and she comes to that particular restaurant about two or three times per week to get out. When I said goodbye, she thanked me for coming to her table to visit. This divine appointment blessed us both.

And I still made it to my optometrist and lunch with my friends! It felt good to be kind!

Be Unstoppable—Go the Distance with God,

And be kind to one another, tender-hearted, forgiving each other, just as God in Christ also has forgiven you.
Ephesians 4:32

CHAPTER 29

DEALING WITH IMPERFECTIONS AND REGRETS

> *Leave the broken, irreversible past in God's hands, and step out into the invincible future with Him.*
>
> Oswald Chambers

Revealing Imperfections

Living in a house for any duration of time reveals its hidden flaws—the unnoticed chips on wooden floors, the water stains on the ceilings, or the light fixtures we avoid due to electrical issues. I call them imperfections. Just as a house has hidden "dents and dings," so do we.

Sometimes, we try to conceal our imperfections from others. Many times, we succeed. But hiding them from God is futile because he knows everything about us. He knows our vices, our sins, and our thoughts. Our heavenly Father even knows our personality and our temperament. He knows who we like and who we don't like. He even knows our future.

In Psalm 139, we learn that God formed our inward parts and wove us in our mother's womb, so he knows our frame. Because he knows everything about us. He knows what is best for us. While leading and guiding us, he also disciplines and lovingly shows us how to bring glory and honor to his holy name. We may love our house—imperfections and all—but do these spots and blemishes make it on to someone else's "to-do" list for fixing? Of course they don't! Allow God to work within you, revealing and addressing imperfections and our responsibility toward them. Confronting ourselves can be extremely hard, but keep working on it. Don't give up.

Navigating Regrets

Regret is a universal experience. While regrets may come in the form of our sinning, there are times when our regrets come from our foolish, apathetic, or unfortunate situations or choices. Reflecting on the Book of Matthew, I find parallels between myself and the three disciples who slept while Jesus prayed fervently before his crucifixion. I do and have struggled with the Christian issue of regret! Regret happens, but by understanding that our heavenly Father knows our failures and desires for us to live a life honorable to him from this moment on, we should take to heart God's longing for us to live a pure and holy life.

In the Book of Matthew, we see Jesus urging his disciples to stay awake and pray with him during his agonizing struggle. Yet, they slept and could not support him in his hour of need.

Then he said to them,

> *My soul is deeply grieved, to the point of death; remain here and keep watch with Me. And he went a little beyond them, and fell on His face and prayed, saying, My Father, if it is possible, let this cup pass from Me; yet not as I will, but as You will. And He came to the disciples and found them sleeping, and He said to Peter, So, you men could not keep watch with Me for one hour? (Matthew 26:38-40).*

He asked, "Couldn't you men keep watch with me for one hour?" In these short verses, Jesus wanted his three disciples close by, praying for him as he went through a deep, unbearable struggle before being arrested and facing death on the cross. But physically, Peter, James, and John could not stay awake. I relate to the three disciples who slept while Jesus prepared himself for his death on the cross. On the day my mother passed away, despite my desire to be by her side, fatigue overcame me, and I fell asleep. The inability to stay awake weighed heavily on me as I longed to be right by her side in her last moments. Gratefully, I am left with loving photographs of when I held and cuddled Mom earlier in the day. Though regrets may linger, I find comfort in the cherished memories I shared with Mom before her passing. These tokens remind me that my love for her endures while she is not with us anymore. Bible verses help us when we encounter regrets—when we hurt, cry, and plead with the Lord to reduce the pain.

In all probability, the disciples didn't intentionally want to fall asleep. I suppose their physical exhaustion overshadowed their intention to stay awake, and they could not fight their weariness. But we can tell by Jesus' words in Matthew 26:40b that he was disappointed when he found them and said, "Couldn't you men keep watch with me for one hour?"

Be Unstoppable—Go the Distance with God,

Jesus said, "Come to Me, all who are weary and burdened, and I will give you rest."
Matthew 11:28

CHAPTER 30

LEARNING FROM LIFE'S MISHAPS AND MISTAKES

> *Great and small suffer the same mishaps.*
>
> Blaise Pascal

Living Life

We've all experienced mishaps, or as I like to call them, mistakes. They came due to poor judgment or being swayed by emotions. As we navigate these moments, turning to faith can offer guidance through the repercussions. And sometimes laughter gets us through! These mishaps may raise eyebrows. Words like bird-brained, dim-witted, empty-headed ,and many others come to mind. Sometimes, "stupid" is the only one that works. But to avoid offending anyone, I will substitute more neutrally accepted words to describe our experiences.

On January 12, 2016, CNN reported on an Ohio fugitive who texted the police a more flattering selfie after seeing an unflattering mugshot of himself. Forty-five-year-old Donald 'Chip' Pugh, texted, 'Here's a better photo. That one is terrible.' His snapshot was shared on the police department's Facebook page, leading to his arrest."[1]

My Unwise Misstep/Mistake

Speaking of half-witted antics, let me share a personal tale from one hectic December day several years ago. Rushing to meet my friend Dee for our annual Christmas gift exchange luncheon, I panicked when I realized I had left my cell phone at home. Frantic about being late, I passed by the entrance and ultimately had to decide what to do. I absent-mindedly drove past the Cheddar's restaurant's only entrance. "My" Cheddar's is a restaurant situated on a busy frontage road off Interstate 10 in the Houston area. My options were limited as I had to decide what to do quickly. I couldn't back up or hang a U, so I decided to pull into the next parking lot belonging to the Olive Garden restaurant and hike across a drainage ravine between the restaurants to reach my intended destination. The big problem was the giant drainage gully between the two restaurants, which included steep grassy slopes on both sides with muddy water connecting the two at the bottom of the hill. A right-thinking person would have gotten back into the car, and driven to the next exit, do a U-turn to Cheddar's, and arrive fashionably late but still in relatively good shape. "I," however, made the impulsive decision to cross the treacherous drainage ditch sloping down at least fifteen feet between the eateries. Convinced I could cross, I plunged down the muddy slope. As I navigated the thick grass, I suddenly felt my foot slip into muddy quicksand of the ditch, threatening to trap me. I purposely fell to the left, quickly dragging my right leg out of the muddy, putrid water, and pulled myself to a wobbly standing position, all the while thinking of the drainage culvert that I had seen on the local news where folks had been sucked into a culvert and died. My right sandal was stuck in the dark sludge three feet down; I looked back, like Lot's wife, and saw my left shoe floating a few feet away. I was scared to retrieve it, but (in another half-witted decision) I did so anyway. I quickly ran up the other side of the drainage ditch like a mad woman, leaving my right sandal at the bottom of the cloudy water. Miraculously, once at the top of the ditch, I pulled myself together, crossed the Cheddar's parking lot, and walked into the restaurant barefoot, muddy, freezing, and soaking wet. I hoped no one would notice my disheveled appearance and ask me to leave. Thankfully, no one said anything.

When I entered, I saw Dee. She was waiting by the front entrance, doubtless wondering what happened to me. Once seated, I shared the story with her.

Dee picks up the story at this point:

I was waiting near the door when I saw you all wet and muddy. I stood by the front entrance waiting for you, to spare you the effort to try to find me in the crowded restaurant. I was definitely surprised when I saw you, but I don't recall what I said. I was trying to help keep the situation under the radar and not call attention to the fact that you had no shoes on, so I didn't acknowledge my shock. You explained what happened and that you couldn't call because you didn't have your phone on you. Your hair was fine. I remember we quickly walked to the table to hide the fact that you were barefoot. We really wanted to have lunch together! I thought it humorous, rather than embarrassing, although I do not really know what you thought. I knew I had a trunkful of donations to give to a Christian charity in my car. I remember thinking it was a "divine intervention" moment. After we ordered, we left our Christmas gifts at the table so the waitstaff wouldn't think we had just left. We went to my car because you were shivering, and there was no way you would enjoy lunch in that condition. You picked some garments out of the trunk. You went to the restroom and put on a pair of overalls, some socks, and a warm sweatshirt. There weren't any shoes that fit you in the trunk, but I don't remember for sure. When you returned and approached the table where I was waiting, I remember noticing the hems of the overalls were extremely short way too small for you. We put our gift bags on the [floor] to hide the fact that you had no shoes on.[2]

From my perspective, I felt like a poor Samaritan being helped by a kind-hearted person passing by. After taking my stack of clothing from Dee's stash, I proceeded to the restroom to change. I had to walk to the other side of the restaurant, pass by waitpersons and servers, to get to the restroom where I could change. No one mentioned my condition, bare feet. or smell. I was fortunate — I could put the tight overalls up to my waist when I unbuttoned all the buttons; I let the bib and straps hang down and put the sweatshirt over me. Then, Dee and I had a lovely Christmas lunch!

I do not believe it was a coincidence that Dee happened to have extra clothes packed in her car at the exact time I needed them. Instead, I believe God, who had a greater view of the situation and the power to address it, lovingly anticipated my blunder and provided a mildly ill-fitting (pun intended!) solution. That is what a loving God does. It was also a tremendous act of mercy for no one to comment on my disheveled appearance while I walked through the restaurant on the way to change into fresh clothes.

The Secular Moral of This Story

At the time, I was sixty-one-years old. I learned that females should never run down a fifteen-foot drainage culvert without expecting some trouble. Neither should males, for that matter! It is just plain stupid, or should I say half-witted? Fortunately, besides losing a sense of composure, dignity, and a pair of shoes, I survived. However, even in my unkempt state at the time, I knew I needed to use more common sense in the future. Just like we have consequences in our physical realm, we have consequences in our spiritual realm. And those consequences might be a lot more catastrophic.

The Spiritual Moral of This Story

The Bible reassures us of divine grace and guidance, especially in our times of trouble. I've experienced this firsthand and have come to appreciate the comfort God offers us, reminding us that we're never alone on our journey, no matter where it leads. As Christ-followers, we all do foolish things at times. Temptation is always lurking, and our choices can have real consequences. It's important to remember that God isn't caught off guard by our mistakes—he knows when we act foolishly or make poor decisions. What's remarkable is that he is forgiving and compassionate, using our blunders to shape our character. He understands our motives and wants us to learn from our missteps so we draw closer to him, depending on his guidance through everything. Yet, we must also acknowledge that there are consequences to our actions, especially when we stray from his path. Take my drainage ditch incident, for example. I showed up at a restaurant covered in mud, yet my friend didn't panic. Surprisingly, the other guests didn't gawk or whisper, and the staff didn't toss me out the door. Instead, Dee offered me a change of clothes to ease my discomfort. It was a moment of grace I'll never forget.

How to Learn from Your Mishaps/Mistakes

1. Reflect on the experience.
2. Take time to analyze what went wrong and what you can take away from it.
3. Don't let your mistakes define you.
4. Remember, everyone makes mistakes. They don't determine your worth or future.
5. Learn and move on.
6. Use the insights gained to grow and avoid repeating the same pitfalls.
7. Use your failure as a means to discover your weaknesses.
8. Embrace failure as a powerful tool to identify areas for improvement.
9. Pressures come but stay calm.
10. Keep your composure when challenges arise; it helps you think clearly and respond effectively.
11. Get in front of a situation before it spirals.
12. Address issues proactively to prevent them from escalating.
13. And remember, trusting God throughout this journey can provide peace and guidance as you navigate your mistakes. Embrace faith, knowing that there's purpose in your learning process.

Though our mistakes may deserve harsh consequences, our God stands as a protector for those who love him. He shields us from penalties and generously bestows unexpected, unearned blessings. So, when impulse or temptation tries to take the reins, let's proceed with caution. Let's learn from our missteps, ensuring we only risk losing what's minor—like my sandals and pride—rather than the much greater things that truly matter—our relationship with the Lord.

Be Unstoppable—Go the Distance with God,

Therefore, be careful how you walk, not as unwise men, but as wise, making the most of your time, because the days are evil. So then do not be foolish, but understand what the will of the Lord is.
Ephesians 5:15-17

CHAPTER 31

THE PERILS OF DISOBEDIENCE

The golden rule for understanding spiritually is not intellect, but obedience. If a man wants scientific knowledge, intellectual curiosity is his guide; but if he wants insight into what Jesus Christ teaches, he can only get it by obedience.

Oswald Chambers

As a member of the Baby Boomer generation, I grew up believing that disciplining children with a switch or a similar object was acceptable. However, looking back as a mother, I now regret using a wooden spoon—also known to everyone in the family as the "discipline stick," which was used to discipline our kids when they were younger. Of course, discipline was used sparingly and always followed with a big hug. I needed the hug more than they did most days! I remember a particular incident while I was stirring a bowl of ingredients making a cake. One of the boys was appalled and asked why I was using a discipline stick for cooking. It was then that I realized I had relied too much on punishing my children with the wooden spoon, and they needed to understand that a wooden spoon was meant for the kitchen, not for punishment.

Reflecting on my experience as a parent, I found disciplining my children challenging and painful. Despite my efforts to address disobedience and disrespectful behavior, I realized that ignoring the issues didn't help raise kind, forgiving, and godly children. However, imposing consequences, whether it was a time-out, denying them a candy treat, or using the discipline stick, their behavior was significantly impacted for the good. I'm happy to report that they have all grown up to be successful adults with happy families of their own. Parents are not perfect.

While the circumstances differ, it reminds me of a time when the people of Judah faced dire consequences due to their disobedience. In Jeremiah 44:11-14, the people's refusal to repent led to the destruction of Jerusalem and their eventual exile into Egypt where God punished them with war, hunger, and disease. By not listening to God, only a few survive to return to Judah.

But before delving deeper into this narrative, let's lay the groundwork.

God is a just and loving God. He loves everyone and does not want any harm or affliction to come upon them (2 Pet. 3:9). Many nations have disregarded God's love and his desire to bless them. In Deuteronomy 28:15-68, when nations and people rejected the Lord and his commandments, suffering, sickness, and plagues came upon them. Before Jeremiah, the Northern Kingdom, which consisted of ten tribes, was destroyed by the Assyrians. Thus, Jeremiah, the weeping prophet, was a prophet to the Southern Kingdom of Judah, which consisted of the two remaining tribes. Jeremiah was present when Jerusalem and the temple were destroyed in 586 BC. Jeremiah states over and over again that without people repenting and turning to God, consequences will befall them. During the time of Jeremiah's unpopular message, the people and leaders were actively participating in many sinful behaviors such as idol worship, sacrificing their children to the gods, stealing, adultery, and more. The people had two choices they could have pursued – To be obedient to God and receive his blessings or continue in their sin and await judgment. Steeped in sin, they decided to remain in it. Jeremiah came upon this scene, and for almost fifty years, he pursued his calling to warn the people that if they did not turn to God and worship him, God would judge them. And, for all those years, he saw minimal, almost nonexistent, change in their lives.

Jeremiah was treated horribly during his ministry:

- The people did not listen to him (Jeremiah 7:25).

- They wanted to kill him (Jeremiah 11:19, 21-23).

- He was beaten (Jeremiah 20:2).

- He was put into the king's prison (Jeremiah 32:1-5).

- He was put into a muddy cistern and left to starve to death (Jeremiah 38:6-10).

However, being encouraged by the Lord, Jeremiah continued his call to preach the message with sadness and tears; thus, his name became the "weeping prophet."

God had sent numerous prophets to the people of Judah, calling for their repentance, and he had given them grace over and over. But God had finally had enough. He instructed Jeremiah to cease praying for the people. When I first read this in the Bible many years ago, I was shocked that God told someone to stop praying for the people until I realized God was genuinely ready to enact his judgment on them. Prayer was delaying the judgment, and God was prepared to act. It is interesting to note that God did not tell Jeremiah to stop preaching the message of repentance.

> As for you, do not pray for this people, or lift up cry or prayer for them, and do not intercede with Me; for I do not hear you (Jeremiah 7:16).

> Therefore, do not pray for this people, nor lift up a cry or prayer for them; for I will not listen when they call to Me in the time of their disaster (Jeremiah 11:14).

> So the LORD said to me, "Do not pray for the welfare of this people" (Jeremiah 14:11).

In our lives, God gives us chance after chance to repent. But, at some point, he may say, "Enough is enough," and he is ready to disperse judgment. And that is a scary place to be.

God decided to use the Babylonians to punish their sin and assign consequences to their behavior. The Babylonians destroyed Jerusalem and Solomon's temple in 586 BC. The people of Judah, who were living amid the destruction, asked Jeremiah to ask the Lord if they should leave and go to Egypt or stay in Jerusalem. The people promised to obey God whether God said to go or stay. Jeremiah did not respond right away. He prayed for ten days. Finally, he told the people what he heard from God.

⁷Now at the end of ten days the word of the Lord came to Jeremiah. ⁸ Then he called for Johanan the son of Kareah and all the commanders of the forces that were with him, and for all the people from the small to the great, ⁹ and said to them, "This is what the Lord says, the God of Israel, to whom you sent me to present your plea before Him: ¹⁰ 'If you will indeed stay in this land, then I will build you up and not tear you down, and I will plant you and not uproot you; for I will relent of the disaster that I have inflicted on you. ¹¹ Do not be afraid of the king of Babylon, whom you are now fearing; do not be afraid of him,' declares the Lord, 'for I am with you to save you and rescue you from his hand. ¹² I will also show you compassion, so that he will have compassion on you and restore you to your own soil. ¹³ But if you are going to say, "We will not stay in this land," so as not to listen to the voice of the Lord your God, ¹⁴ saying, "No, but we will go to the land of Egypt, where we will not see war, or hear the sound of a trumpet, or hunger for bread, and we will stay there"; ¹⁵ then in that case listen to the word of the Lord, you remnant of Judah. This is what the Lord of armies, the God of Israel says: "If you really set your minds to enter Egypt and go in to reside there, ¹⁶ then the sword, of which you are afraid, will overtake you there in the land of Egypt; and the famine, about which you are anxious, will follow closely after you there in Egypt, and you will die there. ¹⁷ So all the people who set their minds to go to Egypt to reside there will die by the sword, by famine, or by plague; and they will have no refugees or survivors from the disaster that I am going to bring on them."'" ¹⁸ For this is what the Lord of armies, the God of Israel says: "As My anger and wrath have gushed out on the inhabitants of Jerusalem, so My wrath will gush out on you when you enter Egypt. And you will become a curse, an object of horror, an imprecation, and a disgrace; and you will not see this place again." (Jeremiah 42:7-18).

The Israelites were warned not to go to Egypt. Furthermore, in Jeremiah 42:21-22, the Israelites were told that because of their disobedience, they should clearly understand they would die by the sword, by famine, and by pestilence in the place they wished to reside. But the people of Judah chose not to obey God's voice and went to Egypt.

The consequence of the people's disobedience was again judgment from God as promised in the form of the destruction of their homeland and their chosen exile to Egypt. The people did not believe or chose not to believe what Jeremiah said about not going to Egypt.

This story reminds me of when our eight-year-old son Jimmy asked me if Santa Claus was real. I kept saying, "Do you really want to know." He stated, "Yes!" This continual bantering went back and forth until I finally decided to tell him Santa Claus wasn't real. His immediate and firm response was, "I DON'T BELIEVE YOU!" Sometimes people believe what they want to think, and you can do nothing about it.

Let's remember that God's genuine desire for his people was to be obedient so he could shower them with blessings—not suffering and trials. How is this story relevant to us today? This story addresses the nation of Judah. However, if we continue our disobedience after many warnings and exhortations, we can end up in a difficult situation, suffering the terrible consequences of sin. Amid sin, we lose his blessings and our relationship with him. God may wait many years for our repentance while we live lives of deceit, immorality, drunkenness, corruption, dishonesty, and lies. Do not let that happen. Allow God to rule your life NOW! Return to the Lord today and accept his love and acceptance by confessing your sins and asking Jesus Christ to be your Lord and Savior.

And as Joshua previously suggested the people do, we should "fear the LORD and serve Him in sincerity and truth" . . . and choose for ourselves today whom we will serve (Josh. 24:14-15).

Be Unstoppable—Go the Distance with God,

But it shall come about, if you do not obey the LORD your God,
to observe to do all His commandments and His statutes with which I charge you today,
That all these curses will come upon you and overtake you:
Cursed shall you be in the city, and cursed shall you be in the country.
Cursed shall be your basket and your kneading bowl.
Cursed shall be the offspring of your body and the produce of your ground,
the increase of your herd and the young of your flock.

Cursed shall you be when you come in, and cursed shall you be when you go out. The LORD will send upon you curses, confusion, and rebuke,
in all you undertake to do, until you are destroyed and until you perish quickly, on account of the evil of your deeds, because you have forsaken Me.
Deuteronomy 28:15-20

CHAPTER 32

EXPLORING MOTIVES
AND INTENTIONS

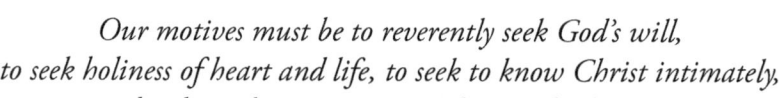

> *Our motives must be to reverently seek God's will,*
> *to seek holiness of heart and life, to seek to know Christ intimately,*
> *and to learn how to instruct others to do the same.*
>
> A.W. Tozer.

When my husband proposed relocating to Lagos, Nigeria, I instinctively understood his motives for wanting an overseas expat assignment. My "YES!" stemmed not from deep analysis but from recognizing his desire to live abroad. In the same way, we can gain insight into God's motives through a close relationship with him. I also remembered that this proposal occurred only six months after the Lord impressed me to leave my job. So, I was preprepared to answer positively, quickly. Yet, navigating our own motives and intentions can sometimes be perplexing.

Defining Motives and Intentions

According to the Merriam-Webster Dictionary, a motive is "something (such as a need or desire) that causes a person to act."[1] Conversely, intentions refer to the plans or purposes behind our actions.[2] While both concepts are closely intertwined, they hold distinct meanings. Motives reflect the underlying reasons for our actions, whereas intentions are the objectives we hope to achieve. Recognizing the differences helps in navigating our spiritual journey, fostering self-awareness, and aligning our actions with God's will.

We often question if our motives are right or wrong. While we may recognize when our motives produce an unrighteous spirit within us, understanding how others perceive our motives can also be complex. One person may think our motives are justified, while another may perceive them differently. Similarly, we wrestle with discerning the motives of others: some may appear virtuous while others may seem flawed. Ultimately, knowing our true motives—and those of others—creates a richer understanding of ourselves, each other, and God.

Absalom's Saga

Absalom's saga in 2 Samuel 15 starkly illustrates how entitlement and power can lead to destructive actions. King David's son Absalom sought to overthrow his father's throne. His charisma allowed him to persuade many that he should reign in Hebron, even recruiting Ahithophel, one of King David's loyal advisors, to support him. Absalom's motives were twofold: an overwhelming sense of entitlement and an insatiable thirst for power. Unfortunately, these motives led him to disrespect his father's authority, demonstrating how misguided motives can result in catastrophic actions. I often wonder how differently the story might have turned out had Absalom turned to God, seeking divine clarification on his motives and intentions. His deliberate choice to betray his father not only severed familial ties but also led to his tragic downfall. He advanced personal ambitions with little regard for the collateral damage—relationships and trust that were irreparably lost due to pride and jealousy.

Such issues highlight how harmful motives can lead to regrettable outcomes. For example, pride might harm one's relationship with God, the desire for approval can lead to dishonesty, a sense of entitlement may breed unhappiness and ungodly behavior, jealousy may incite revenge, while criticism may spring from hurt feelings.

Absalom used his outward charm and likability to garner support, but his ulterior motive was to amass popularity for the nefarious purpose of dethroning his father. Absalom's legacy serves as a cautionary tale; had he considered the broader implications of his actions, perhaps he would have approached life differently—one that didn't lead to estrangement from his father or the devastation of family relationships. In sum, while motivations drive our actions based on internal desires, intentions articulate the goals we seek through those actions. Both demand introspection and alignment with the will of God for spiritual growth and maturity.

Questioning Our Motives

Let's face reality: first impressions matter. Whether it's for a job, social interactions, or church activities, we strive to present ourselves positively. However, we must ask ourselves this: are we acting out of genuine goodness, or are we seeking validation through our actions? Consider the following questions:

- Do you act differently at home than at church?

- Do you volunteer for nonprofit organizations solely to appear virtuous?

- Do you help others only to receive recognition or rewards?

- Do you attend church merely to network?

- Do you treat others to meals to display your wealth?

- Do you boast about your spiritual gifts?

- Do you crave the spotlight at home, church, or work?

- Do you spend beyond your means to impress others.

If you answered "yes" to any of these questions, it suggests that our motives may not be pure. Recognizing our motivations is the first step toward transformation. Often, our actions are less about genuine kindness and more about influencing others' perceptions of us. As Christians, it's imperative that we reflect the light of Christ rather than seek our own glory. Turning our hearts towards the Lord through Scripture and prayer becomes essential for understanding our motives and intentions.

What to Do When Questioning the Motives of Others?

Let's face it—we are human beings, and we sometimes wonder about other's motives. This may be a cursory glance or a scrutinizing in-depth evaluation.

Some guidelines are:

- Don't rely on preconceived notions about others. People change. God does change people,

- Don't depend exclusively on first impressions or our intuition,

- Find out all the facts before judging a person's motives (and especially before addressing them),

- Put yourself in someone else's shoes, and

- If you have misjudged someone, apologize and reconcile as soon as possible.

Although a person's background, personality, and life experiences may clash with yours, that doesn't always make you right and them wrong.

Having been raised for most of my formative years in London, England and the northeastern part of the United States in Pennsylvania, I may think differently from some of my friends raised in the deep South. My life experiences and spiritual experiences are different from others. Still, I hope and pray that my friends and acquaintances will look at me through the eyes of God—instead of through my idiosyncrasies. And especially not in a judgmental way.

> *Therefore, do not go on passing judgment before the time, but wait until the Lord comes, who will both bring to light the things hidden in the darkness and disclose the motives of men's hearts; and then each man's praise will come to him from God (1 Corinthians 4:5).*

Seek God's Input

As mentioned, God's input about our motives is a fantastic place to start—but it is usually quite challenging. We live in our dreams and desires, and they are hard to replace, especially if you are ruminating person. God wants us to put him above all else. When we reach the place of total surrender (or as close as we can), we move on to pleasing him. We sometimes don't know how God will answer our prayers, but no matter what, know that he is working, and all our prayers are heard by him. No prayers are wasted. Although it is tough to accept, there are times when we need to bow down and tell God that we are too close to the situation to discern his direction, guidance, or will. At these times, continue to depend on him, and if it is appropriate, share with your friends or family, and rely on their intercessory prayers. No one, but God, can understand the extent of what we are undergoing. We may wonder if our thoughts are from our intellectual brain or God. We may wonder if we are operating according to a satanic attack, our fleshy desires, or sin. We may agonize over our motivations, causes, purposes, intentions, and even our spiritual aptitude to discern. Discovering our true motives can be complex as we may be dealing with strongholds in our lives. Satan is always prowling around seeking who he can devour. Even strong, spiritually minded Christ-followers should pray about their motives, because we seek clarity to ensure our motives are acceptable to God. This desire stems from a longing to fully grasp what God wants to convey and submit wholeheartedly to his plan for their lives. Occasionally, a Christ-follower's heart becomes so impressed with a passage of Scripture that he feels God is declaring his plan or words to him. If that is your case, take that verse, meditate upon it, look at the context, and talk to the Lord about what it means for you and this situation. And treasure those special verses.

"Dear God" Letters

I write "Dear God" letters when I have something important that I want to articulate to the Lord, but I don't know how to put my thoughts into words for the Lord. I've been doing it for half a century now. One deep-rooted and sincere prayer stated,

Dear God,

Why am I praying for this particular desire over and over? What are my motives, and what are your motives? It sounds ridiculous to pray that this could come true, but I hope for it. I am waiting patiently. I ask you to remove the desire and correct my prayer if it isn't your will. I am at wit's end, trying everything to know your will. I don't know if it is a sin, a glimpse into the future, or a thought from Satan. Lord, I don't

*understand my motives. Correct me, Lord. I don't understand.
I need relief. Is it time for me to stop praying about this? Lord
Jesus, my spirit is heavy. Search me, O Lord. I want to be in
your absolute will, but how can I be until you answer this
prayer?*
God: I love you.

Patti

Not all my "Dear God" letters are quite as brutally honest. Sometimes, I praise God when writing them, but I share this letter with you because many times, there comes a point where we must stop saying the general prayers that we so often pray and start praying honestly to God. Tell God you don't understand why you are experiencing a problem. Tell him you need his wisdom and discernment. Tell him you need his power to know his motives. Why? Because he knows us better than we know ourselves. Jeremiah 29:11 reassures us that he knows the plans he has for us because they are plans for welfare and not calamity, to give us a future and a hope.

When we depend on the Lord, our thinking about others and their motives will be guided by his light and wisdom. When we pursue God, he will show us any behaviors or actions he wants us to address. Christian love and compassion should rule in our hearts—not negativity or criticism.

Tips to Discern Our Motives

The next time you question your motives, remember that God loves each of us and desires honest, heartfelt communication.

When you talk to Him:

- Be specific in your prayers.

- Be bold in your inquiries.

- Be honest with God about your thoughts and feelings.

- Be committed to seeking him daily for direction and understanding.

- Let him know that you want to understand his and your motives clearly, because you don't want to misinterpret them, and

- Engage with the Lord in a genuine way, and watch your relationship grow.

Our Lord does not want his people to proceed with an unsettled or perplexed mind but with confidence and clarity of spirit.

In his blog entry about motives, Joshua Kennon warns: "A final word of caution: I would urge you to consider keeping your thoughts on another person's motivation to yourself."[3] That's wisdom.

Until Jesus gives you the spiritual wisdom to discern where a person is coming from, keep your ears and eyes open for when, how, or even whether or not you should speak. When God gives us his wisdom, he will also guide us to learn how to spur a person to hear God's voice and experience a deep passion to follow Christ's will.

Now, that is not being "judgmental." Far from it! It's being a servant of God.

It is hard to imagine what life would have been like if Absalom developed a godly camaraderie and an alliance with King David. But I daresay that our world history books would be different if Absalom's motives were wholly surrendered to God, which is always the preferred method.

Be Unstoppable—Go the Distance with God,

For the Word of God is living and active, and sharper than any two-edged sword, even penetrating as far as the division of soul and spirit, of both joints and marrow, and able to judge the thoughts and intentions of the heart. Hebrews 4:12

Chapter 33

PURAH:
AN OLD TESTAMENT SERVANT

> *At the end of your life, only two words matter: Well done.*
> *That's all you want to hear. Nothing else matters*
> *—the status of your position at work, your income,*
> *the breadth of your fame, the accolades of your peers—just those two words.*
> *Faithful servants do what they are supposed to do*
> *and go where they are called—to the very end.*
>
> John Bisango

Grateful

Do you have a Purah in your life? I do. It is my husband. A Purah is the one person who is always loyal to you, who shows up just when you need them, and who always wants the best for you. Your Purah might be a parent, a mentor, or a friend. As I was reading Judges 7:10, I ran across this man named Purah. He is mentioned only once in the Bible, so most consider him insignificant. Upon further exploration, I discovered that Purah, despite his lack of recognition, played a significant role in Gideon's journey and in achieving God's desired outcome.

The word "grateful" does not express how the support my husband has given me to follow the Holy Spirit's leading has affected me positively. His support parallels Purah's support for Gideon—behind the scenes but needed and cherished. He truly is my most significant Purah. He always wants the best for me and quietly encourages me to follow God's leading, like starting my master's degree in Theological Studies at age 66!

The Man behind the Scene

The Midianites were oppressing Israel while Israel was doing what was evil in the sight of the LORD. An angel of the LORD came to Gideon and told him that the LORD was with him. Then, after Gideon asked why all these bad things had happened to the Israelites, the LORD said, "Go in this your strength and deliver Israel from the hand of Midian. Have I not sent you?" (Judg. 6:14).

God called Gideon into the ministry of saving Israel. Gideon destroyed the altar of Baal, and then he asked for signs from God to be sure of his call. When God reduced Gideon's army of 22,000 men to only 300, the LORD said to Gideon,

> *I will save you with the three hundred men who lapped, and will hand the Midianites over to you; so have all the other people go, each man to his home. So the three hundred men took the people's provisions and their trumpets in their hands. And Gideon dismissed all the other men of Israel, each to his tent, but retained the three hundred men; and the camp of Midian was below him in the valley (Judges 7:7-9),*

God knew Gideon was encountering fear. How would you feel defeating an entire army with only 300 men? However, God loved Gideon and gave him a strong, wonderful man called Purah to offer encouragement, comfort, and protection. Purah was there for Gideon. Those ministering for the LORD often become discouraged, fearful, depressed, weak, and needy; when these times occur, they need a Purah. Are you available and in the right spiritual mindset for God to use you in that capacity? Maybe you are the Purah someone else needs.

Your calling may be working with someone in a complex or challenging situation. Or you may need a Purah yourself. Has God called you to do an impossible task that seems too overwhelming to tackle alone? If so, keep your eyes open for God to encourage you to pursue it. God may help you through someone who will comfort and urge you to be all God wants you to be. The LORD knew Gideon needed strength to fulfill God's call. And God provided it through Purah.

But why Purah?

In *The Wisdom of Purah: Gideon's Mentor,*[1] Blogger Penman Tarisai states that Purah was more experienced, older, and mature than Gideon. He was loyal to Gideon and enjoyed seeing Gideon get credit for Purah's actions.[1] We discover a treasure when we find a spouse, friend, or employee like that!

How to Be a Purah

To be a Purah, we must depend on the Word of God. The Bible is our instruction book on how Christians should live. Praying for opportunities to be used by God keeps our eyes open to recognizing occasions for service. In addition, pray for yourself to acknowledge and fulfill his will in all areas of life. What he might show you may be more than you ever thought possible.

Being a Purah to others means being a loyal friend, family member, and employee. It means being a confidant to others and thinking of them before yourself. Moreover, how we treat people is essential. Be humble, don't harbor jealousy, be available, and be grateful for whomever the Lord places in your life.

As you read the following summary from Judges 7:1-19 regarding Gideon's 300 Chosen Men, be conscious of Purah, the man behind the scenes. Often, the mighty works of God's servants have the support and prayers of others ministering to them behind the scenes, like a spouse supporting a spouse, a CEO supporting the employees, or a minister supporting his staff.

What the Bible Says about Gideon's Three Hundred Men in Judges 7:1-19: A Summary

> Gideon took his fighting men and camped south of the Midianite army, which was camped in the Valley of Jezreel. When they arrived, God told Gideon he had too many men. God wanted to reduce the number of Israelites so they wouldn't foolishly believe they won the battle by their own strength. God wanted it to be undeniable that it was His power that gave them victory. Gideon was told to allow all the men who were scared to return home. This

reduced Gideon's army from 32,000 to 10,000. Next God told Gideon to take the army to the stream to get a drink. Based on the way each man drank, he was to be separated into one of two groups. If the man kneeled and drank directly from the stream, he was put into one group. If the man took a handful of water and brought it to his mouth, he was put into the other group. God told Gideon to dismiss all the soldiers who drank directly from the stream (the 1st group). After doing so, Gideon was left with only 300 men.

God reassured Gideon He would overcome the entire Midianite force with his small band of 300 men. He told Gideon, if he still had doubts, he could sneak into the Midianite camp that night and he would find the strength he needed. So, that night, Gideon took a servant to a Midianite outpost. While there, he overheard a man telling another man about a dream he had. "Behold, I dreamed a dream, and behold, a cake of barley bread tumbled into the camp of Midian and came to the tent and struck it so that it fell and turned it upside down, so that the tent lay flat." His comrade interpreted the dream by saying, "This is no other than the sword of Gideon, the son of Joash, a man of Israel; God has given into his hand Midian and all the camp."

As soon as Gideon heard the dream and its interpretation, he worshiped God, returned to his army, and rallied them for battle. He divided them into 3 groups, gave each man a trumpet and a torch, and had them spread out around the outskirts of the enemy camp. Simultaneously the 300 soldiers revealed their torches, blew their trumpets, and cried "A sword for the Lord and for Gideon!" The Midianites and their allies panicked and ran. God caused them to become confused and they started fighting one another. Gideon's men pursued them and sent messengers to the men of Ephraim for help. They captured and killed 2 Midianite princes, Oreb and Zeeb.[2]

Being Purah's sidekick enabled Gideon to have the support and courage to do what the Lord called him to do: deliver the Israelites from the Midianites and Amalekites. Have you ever been in a challenging situation? Have you ever been afraid? Has God ever put a particular person in your path to help you when you are fearful? Not only was Gideon called to do work for the LORD, but Purah was also called to be instrumental in getting God's work done by encouraging Gideon. Both men were essential to the task at hand.

Be Unstoppable—Go the Distance with God,

Servants, be subject to your masters with all respect,
not only to those who are good and gentle, but also to those who are harsh.
1 Peter 2:18

CHAPTER 34

PETER'S TRANSFORMATION: FROM HOT-HEADEDNESS TO SPIRITUAL MATURITY

Between the day we were saved (justification)
and the day we shall be transformed into His image (glorification),
we are in the second stage, called sanctification.
We are slowly but continually being made more and more holy,
more Christ-like every day.
To be sanctified is to be "holified."

John Bisango

We all have different personalities. Most of our character and personality traits develop in childhood or are given to us by the Lord for a purpose we may or may not see. Let's look at Simon Peter, also known as the Apostle Peter in the New Testament. Peter was a fisherman who later became Jesus' disciple. He is one of the twelve disciples chosen by Jesus. Peter was a strong personality who, to outsiders and insiders, could appear inconsistent in his Christian walk. He could be a boastful, reckless, impulsive hothead at times. Some say Peter exhibited a lot of the characteristics of a person with Attention Deficit Hyperactive Disorder (ADHD). In John 18:10, we see Peter's impulsiveness when he quickly draws his sword, strikes the high priest, and cuts off his right ear. In John 21:7, when Jesus appeared to his disciples after his resurrection,

Peter heard another disciple say, "It is the Lord." Immediately, he threw off his outer garment, stripped for work, and threw himself into the sea. In Matthew 26:33, we see an example of his pride when he says to Jesus, "Though they all fall away because of you. I will never fall away."

Throughout our Christian journey, we experience ups, downs, passivity, assertiveness, or even denial, as Peter did when he denied Jesus three times before the cock crowed. But what Peter did when he realized he denied his Lord was heartfelt. He wept bitterly and was so sorrowful he had hurt his Lord and discredited Jesus' name. He showed his sensitivity when he thought he had made a shipwreck of his life by dishonoring God.

Paul charges people to wage a good warfare, saying,

> *Cling to your faith in Christ, and keep your conscience clear. For some people have deliberately violated their consciences; as a result, their faith has been shipwrecked.*
>
> *But Peter changes (1 Timothy 1:19 NLT).*

In the Book of Acts, after Pentecost, we see Peter changing and becoming more steadfast. He is continuing to develop a Godly character. He is not so self-centered or proud. We see him growing in his Christian faith. Sin can lead us to doubt God. But Peter is keeping his faith strong and learning from his experiences. He is growing and maturing in the Lord.

Faith

How can we follow Peter's example in this area of faith when our faith encounters discouragement? And we don't see answers or God's directions fast enough? Romans 10:17 ESV states, "Faith comes from hearing, and hearing through the word of Christ." We can put ourselves under the teaching of God's Word by listening to sermons, personal Bible study, and Christian fellowship. Our faith does matter to God. And, even when we are faithless, remember that God remains faithful (2 Tim. 2:13). By becoming a lifelong learner of God's ways, our faith and trust in the Lord grows, and we become more mature Christ-followers. Our maturity will show, and our fellow man will see the presence of God in actively living in us. And might I add, we are never too old to start our journey with God. Accepting Jesus Christ is just the beginning of the Christian journey; ongoing growth in the Lord is essential.

Mentoring

It is hard to believe that this hot-headed disciple from the gospels is now a great leader of love, humility, and respect for authority. After maturing, Peter is now writing 1 and 2 Peter. He imparts wisdom to others by mentoring and teaching them how to be born again to a living hope.

- be holy
- be Godly husbands and wives
- be stewards of God's grace
- be discerning of false prophets and teachers, and
- be wise in the Last Days

Maturing in faith takes place in many forms: church, Bible study, individual study, friendships, experience, and person-to-person mentoring. Regardless of the method, having someone or something to guide you in your spiritual walk is invaluable for your sanctification and growth. While the specific booklets I used are out of print, you, your family, and your friends can deepen their faith with numerous other available resources. Welcoming and adopting all forms of spiritual growth will significantly enhance a believer's spiritual journey.

My Spiritual Journey

I experienced spiritual growth through the *Introduction* and *Ten Basic Steps Toward Christian Maturity* booklets by Campus Crusade. Although I didn't have a personal mentor, these resources taught me vital concepts that shaped my faith. Through these booklets, I learned about:

1. The Christian adventure
2. The abundant life
3. The Holy Spirit
4. Prayer
5. The Bible
6. Obedience
7. Witnessing
8. Stewardship
9. Highlights of the Old Testament, and
10. Highlights of the New Testament.[1]

Peter's life is an example of growing in the Lord. Jim Scott Orrick, a writer for the *Holman Illustrated Bible Dictionary*, gives three defining features about God's free grace where we are made more and more into the image of God through our sanctification, another word for growing and maturing. "First, sanctification is an ongoing process. Second, sanctification is a work of God's free grace . . . [and] God chose you as first fruits to be saved through the sanctifying work of the Spirit and through belief in the truth .. [and believers] ought eagerly to cooperate in the process of sanctification by taking advantage of all the means of grace that God has appointed in His Word. Third, this process of being renewed after the image of God is summarized as our being abled more and more to die unto sin and live unto righteousness."[2]

Be Unstoppable—Go the Distance with God,

You therefore, beloved, knowing this beforehand, be on your guard so that you are not carried away by the error of unscrupulous people and lose your own firm commitment, but grow in the grace and knowledge of our Lord and Savior Jesus Christ. To Him be the glory, both now and to the day of eternity. Amen.
2 Peter 3:17-18

CHAPTER 35

THE SPECK AND THE LOG

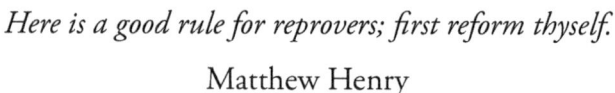

> *Here is a good rule for reprovers; first reform thyself.*
>
> Matthew Henry

> *Judge not, that you be not judged. For with what judgment you judge,*
> *you will be judged; and with the measure you use,*
> *it will be measured back to you.*
> *And why do you look at the speck in your brother's eye,*
> *but do not consider the plank in your own eye?*
> *Or how can you say to your brother,*
> *'Let me remove the speck from your eye'; and look, a plank is in your own*
> *eye? Hypocrite! First remove the plank from your own eye, and then*
> *you will see clearly to remove the speck from your brother's eye.*
>
> Matthew 7:1-5 NKJV

Many reasons abound as to why we enjoy judging others and take secret delight in seeing the speck (fault) in our brothers. We can blame it on human nature: we like to revel in gossip, pride, or anger, to name a few. Often, when we judge others, we are justifying ourselves and our actions. A fine example of this type of justification appears in Luke 18 between the Pharisee and the tax collector.

> *Two men went up to the temple to pray, one a Pharisee and the*
> *other a tax collector.*

The Pharisee stood and prayed thus with himself, 'God, I thank You that I am not like other men—extortioners, unjust, adulterers, or even as this tax collector. I fast twice a week; I give tithes of all that I possess.' And the tax collector, standing afar off, would not so much as raise his eyes to heaven, but beat his breast, saying, 'God, be merciful to me a sinner! (Luke 18:9-13 NKJV).

Speck and the Log: Mote and Beam/Plank

Different versions of the Bible call a speck a "mote" or a "speck of sawdust" while a log may be called a "beam" or a "plank." No matter what synonymous term appears, a speck defines itself along the terms of a minor fault (comparing it to something that might fly into your eye), and a log compares to a beam that could support an entire building. If you are like me, you might see "specks" in your children, spouse, so called friends, bosses, co-workers, and even people you don't know, like public speakers or preachers. I even hate to admit this, but a newscaster really bothers me because she tilts her head back and forth in both directions. What we do with our perceived faults/specks of others is interesting. Sometimes, we do nothing; occasionally, we hastily utter their faults to them or others; sometimes, we hold our thoughts in and let the annoyance grow and grow; and sometimes, we pray about it. And, through our meditation and Bible reading, we ask the Lord what, when, if, and how God wants us to deal with another without being an unrighteous judge! We often see a reflection of us in others, and God uses that annoyance/fault/sin to show us our log.

When I pondered this chapter's introductory Bible verse—Matthew 7:1-5—a series of thoughts and questions flooded my mind. This train of thought led me to consider whether there was a right way for others to point out someone else's faults.

Questions about

Our Log

1. Who is supposed to tell me about my logs? Kids? Spouse? Parents? Friends? God?

2. How should I prepare myself to hear bad news about myself?
3. Why do we seem to notice the faults (specks) in others but fail to see our own?
4. Where does humility come into play in all of this?

Others' Specks

1. Why do I feel the need to judge others for their faults?
2. Is it okay to tell someone about their speck, if I perceive they are in danger?

These questions made me realize that I needed to work on removing the log from my own eye before I could help others with their specks. I wondered if I was a hypocrite. I asked myself if I really wanted to hear what the Lord might tell me. As you can see, these questions brought me many more of these questions than I anticipated. If I thought beyond the few minutes it took to come up with these questions, I could double the number of questions that would quickly come to the top of my head. As I ponder these verses, there are three subjects to consider: (a) judging others, (b) our brother's speck, and (c) our log. It does not address our speck or our brother's log. While I am not a theologian, I suspect that speck and log are used in the singular vernacular because the Lord may want us to concentrate only on one speck or log at a time. However, a theologian scholar would be best able to answer that question as my cursory research into Bible commentaries and "Google" gave no answers. As for this chapter, the words speck, and log will be used uniformly throughout. In addition, *Strong's Concordance* defines a brother as a member of the same religious community, especially a fellow Christian.

Judging Others

Jesus said,
Do not judge so that you will not be judged. For in the way you judge, you will be judged; and by your standard of measure, it will be measured to you (Matthew 7:1-2).

Paul said,
Brethren, even if anyone is caught in any trespass, you who are

spiritual, restore such a one in a spirit of gentleness; each one looking to yourself, so that you too will not be tempted. Bear one another's burdens, and thereby fulfill the law of Christ (Galatians 6:1-2).

These two verses seem paradoxical. On one hand, we shouldn't judge others; on the other hand, we should aim to restore a person. Jesus tells us to first examine ourselves and repent of our sins before we confront others. We can only help others after cleansing ourselves, and we must do so gently. For instance, if we're having a marital affair ourselves, it would be hypocritical to tell someone else not to have one.

Specks Hurts

Think about how you feel when you get something in your eye. Eye doctors know that even small objects in someone's eyes can cause scratches or abrasions on a cornea. While usually just rinsing your eye can alleviate the symptoms and discomfort, these small objects can occasionally cause an infection or cause one to lose their eyesight.

Our son Jimmy once experienced extreme pain in his eyes. He tried driving to work but had to turn around and come home after driving only a mile from our house. He couldn't see; the pain was excruciating, and he couldn't even keep his eyes open. This eye problem became an emergency, necessitating immediate treatment. Pain, attentive parenting, excellent doctors, and medicine restored our son's eyesight. Thus, the problem was that he slept with his contacts in, against his ophthalmologist's recommendations. He did not follow the suggested "rules" for contact wearers, so he put himself in harm's way. When we do not follow God's biblical "rules" outlined in the Bible, we can easily and quickly produce a speck that needs immediate attention. And the one who has already taken the log out of their eye is usually the one to come to peoples' rescue. If we had told our son that he was responsible for his eye situation and that he put himself in this dire situation but didn't offer any solutions to help him, his life could have changed dramatically.

Sometimes, God will call us to confront people about their speck expeditiously – because it could be an emergency, and God does not want their condition to worsen.

Someday, someone may bring to our attention a flaw in our behavior, like an issue we might be overlooking. This could happen if we are at risk of committing adultery, drinking excessively, engaging in pornography, or gossiping. When this occurs, it's important to listen carefully. God may be using that person to guide us back to the right path or to protect us from more severe consequences.

Our Log

Now, let's talk about our log. Remember, our log is like a giant beam—something we have difficulty seeing ourselves. Confronting our log is painful. We often don't even think about what log or logs we have in our own eyes. I read once that when you want to know what your log is, you should ask someone close to you, someone who would be honest with you.

So, as I was writing this chapter, I asked my husband, John, if he would tell me what log I have in my life. His immediate response was, "Just one?" Not exactly what I was expecting, but as he contemplated how to answer me, he couldn't pinpoint what to tell me that day. Wise man! But, when I asked him again the next day, he gave me an answer after he prayed about it. I was shocked at his answer. I never thought of myself in the words he described. And no, I am not telling you, my readers, what he said. However, I asked John with a genuine desire to know.

We usually don't think about the log in our eyes. While I have read Matthew 7 multiple times, I was unsure how I felt about my log until I started writing this book. Some might not want to confront their log because it might cause them to change, disrupt their lives, confront their sins, or recognize their pride. That is something to think about.

Constructive Guidelines for Discussing Someone's Specks

Our DNA presents imperfection, not perfection. We are not perfect, but our willingness to be clean vessels for God does not go unnoticed by God. The Lord might prompt us to speak to others about their speck; but only after the log is out of our eyes. It is not loving to criticize others and call attention to their faults without ensuring our log has been laid at the feet of Jesus. If we feel a holy hutch to discuss this very sensitive topic with another person, take the following guidelines to heart first.

1. Pray for Wisdom and Discernment: Begin by praying until the Lord confirms that you should address a person. Ask if you are indeed the right person to discuss someone's struggles.

2. Develop a Loving, Humble, and Honest Heart: Cultivate a heart full of love and humility. Cleanse yourself from any known sin and take time for personal reflection.

3. Seek God's Perspective: Pray to see the person through God's eyes. Foster compassion and understanding as you prepare for the conversation.

4. Familiarize Yourself with Scripture: Understand relevant Scripture that pertains to the situation. This will help ground your approach in truth.

5. Identify the Sin: Clearly identify the exact or potential sin the person is committing. Ensure you are not grappling with a similar sin that would hinder your ability to provide constructive reproof.

6. Prepare to Approach with Humility: Approach the situation with humility, avoiding any sense of pride or superiority. Always remember the golden rule—treat others as you would want to be treated.

7. Communicate with Kindness and Respect: When the time comes to speak, do so with kindness and respect. Be prepared to share truth with love, addressing the issue with righteousness and compassion without making accusations based on assumptions.

8. Be Open to Fasting: Consider fasting if it helps you seek deeper clarity about the conversation and the person involved.

9. Focus on the Issue at Hand: Stay focused on the issue being discussed and remain sensitive to the Holy Spirit's leading throughout the process.

10. Provide Encouragement and Guidance: Finally, offer encouragement and guidance as you navigate this difficult but necessary conversation.

Following these guidelines will help ensure that your discussion is spiritually grounded and respectful. Remember, you might one day be on the receiving end of the stick.

Be Unstoppable—Go the Distance with God,

My brothers and sisters, if anyone among you strays from the truth and someone turns him back, let him know that the one who has turned a sinner from the error of his way will save his soul from death and cover a multitude of sins. James 5:19-20

SECTION 4

**Pioneering Leadership
Principles and
Characters**

CHAPTER 36

BARNABAS: THE HEART OF NEW TESTAMENT SERVICE

> *To lead like Christ, we must carry about us the attributes of Christ that are reflected through our ministry.*
>
> A.W. Tozer

Following Christ means embracing self-denial to follow in his footsteps. Jesus emphasized, "If anyone wishes to come after Me, he must deny himself, take up his cross daily and follow Me" (Luke 9:23). This verse serves as a cornerstone for believers and church leaders.

During Barnabas' years in ministry, Christ-followers possessed their heart's intent on following Jesus and a profound commitment to following Jesus' servant leadership model. This goal was accomplished using Jesus' style of leadership—servant leadership. Born and raised in Cyprus, and named Joseph (Joses). His training and upbringing stemmed from him being a Levite of Jewish descent. His name appears twenty-three times in the Book of Acts and five times in Apostle Paul's letters. The Apostle Luke interprets Barnabas into the Greek words *huios paracletes*, which translates as "son of encouragement," "son of comfort," or "Son of Exhortation." Some say it could mean "son of a prophet," but then doubts are cast about why Luke calls him the "Son of Encouragement" (Acts 4:36)[1]

Barnabas' Qualities, Strengths, and Weaknesses

Throughout the Book of Acts, we see generosity, encouragement, leadership, loyalty, friendship, consistency as a team player, and a love for God. His focus on the mission God had prepared for him is evident through his words and actions. Barnabas' illustrations of his strengths include selling property, giving the profits to the Jerusalem church, meeting and introducing Paul to the church in Jerusalem, being commissioned to travel to Syrian Antioch to evaluate what was happening with the preaching and Christianity there, leading the first missionary journey with Paul, setting out on a missionary journey with his cousin John Mark, and an instrumental leader in Cyprus, Antioch, and Jerusalem.

Godly character and behavior remained pivotal throughout Barnabas' life. His strong personality was developed by his love and dedication to salvation and God's call upon his life. Barnabas naturally had multiple strengths. They serve as a blueprint for ministry leaders, emphasizing the importance of humility, integrity, and a relentless pursuit of God's call upon a person.

Personal Qualities Affecting Barnabas' Reputation

1. **Big-hearted:** When Barnabas sold his land to give to the early Christian community, that behavior was rare then. Could this be one of the first relief work missions that one sees from the New Testament?

2. **Persuasive:** In Jerusalem, Barnabas received a distant reception because the disciples could not believe that Paul had changed from a persecutor to a follower of Jesus. Barnabas persuaded them, and they eventually believed Paul was a disciple of Christ.

3. **Loyal:** Barnabas was faithful to John Mark when he abandoned his work on the first missionary journey. He did not allow the disagreement when Paul refused to have John Mark participate in the second missionary journey to affect their relationship. Due to Barnabas' encouragement, vital contributions from both Paul and Mark impacted the Christian faith and the New Testament.

4. **Exceptional evangelist:** Many souls accepted Christ as he traveled from city to city, church to church.

5. **Discerning:** Barnabas discerned that Paul's character transformed from a sinner to a believer in Jesus Christ.

6. **Humble:** Barnabas followed wherever invited or led. He did not show one-upmanship or comparison to others as he lived.

7. **Filled with the Holy Spirit:** Barnabas would not have been able to minister as he did without the Holy Spirit leading and guiding him.

8. **Encouraging:** As an encourager, he could keep peace with Paul through a lasting friendship and inspire those he met along his life journey.

However, hypocrisy was a weakness mentioned by the Apostle Paul regarding Peter and Barnabas. Paul accused Peter and Barnabas of being hypocrites because they separated and feared the circumcision party. Paul mentions that "even Barnabas was carried away by their hypocrisy" (Gal. 2:13). Not knowing the heart of Barnabas on this matter, this weakness may or may not be accurate since we should never judge others primarily based on the word of only one person and this one incident.

Principles and Issues on Leadership

Over the years, many secular scholars have tried to conceptualize and define leadership. Peter G. Northouse defines leadership as: "a process whereby an individual influences a group of individuals to achieve a common goal."[2] While that is a helpful definition, Jesus' life and lifestyle would be more appropriate if one were to look for the biblical description and qualities a leader should possess. In *Jesus on Leadership*, C. Gene Wilkes discusses seven servant leadership principles. These principles are demonstrated to one degree or another in Barnabas.

Barnabas' Servant Leadership Qualities in *Jesus on Leadership*

First, Barnabas' humility and generosity are recognized in Acts 4:37, where he sold a tract of his land, brought the money, and laid it at the apostle's feet to be appropriated as needed in the Jerusalem church. Second, Barnabas' belief that people can change for good is noted in Acts

9:26-27 when the disciples feared Paul. Barnabas told the apostles that he had talked to Paul and spoken out boldly for Jesus. Third, In Acts 15:35, Barnabas is regarded as a leader proclaiming the words of the Lord. His leadership is shown in his involvement with the Council of Jerusalem. There, Paul and Barnabas afforded "the right hand of fellowship, that we might go to the Gentiles" to proclaim God's message of salvation (Gal. 2:9). Fourth, Barnabas continued in Jesus' footsteps by being a risk-taker. When Paul would not allow John Mark to accompany him on his second missionary journey, he took John Mark under his wing, and they proceeded to proclaim the Lord to the world, even though John Mark deserted them on the first missionary journey. Fifth, serving others through his preaching, teaching, and mentoring was Barnabas' everyday behavior. In Acts 13:42-43, the people in the synagogue begged Paul and Barnabas to continue to speak to them. Both these men served the Lord by encouraging them to persist in the grace of God. Sixth, Barnabas loved God and recognized God's authority over his life. *In Jesus on Leadership*, Wilkes says, "Barnabas' relationship to God helped him see past the fear of others and come alongside Paul who would ultimately take the message of Jesus to all people groups."[3]

Finally, Barnabas built a close-knit team by mentoring Paul and John Mark. However, he also left the mark of Jesus upon all the churches and cities he traveled to share the Good News of Jesus Christ.[3]

How Barnabas' Leadership Applies to Ministry Settings

Studying the life of Barnabas brings many principles that one can apply to a servant leadership style. Values arising from these principles may be valuable to any Christ-follower working in a secular or Christian environment.

Like Barnabas did, striving, desiring, and working toward a life of holiness is essential to one's spiritual growth and ability to lead. His lifestyle of character, integrity, and submission to the Lord represents a true disciple of God. His determination steered him to possess and retain God's heart. He lived and served as Jesus did, and Jesus' influence led him to behave and interact lovingly with others. Standing up for what is right and acknowledging God as our strength in our ministries creates a life that others will want to emulate. Honesty and honest work are vital. Leading like Christ and behaving like Christ is how ministry workers should behave and lead. Just as Barnabas served people, so must those in ministry.

However, how is that done? Wilkes says, "Servant and leader stand together as a model for those entrusted with the well-being of a group. Leaders who follow the example and teachings of Jesus will lead first as servants."[4] My personal goal for ministry leadership aligns with Wilkes' beliefs: to pray for humility, patience, a desire to put others before me, take risks, and equip others well. Pressing on toward the upward call of God in Christ Jesus is a worthy goal. When that goal is at the forefront of a believer's mind, as it was with Barnabas, servant leadership will follow.

Legend says this Barnabas died a martyr's death at Salamis in AD 61. His legacy includes possibly one of the seventy mentioned in Luke 10:1 and the traditional founder of the Cypriot Church. Most would agree with Norman Blackaby and Wilkes that Barnabas' leadership and character "made a lasting difference in the lives of millions because he demonstrated the heart of God."[5]

Jesus as the Model of Servant Leadership

Barnabas' leadership qualities are reflected in various locations in the Bible that closely mimic the same leadership model of Jesus. Jesus played a significant role in shaping our understanding of both servanthood and leadership. He exemplified humility by submitting to God's will instead of pursuing personal status or recognition. In his teachings, Jesus redefined greatness, emphasizing that true significance lies in serving others. He demonstrated this principle by choosing to serve even in humble circumstances, trusting fully in his identity as God's Son. By stepping away from his prestigious position as God's son to serve in his humanity role to meet the needs of those around him, Jesus showcased servant leadership. Furthermore, he shared responsibility and authority with his followers, empowering them to lead, while building a cohesive team dedicated to fulfilling a global mission. Through these actions, Jesus illustrated that effective leadership is rooted in the willingness to serve.

Reflecting on Spiritual Growth

People mature and grow in their faith in their own unique ways. We all grow at various times and through multiple means. I've been thinking about that dreaded feeling I experienced when I realized a painter had painted over all the markings on our "kid's growth chart." Before the days of professionally made wooden and personalized growth charts, I used to mark our kids' height and growth on the inside of the pantry door in our home but when the "chart" ended its presence, I felt like their growth topped out, as irrational as that sounds.

As individuals, we all strive towards achieving spiritual growth and development. One way to measure our progress is by assessing our spiritual growth chart. It helps us understand whether we are on track, short, tall, or healthy in our journey. We must ask ourselves," Are you in a season of mighty growth?" to evaluate our progress and identify improvement areas. By consistently examining our spiritual growth, we can continue to grow, develop and reach our full potential in all aspects of life. Or could it be possible that our growth is no longer visible, just like how our kid's pencil and pen growth chart no longer prevailed?

Unfortunately, our growth chart patterns sometimes signal a spiritual problem, affecting the call the Lord intended for our lives—especially in leading God's way. Christ-followers are all sinners—even Barnabas. But his growth and love for the Lord is depicted throughout his service life, as should ours.

Be Unstoppable—Go the Distance with God,

Brethren, I do not regard myself as having laid hold of it yet; but one thing I do: forgetting what lies behind and reaching forward to what lies ahead. I press on toward the goal for the prize of the upward call of God in Christ Jesus. Philippians 3:13-14

CHAPTER 37

NEHEMIAH: THE UNLIKELY LEADER WHO BUILT WALLS AND HEARTS

> *It doesn't matter if your job is secular or if your job is ministry. Ultimately, you still work for the Master, so don't make excuses.*
>
> John Bisango

Nehemiah, often mistaken as a prophet or priest, was a regular person like most of us, serving the Lord in a layman's capacity. His remarkable story begins in the ancient city of Shushan, where he served the Persian King. But his legacy transcends his role as a cupbearer, as he emerges as a symbol of determination and leadership, rebuilding the walls of Jerusalem and fortifying the city. His unique leadership skills, such as determination and the ability to inspire others, are worth emulating. Most scholars suggest the book starts around 444 and 445 BC. The temple had been rebuilt, but there were no walls to protect or fortify the city. Nehemiah traveled to Israel, leading the third Jewish journey back to Israel after being in Babylonian captivity for 70 years. His reputation was that of a humble man with an upright character. He exhibited determination and leadership to fulfill the calling the Lord bestowed upon him. He talked to nobles, rulers, and the people, and planned to prevent injustice. This steadfast commitment to stand up for what is right is a crucial aspect of leadership.

Each one of us has a leadership role. It might be as a minister, a church member, a boss, a teacher, a parent, a politician, or a business owner. My husband was a manager in the corporate real estate profession. If you asked him how difficult it is to start a building project, he would tell you that it is not the easiest thing to accomplish. There are a lot of factors involved, like which country you are going to build in, the legal laws of the land, how much money is needed, who should be involved, how obstacles should be handled, the leadership of the people involved, and the timeline for completion.

Let's examine ten leadership skills using Nehemiah as our model. We can be masterful leaders in the various positions God has called us, whether in the office, ministry, or home.

Leadership Skills

1. Make Your Voice and Presence Known to Those Who Count.

Nehemiah sat down and wept when the wall of Jerusalem and its gates were found destroyed. He mourned for days and prayed to God. It was the Lord to whom Nehemiah first made his voice and presence known. Then, in the first part of Nehemiah 2, he addresses the King. Notice that when Nehemiah fervently prayed over this need, God put it in his heart to be the person to meet that need, as it often happens with us. After praying about a situation or issue, we often find ourselves the one or part of a group to help with that matter. As did Nehemiah, we all have projects or goals the Lord has given us or wants to accomplish. Let's accept God's calling and see if we can utilize some of Nehemiah's strategies to succeed.

> *Let your ear be attentive and your eyes open, to hear the prayer of your servant that I now pray before you day and night for the people of Israel your servants, confessing the sins of the people of Israel, which we have sinned against you. Even I and my father's house have sinned (Nehemiah 1:6 ESV).*

2. Spend Time Planning Your Project(s).

Nehemiah arrived in Jerusalem with a good reputation from his time in Shushan. His reputation followed him, and the people already respected him. He could have immediately told his workers what to do. But, as a leader, he understood the importance of evaluating the situation, spending the time planning, and evaluating how to approach others. This emphasis on planning is a key aspect of effective leadership. How often do we involve ourselves in a project without adequate preparation? It's too frequent. In this chapter, we see Nehemiah laying out his strategy for meeting the goal of restoring the wall around Jerusalem.

> *I went out by night by the Valley Gate to the Dragon Spring and to the Dung Gate, and I inspected the walls of Jerusalem that were broken down and its gates that had been destroyed by fire (Nehemiah 2:13 ESV).*

3. Stand Up for What is Right.

While being a Godly man, Nehemiah became angry when he heard about the injustices in Jerusalem. He experienced ridicule by Sanballat, Tobiah, the Arabians, Ammonites, and Ashdodites. They were angry because God had proposed his plans in Nehemiah's heart to restore the wall. Nehemiah prayed while his enemies were conspiring to go to Jerusalem to persecute, hinder, and try to stop the progress on the wall. But Nehemiah was confident in what God had called him and his men to do. He talked to the nobles, the rulers, and the people and planned to prevent injustice from occurring. This steadfast commitment standing up for what is right is a crucial aspect of leadership.

In our leadership roles, do we ever see injustices? If so, we would be well-advised to follow Nehemiah's example—to pray—and then talk to the right people about it.

> *And we prayed to our God and set a guard as a protection against them day and night . . . And I looked and arose and said to the nobles and to the officials and to the rest of the people, "Do not be afraid of them. Remember the Lord, who is great and awesome, and fight for your brothers, your sons, your daughters, your wives, and your houses (Nehemiah 4:9, 14).*

4. Set Clear Expectations for Performance

Even while men plotted against Nehemiah, we can deduce that Nehemiah had his game plan in motion. His men knew what to do. How do we know this? We understand this because his men finished the project in fifty-two days. That was a fantastic feat! Nehemiah needed direction to leave his men to fend for themselves. He gave them specific and sensible instructions. The men of Jericho, the Levites, the Priests, and the other builders knew what part of the wall was assigned for them to build. These workers enjoyed working for someone they respected and who had clear plans and guidelines in place. As leaders, we should make our expectations clear to those working with and alongside us.

> *The wall was finished on the twenty-fifth day of Elul, in fifty-two days. And when all our enemies heard of it, all the nations around us were afraid and fell considerably in their own esteem, for they perceived that this work had been accomplished with the help of our God (Nehemiah 6:15-16 ESV).*

5. Surround Yourself with Good Talent.

After the wall and all the gates were built, Nehemiah gave his brother Hanani and Hananiah charge over Jerusalem. But why? He gave them the job because they had already proven they could handle the mission. Nehemiah was honoring the hard work and trustworthiness he had already observed in them. When you need to ask someone to take charge of a job or project, do you find yourself asking the person you think is the most capable and dependable? Most of us do. However, sometimes, leaders try to do too much themselves without delegating. When we reach the state of being an overseer, it is time to move away from being the specialist and become the generalist who sees the big picture using the talented people you have charge over. Nehemiah did.

> *Now when the wall had been built and I had set up the doors, and the gatekeeps, the singers, and the Levites had been appointed. I gave my brother Hanani and Hananiah the governor of the castle charge over Jerusalem, for he was a more faithful and God-fearing man than many (Nehemiah 7:1-2 ESV).*

6. Be Humble and Acknowledge that God is Your Strength.

Many believe the books of Nehemiah and Ezra to have originally been one combined book in the Bible. It is obvious that Ezra, the priest and scribe, and Nehemiah, governor in Jerusalem and re-builder of the city wall, were colleagues. After the completion of the wall, the people needed some reconstruction of their own. We find Ezra and other Israelites gathering by the Water Gate, worshiping, reading the Law, teaching the people to acknowledge the Lord, and encouraging them to study and understand the words of divine instruction. Then, on this HOLY DAY, we see Nehemiah, Ezra, and the Levites rejoicing.

If you are in a ministry role, like Vacation Bible School, the workers must regroup and be encouraged again to stay working for the Lord and seek to please him as they move forward. Do you encourage your employees (or volunteers) to worship humbly, read the Bible, enable them to study God's Word, and reiterate that God is their strength, especially after a major project? If so, then leaders can mitigate the post-ministry slump by focusing on upcoming projects, ministries, or learning opportunities.

In a work environment, when your employees perform remarkably well by completing a complex project, do you just let their "high" accomplishments go unnoticed, or do you praise them and encourage them to continue with their excellent work?

> *And Ezra blessed the Lord, the great God, and all the people answered, 'Amen, Amen,' lifting their hands. And they bowed their heads and worshipped the Lord with their faces on the ground (Nehemiah 8:6 ESV).*

> *And Nehemiah, who was the governor, and Ezra the priest and scribe, and the Levites who taught the people said to all the people, 'This day is holy to the Lord your God; do not mourn or weep.' For all the people wept as they heard the words of the Law. Then he said to them, 'Go your way. Eat the fat and drink sweet wine and send portions to anyone who has nothing ready, for this day is holy to our Lord. And do not be grieved, for the joy of the Lord is your strength.' So the Levites calmed all the people, saying, 'Be quiet, for this day is holy; do not be grieved.' And all the people went their*

way to eat and drink and to send portions and to make great
rejoicing because they had understood the words that were declared
to them (Nehemiah 9-12 ESV).

7. Correct and Admonish When Needed.

The time will come when someone who works for you needs correction and admonishment. It is a thorny and sensitive issue that leaders face. Nehemiah could lessen the load by pre-handling this, giving his men an example from the Book of Deuteronomy, which they all understood. Moses explained to the gathered rebellious children of Israel the consequences of their disobedience (namely, arousing God's ire and where that may lead). What better way to lead than to pre-warn people of situations that may arise, where correction, admonishment, or even firing may result, by talking about it beforehand? How wise!

In Nehemiah 9:28-29, after they rested, they did evil again, and evil had power over then. When they cried out to God, they heard from heaven. God heard their cries, and he delivered them according to his mercies. Unfortunately, they did not obey God's commandments and sinned against the law. Their stubbornness would not obey God!

8. Obey the Company or Ministry Policies.

Companies, churches, organizations, and families have policies and rules of ethics. They are there to be abided by unless they are against God's laws; in that case, decisions and prayerful considerations need a course of action. If your ministry (individual or group) does not have policies, it may be time to develop them. Many ministries have or are developing boards or foundations to oversee their activities to ensure they operate under an authoritative source.

In Nehemiah 10, the purpose was to join and bind the people with an oath to follow God's laws, commands, regulations, and decrees. Rules and codes of behavior are fundamental in corporate offices, ministries, and even within homes where children are growing up under their parents' instructions.

The rest of the people, the priests, the Levites, the gatekeepers, the
singers, the temple servants, and all who have separated themselves

from the peoples of the lands to the Law of God, their wives, their sons, their daughters, all who have knowledge and understanding (Nehemiah 10:28 ESV).

And if the peoples of the land bring in goods or any grain on the Sabbath day to sell, we will not buy from them on the Sabbath or on a holy day. And we will forego the crops of the seventh year and the exaction of every debt (Nehemiah 10:31 ESV).

9. Celebrate the Achievements of Others.

Nehemiah celebrated the dedication of the wall with gladness. We see achievement awards, 10-year anniversary recognitions, and "Good Job" certificates in both businesses and churches. All these play an important role among those who have worked with you to achieve the goals the Lord has given you. You may not even be aware that those working for you are inwardly proud of their personal accomplishments through "your" project. If you close a deal at work, how about a party to acknowledge your employees' excellent and steadfast work? How about throwing a dinner to thank those who volunteer their time and effort in the ministry? And what's wrong with some ice cream for good grades?

At the dedication of the wall of Jerusalem, the Levites were sought out from where they lived and were brought to Jerusalem to celebrate joyfully the dedication with songs of thanksgiving and with the music of cymbals, harps and lyres (Nehemiah 12:27 ESV).

10. Define Roles and Responsibilities AGAIN.

Defining roles and responsibilities is a process in ministry and work. People must be taught and retaught. Just as in our lives, we must perpetually be in the Word of God and frequently hear God's expectations. It isn't just going to church on Sundays. It isn't just going to a conference. It isn't praying only in our time of need. Our bosses or ministers will not always be around to instruct us, as was the case with Nehemiah; when he wasn't there, the people turned to ungodly activities.

Finally, in Nehemiah 13:6-7, we see that Nehemiah had left Jerusalem during the thirty-second year of King Artaxerxes' reign. But, when he returned, he found the house of God in disarray. Widespread shenanigans were going on in his absence. Upon arrival in Jerusalem, Nehemiah commanded that the chambers be cleaned. He contended with the officials and asked them why the house of the Lord had been neglected and forsaken. Nehemiah reproved the nobles and warned them. He cleansed them from everything heathen and started all over again with defining roles and responsibilities.

We, as individuals, must remember that we must stay in contact with the Lord. We can't live in someone else's shadow. And, as leaders, we need to constantly remind those working with us to be responsible and obedient, with or without "the leader or boss" around. This chapter reminds me of the idiom, "When the cat's away, the mice will play." Let's be responsible and teach those under our leadership to always act with integrity and honesty.

Nehemiah's contributions, administrative skills, and ability to face obstacles were honorable, and he acknowledged his strength came from the Lord. He completed the work God assigned to him. He faced obstacles honorably. He admitted his strength came from the Lord. If only he were here, I'd throw him a party of grain, legumes, and domesticated beasts to celebrate the legacy he left behind to the family of God, because as Psalm 78:72 foretold the principle of shepherding, "he shepherded them according to the integrity of his heart and guided them with his skillful hands."[1][2]

Be Unstoppable—Go the Distance with God,

Then I will give you shepherds after My own heart,
who will feed you on knowledge and understanding.
Jeremiah 3:15

CHAPTER 38

EXPLORING LEADERSHIP
THROUGH
THE WISDOM OF PROVERBS

Conduct flows from faith just as a stream flows from a fountain.

A.W. Tozer

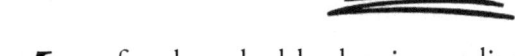

Most of us have had leaders in our lives. They come from parents, employers, mayors, pastors, principals, and presidents. The Book of Proverbs delves into the qualities of both good and bad leaders. Both testaments mention good/wise leaders and bad/evil leaders throughout the Old and New Testaments. Today, in all occupations, we find leaders from both extremes and some in-between. As in the Bible, today's leaders can change: There are good leaders who remain good, bad leaders who remain bad, bad leaders who turn good, and good leaders who turn bad.

As a point of trivia, it is interesting to note that the House of Israel had more bad kings than the House of Judah did. But let's look now only at the Southern Kingdom—The House of Judah. The Southern Kingdom consisted of two tribes, Judah, and Benjamin. The Kingdom extended in the north of Israel as far as Bethel, while in the south, it ended in the dry desert area known as the Negev. Its eastern and western boundaries were the Jordan River and the Mediterranean Sea, respectively. Jerusalem was its capital, and it lasted from about 922 to 586 BC.

During this period, eight kings were considered good, and eleven were considered evil in the sight of the Lord. Two of the eight good kings bounced between extremes during their lives. Kings Asa, Jehoshaphat, Uzziah, Jotham, Hezekiah, and Josiah are noted in most commentaries as "good" kings. At the same time, Joash and Amaziah are recognized as kings who did right in their youth but evil in their old age.

King Jehoshaphat was an example of a good king. He ruled the House of Judah between 873 and 849 BC. When Jehoshaphat was twenty-five years old, he ascended to the throne. He established peace between the Northern and Southern Kingdoms and eliminated Baal worship in Judah. He sought God's approval when attempting to recover Ramoth-Gilead from the Syrians. Jehoshaphat had a highly successful military career. He encouraged the worship of God and reformed the justice system. He died at the age of sixty, leaving a kingdom that loved him.

While the list below is far from exhaustive, it is still instructive to enumerate the leadership qualities of a good leader taken directly from *The Holy Bible English Standard Version*.

Chart 1

Good Leaders: Book of Proverbs

Knows wisdom and instruction	Proverbs 1:2
Receives instruction in wise dealing in righteousness, justice, and equity	Proverbs 1:3
Gives knowledge and discretion to the youth	Proverbs 1:4
Listens and increases in learning	Proverbs 1:5
Obtains guidance	Proverbs 1:5
Fears the Lord	Proverbs 1:7
Walks in the way of righteousness	Proverbs 8:20
Embraces God's instructions	Proverbs 8:32-33
Walks with integrity	Proverbs 10:9
Gives thought to his steps	Proverbs 14:15
Acts cautiously and turns away from evil	Proverbs 14:16
Their prayers are acceptable to God	Proverbs 15:8
Speaks with divine wisdom and never judges unfairly	Proverbs 16:10
Commits their work to the LORD	Proverbs 16:13
Life shows in their face	Proverbs 16:15
Acquires and seeks knowledge	Proverbs 18:15
Sifts out the wicked from the good	Proverbs 20:26
Conducts themselves with purity and righteousness	Proverbs 21:8
Possesses strength, and their knowledge enhances their might	Proverbs 24:5
Has an abundance of counselors	Proverbs 24:6
Leads their land [their territory] toward stability	Proverbs 28:2
Understands justice	Proverbs 28:5
Builds their land [their territory/the people]	Proverbs 29:4
Knows the rights of the poor	Proverbs 29:7
Possesses self-control; does not listen to lies	Proverbs 28:12a
Faithfully judges the poor	Proverbs 29:14
Not hasty in words	Proverbs 29-20
Does not drink excessively [or at all]	Proverbs 31:4b
Judges righteously and defends the rights of the poor and needy	Proverbs 31:9

Look at those with a leadership role over us and see how many of the preceding qualities they possess. While we are all human and imperfect, possessing some of these attributes is an excellent start to becoming a good leader in whatever field or occupation we find ourselves today.

Bad Leaders

Just as there are good leaders, there are also bad leaders. Bad leaders come in many varieties. There are bad military leaders, dictators, bosses, presidents, labor leaders, church leaders, business leaders, parents, and more. I use the term bad to explain that they are not functioning in a good capacity—maybe it's their personality, style, or even lack of training. Who knows?

When living in St. Peters, Missouri, our fifth-grade son joined the YMCA's basketball team. It was his very first encounter with team basketball, and he was a novice, while most of the other boys were experienced in the game. One Saturday morning game, two teams were running up and down the court, acting as if they were big-shot basketball players playing like their win would get them into the Basketball Hall of Fame. On a side note, our son was skipping up and down the court. It was cute, but not the most precise pose for an aggressive basketball team.

During the last few seconds of the game, our son just happened to get his hands on the ball, shot it, and it went right through the hoop! His surprise score won the game for his team. He was the hero! He got the applause, the high-fives, and the pats on the back. Then, the fireworks began. There was a more experienced and vigorous fifth grader on the team whose father felt his son should have made the winning dunk. Out in the lobby of the YMCA, this father hit his son and hollered at him for not taking the ball away from our son and making the winning play himself. I will never forget the look on that boy's face while enduring the torrent of belittlement, abuse, and humiliation from his father. The next thing we saw was the father rammed into the back of a police car in the YMCA parking lot. Someone must have called and reported him. Now, this is a real-life example of a poor parental leader. Not only did he belittle and embarrass his son, but he also exhibited jealousy, violence, and arrogance.

Many commentaries call Ahab one of Israel's most wicked kings. Even God said that Ahab did more evil than any other king before him. Ahab was king of Israel from around 869 to 850 BC. While he was an able warrior, he was utterly disloyal to God and embraced his wicked wife Jezebel's paganism. The LORD allowed Ahab the opportunity to redeem himself through the Prophet Elijah, but Ahab refused. His legacy is intermingled with Jezebel's, but Ahab's father, King Omri, taught Ahab to be cruel, and as such, Omri, is remembered as an evil and corrupt king. In Richard R. Losch's book *All the People in the Bible*, the author describes Ahab as being "one of [the Scriptures'] more notorious scoundrels."[1]

Success Magazine mentions in "15 Traits of a Terrible Leader" qualities: a lack of transparency, dismissing ideas other than your own, being egotistical and closed-minded, a lack of empathy, poor communication, and inconsistency.[2]

In biblical history, Herodias, Jehoram of Judah, Abimelech, Herod, and Judas Iscariot were leaders in the Bible known as terrible leaders. In *Worst Presidents: Warren Harding (1921-1923)* by Jay Tolson, Harding was mentioned as one of the worst Presidents of the United States because he was more concerned with his womanizing, poker, and golf.[3] Even Harding himself admitted it, saying: "I am not fit for this office, and should never have been here."[3]

I hope the basketball father mentioned earlier made a turnaround. Watching "bad leadership" in action is not pleasant. I was highly disturbed that our children had to witness this scene unfold.

Bad Leaders: Book of Proverbs

Again, while I wouldn't say I like listing a long, non-exhaustive list of qualities of a bad leader, I will because by looking at them, one might see themselves and improve in one area or another, and balance out the quality listing of good leaders.

As with good leader qualities, the deficiencies following also come directly from *The Holy Bible English Standard Version*.

Chart 2

Bad Leaders: Book of Proverbs

Despises wisdom and instruction	Proverbs 1:7
Hates knowledge	Proverbs 1:22
Can't sleep unless they have done wrong	Proverbs 4:19
Lacks discipline	Proverbs 5:23
Crooked speech	Proverbs 6:12
Lying lips utters slander	Proverbs 10:18
Trusts in his riches	Proverbs 11:28
Ensnared by the transgressions of his life	Proverbs 12:13
Utters deceit	Proverbs 12:17
Reckless and careless	Proverbs 14:16
Quick temper	Proverbs 14:17
Pride	Proverbs 16:18
Seeks rebellion	Proverbs 17:11
Accepts bribes	Proverbs 17:23
Takes no pleasure in understanding. Only wants to express his opinion	Proverbs 18:2
Haughty eyes and a proud heart	Proverbs 21:4
Desires evil	Proverbs 21:9
Puts on a bold face	Proverbs 21:29
Does not understand justice	Proverbs 28:5
Cruel oppressor	Proverbs 28:16
Gives full vent to his spirit	Proverbs 29:11
Listens to falsehoods	Proverbs 29:12
Hasty in his words	Proverbs 29:20
Drinks and forgets what has been decreed	Proverbs 31:5a
Perverts the rights of the afflicted	Proverbs 31:5b

If some of these characteristics resonate with you, there is hope. Hopelessness often comes about with concern for one's future. Anchoring oneself in the promises of God, which are scattered throughout the Bible, helps and motivates us to claim them for ourselves. An example of a promise God would be, "Have I not commanded you?

Be strong and courageous! Do not tremble or be dismayed, for the LORD your God is with you wherever you go" (Josh. 1:9)." Ask the Lord to help you recognize and trust his promises. Many books have been written about the promises of God, and a quick online search on "the Promises of God" will lead to multiple promises to depend on every day. Many say there are over eight thousand promises in the Bible.

Ask the Lord to produce in you a godly character and a life of integrity. He loves you and wants to help.

Be Unstoppable—Go the Distance with God,

But we request of you, brethren, that you appreciate those who diligently labor among you, and have charge over you in the Lord and give you instruction, and that you esteem them very highly in love because of their work. Live in peace with one another.
1 Thessalonians 5:12-13

SECTION 5

**Overcoming Spiritual
Breaking Points**

CHAPTER 39

DEALING WITH A CRISIS

---

*Nowhere does the Bible teach that Christians are exempt from
the tribulations and natural disasters that come upon the world.
Scripture does teach that the Christian can face tribulation, crisis, calamity,
and personal suffering with a supernatural power
that is not available to the person outside of Christ.*

Billy Graham

The 2023 Barna survey reported that "Trauma affects all types of people, cutting across all demographics and faith categories. Being a Christian, even a thriving one, does not prevent a person from experiencing or witnessing trauma . . . [but] Those who are Scripture engaged rate the effects of trauma in their lives at a lower level of severity than those with less connection to the Bible."[1]

Nigeria

Nigeria faces numerous crises. One crisis happened when my husband and I lived in Lagos. During an inspection, customs clearing agents clashed violently with Nigeria Customs Service officials, resulting in severe injuries and terminal closures. This chaotic situation underscores the urgent need for improved airport security as unauthorized access and violence persist. Many people were furious that the terminal buildings were closed, affecting revenues and making goods unable to be distributed. Criminals jumped fences and were privy to illegal access to the gates that were not policed. It was a crisis. On November 28, 2014, *This Day*, a Nigerian news source, published "Taming the Crisis at Lagos Airport Cargo Terminal." The article highlighted inadequate security as a primary concern, emphasizing the necessity for a lasting solution.[2] That happens when dealing with an impossible crisis that has become chaotic and uncontrollable. When a crisis reaches that level, we must identify the weaknesses, find foolproof security, and develop a lasting solution.

Solutions

To find solutions to crises in our lives, first, we must analyze what is coming into our lives causing instability and confusion. Are there ungodly influences in our lives? Have we been involved in any sinful behavior? Are our attitudes toward people or our circumstances entering your mind disrupting how you see your crisis? Second, where is our security? Is our solution to the crisis based on Jesus Christ? Have we confessed our sins and placed our security in the arms of our Blessed Lord and Savior? Doing this addresses our inadequate security. When Jesus Christ leads our lives, our security creates stability and assurance that God will take over and handle our problems. Finally, the lasting solution is to trust God and seek his will and way out. This may involve making changes, requiring apologies, or disassociating from undesirable individuals. Reading the Bible and asking God to speak to you about your problem will bring peace and hopefully a lasting solution, but we must obey his Word and leading, as he has shown us.

Job Loss Illustration

Most people experience a crisis at some point in their life. I define a crisis as a profound event that leaves an indelible mark on our lives. For some, it may be the loss of a child or spouse; for others, it may be a devastating illness or an internal struggle with despair and a fading will to live. For others, it could be the hardship of a job loss. Whatever the nature of the crisis, the path often follows a similar pattern: a journey towards regaining stability, a sense of normalcy, and moving on into a new season. Coping with a crisis is deeply personal, but specific strategies help restore stability and resilience.

In times of crisis, it's crucial to lean on your support systems, which include family and friends, and allow yourself to feel your emotions. Suppressing feelings can lead to more distress when, in these situations, we need to acknowledge our grief, anger, or fear. Even amidst chaos, maintaining a routine through exercise, good sleep, and balanced nutrition is essential. Furthermore, it's wise to limit exposure to distressing news or social anxiety to avoid digging deeper into despair. Some people find solace in journaling, painting, or simply processing their feelings differently.

Recovering from a crisis isn't an instant process; it's about taking one day at a time and breaking things into manageable steps. It's vital to be grateful for any help, as pride and fear often prevent individuals from seeking the support they need to heal. I want to illustrate this point by sharing my husband's perspective on the job loss he experienced.

Job Loss Illustration

About 13 years into our marriage, rumors circulated about mass layoffs at my husband's workplace due to a drop in oil prices and over-hiring. After investing 12 years in a job that he thought would last a lifetime, that dream ended with a single visit from his supervisor. John became one of the 1,500 people being laid off! His initial reaction was shock, filled with questions like, "What should I do?" and "Where should I go?" As a stay-at-home mom with three kids at the time, I had no job to sustain the family.

After the shock came fear. Many people asked him if he felt excited about the opportunity to reset his life, but he confided in one of the counselors, saying, "There's not one thing I'm excited about. I'm scared to death." This prompted him to seek professional counseling, which was crucial for his emotional well-being. Our church also played a vital role in his support system; while it didn't help us financially, it provided encouragement. He contemplated various paths, including returning to teaching, becoming an insurance agent, or attending seminary. John recalled a significant presentation at church, where he learned the advice: "When you don't know what to do, do what you know how to do." This advice helped him refocus his job search on corporate real estate, where he had experience and expertise.

As we navigated this challenging time, I signed the kids up for the government's free breakfast and lunch program at school. They felt special being the only ones who had that benefit.

John also battled anxiety during this uncertain period. After his initial numbness, he found himself in the unemployment line. While it wasn't a good day, he returned home with hope, realizing he wasn't alone in his circumstances. That day, he coined the phrase, "A bad day at [his company] was a better day than a good day in the unemployment line." This is a saying he has passed on to our kids and others when they start complaining about not liking their jobs.

Through it all, John relied heavily on his faith. The crisis was challenging, with four people depending on him, yet he found strength in knowing the Lord. But in the end, he found a job in St. Louis that was the right fit for his skills and experience. and the move was made easier with my support. Through this experience, John learned a valuable lesson: all things work together for those who love the Lord.

Many people react to crises with anger, shame, and frustration, but John never let those feelings overwhelm him.

Years have passed since then, but John is grateful for what he went through, as it taught him essential skills for navigating life's challenges. When I asked him for advice to share with others going through a crisis, he emphasized, "You must pray and trust God. If you are not close to God, do your best to become closer to Him."

God also spoke to John through his Word, and he has remembered the following verses for years. God can do the same for you.

> *I will repay you for the years the locust have eaten—*
>> *The great locust and the young locust,*
>> *The other locusts and the locust swarm—*
> *my great army that I sent among you.*
> *You will have plenty to eat, until you are full,*
>> *and you will praise the name of the LORD your God,*
>> *who has worked wonders for you;*
> *never again will by people be shamed.*
> *Then you will know that I am in Israel,*
>> *that I am the LORD your God*
>> *and that there is no other;*
> *Never again will my people be shamed (Joel 2:25-27).*

But, What about Children in Crisis?

I understand how important it is to teach children how to handle crises while they are still at home. It equips them with essential life skills and resilience to navigate challenges they may encounter in the future. These skills are invaluable.

Hold onto the special moments shared with your children. I cherish the questions and antics of young children, like John Jr's sweet question asking if birds can sit on clouds and his innocent fascination with the scent of money. Through open communication, problem-solving, and emotional support, we can help our children develop the confidence and capability to face adversity that comes their way. John Jr. once wanted to get his hair cut short when he was eight years old. I did not want him to cut all his beautiful curls off, but I allowed it. It was tragic. He abhorred how he looked without his curls. After lots of hugs, his solution was to wear a hat to school the next day. I don't remember if he did, but he took one to school—just in case he needed it. John's emotions ran high: he was embarrassed, he was fearful he would be made fun of; and he was affected by his appearance. He was learning to deal with a crisis but had parental support that encouraged him to move on. Children can learn how to cope. So can teenagers and adults.

Just like children, we can overcome and maintain our crisis that create anguish, sorrow, or fear, by finding the appropriate support needed in Jesus Christ, and trusting that God can provide a long-lasting solution. Trauma is experienced at every age level. Look for lasting solutions, analyze your influences, have open communication with those who genuinely love you and those who can guide you with a spiritual perspective and emotional support.

Be Unstoppable—Go the Distance with God,

Trust in the LORD with all your heart,
And do not lean on your own understanding,
In all your ways, acknowledge Him,
And He will make your paths straight.
Proverbs 3:5-6

CHAPTER 40

NAVIGATING ACCIDENTS

The afflictions of the righteous are many.
But the LORD rescues him from them all.

Psalm 34:19.

In a humorous anecdote, Mark Altrogge in an article titled "There Are No Accidents with God," repeats a story about the cowboy who applied for health insurance. The agent routinely asked him, "Have you ever had any accidents?" The cowboy replied, "Well, no, I've not had any accidents. I was bitten by a rattlesnake once, and a horse did kick me in the ribs. That laid me up for [a] while, but I haven't had any accidents." The agent said, "Wait a minute. I'm confused. A rattlesnake bit you, and a horse kicked you. Weren't those accidents?" "No, they did that on purpose."[1] Now, that makes us laugh, because what the cowboy said sounds like an accident. Accidents, mistakes, and sins share one common trait—their unexpectedness. Accidents in particular can strike without warning, like a bolt of lightning, leading to tragic outcomes such as the loss of a loved one. Despite the sorrow accidents produce, it is crucial to navigate through the suffering.

As we have seen in the last chapter, crises erode our sense of control, but accidents take it away in a heartbeat. The pain and chaos may be similar, yet accidents bring a unique kind of uncertainty. They force us to react quickly, to adapt without warning, and to confront the unexpected. In these moments, survival becomes more than just enduring suffering. It becomes a test of how we pick up the broken pieces and move forward.

Let's look at suffering and pain from the viewpoint of unforeseen accidents such as running into a concrete wall during basketball practice, being hit by lightning, or electrical accidents. First, we must understand that accidents do happen! They can occur because of risky behavior, or they can happen without warning, with or without any ability on our part to avoid them. While we or a loved one may be in unrelenting searing pain, the results are in God's hands. We can pray for support, healing, acknowledge Jesus' empathy in suffering, and express gratitude for the strength to persevere.

We know this because Jeremiah says,

> *For I know the plans that I have for you, declares the LORD, plans for welfare and not for calamity to give you a future and a hope. Then you will call upon Me and come and pray to Me, and I will listen to you (Jeremiah 29:11).*

The Bible does not promise a life free from accidents. We strive to avoid mistakes and sins, but accidents are often beyond our control, However, it is important to remember accidents can serve a purpose in God's plan—they can test our faith, keep us from evil, increase our character, and help someone else walk in their faith. This understanding can bring a sense of assurance and comfort in the face of suffering.

How to React in the Midst of Pain and Suffering

The Barna Group surveyed people about what they would like to ask God. The number one question that people wanted to know is, "Why does God allow pain and suffering in this world?" People usually ask this question when they are in the middle of a crisis or philosophically looking for an answer. Either way, the question is asked frequently.[2] As a believer, when we encounter pain and suffering, how should we react? If you're going through a difficult time, there are some guidelines to help you.

Start by having others pray for you. Even if you're not in a position to pray yourself, having others pray for you is crucial. It encourages others to enter a season of prayer, but God hears the healing prayers of the righteous. I have heard it said, if any among you are sick, pray and take them to a doctor. Remember Jesus himself suffered and understands our pain (Heb.

4:15). Take a moment to thank God for the strength to keep going, even if it's just hour by hour or day by day (Phil. 4:13). Don't blame God for your accident or difficult circumstances. Accidents happen unexpectedly, but God is still in control (Prov. 19:21). Work hard not to become like King Ahaz in the Old Testament, who became more unfaithful to the Lord during his distress (2 Chr. 28:22). Finally, recognize that God allows everything for his glory. Even if it's difficult to see how your circumstances could bring glory to God, trust that he is working all things together for good (Rom. 8:28). Many claim they have become more confident in their walk with the Lord and feel a more profound compassion toward people, during and after a period of pain and suffering.

When explaining the godly results of suffering, Mary J. Yerkes states it best in her article "When We Suffer: A Biblical Perspective on Chronic Pain and Illness." She states:

- Suffering produces intimacy with God (Job 42:5).

- Suffering equips us to comfort others (2 Corinthians 1:3-5).

- Suffering refines us (Isaiah 48:10).

- Suffering produces growth and maturity (James 1:2-4).

- Suffering conforms us [into] God's image (Romans 8:28-29).[3]

Let's look at accidents in this way from now on. As I mentioned, accidents often cause us or a loved one to suffer. Your child may fall off a balance beam and break their arm; you may swallow some coins, or you may flip your bike doing wheelies. Whatever it is, remember that God knows what has happened and is there to get you through your pain.

Quotations

As I look back over fifty years of ministry, I recall innumerable tests, trials, and times of crushing pain. But through it all, the Lord has proven faithful, loving, and totally true to all his promises.
David Wilkerson[4]

I am not a theologian or a scholar, but I am very aware of the fact that pain is necessary to all of us. In my own life, I think I can honestly say

that out of the deepest pain has come the strongest conviction of the presence of God and the love of God.
Elisabeth Elliot[5]

Pain is distressing. There can be nights of agony when God seems so unfair and it seems that there is no possible help or answer. Temporary relief may seem adequate, but the real solution to suffering is not to isolate it in an attempt to do away with it, nor even to grit our teeth and endure it. The solution, rather, is to condition our attitudes so that we learn to triumph in and through suffering.
Billy Graham[6]

Be Unstoppable—Go the Distance with God,

And not only this, but we also exult in our tribulations, knowing that tribulation brings about perseverance; and perseverance, proven character; and proven character, hope; and hope does not disappoint, because the love of God has been poured out within our hearts through the Holy Spirit who was given to us.
Romans 5:3-5

CHAPTER 41

LOVING YOUR ENEMIES

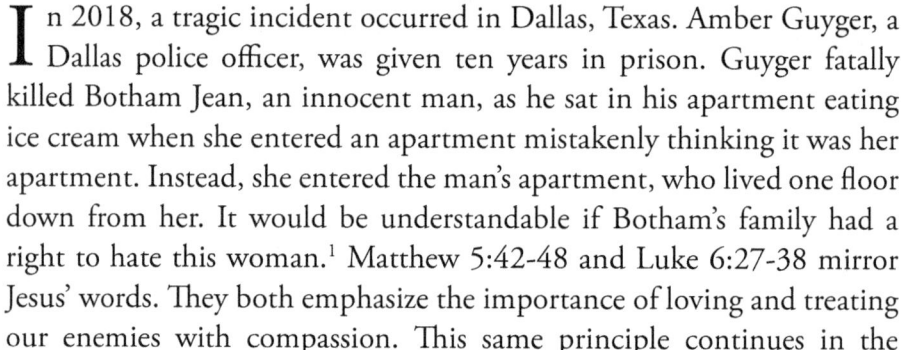

> *Our inclination may be to retaliate or "get even."*
> *But the Word of God always speaks of a different kind of response.*
>
> Billy Graham

In 2018, a tragic incident occurred in Dallas, Texas. Amber Guyger, a Dallas police officer, was given ten years in prison. Guyger fatally killed Botham Jean, an innocent man, as he sat in his apartment eating ice cream when she entered an apartment mistakenly thinking it was her apartment. Instead, she entered the man's apartment, who lived one floor down from her. It would be understandable if Botham's family had a right to hate this woman.[1] Matthew 5:42-48 and Luke 6:27-38 mirror Jesus' words. They both emphasize the importance of loving and treating our enemies with compassion. This same principle continues in the following verses.

> *You have heard that it was said, Love your neighbor and hate your enemy. But I tell you, Love your enemies and pray for those who persecute you, so that you may be sons of your Father in heaven. For He causes His sun to rise on the evil and the good, and sends rain on the righteous and the unrighteous. For if you love those who love you, what reward will you have? Don't even the tax collectors do the same? And if you greet only your brothers, what are you doing out of the ordinary? Don't even the Gentiles do the same? Be perfect, therefore, as your heavenly Father is perfect (Matthew 5:43-48 HCSB).*

In outlining Luke 6:27-38, one can see how Jesus wants his children to act toward their enemies. This passage unfolds from start to finish by giving instructions on loving enemies, how to act toward them, and the results of acting godly toward foes.

- Love one's enemies (Luke 6:27-28).

- Handle physical abuse and give to those who ask (Luke 6:29-30).

- Treat people equally (Luke 6:31). Credit love and lend to others, even to sinners (Luke 6:32-34).

- Do good and lend expecting nothing in return (Luke 6:35-36).

- Do not judge (Luke 6:37).

- Give, and it will be given to you (Luke 6:38).

It is essential to understand whom the Bible refers to as enemies, also called foes or adversaries——the world, the flesh, and Satan. Additionally, by examining Luke's context and historical background, we can gain insight into the intended audience and purpose of his writing.

Context

We must look at Luke's historical-cultural context to fully understand the Book of Luke and Luke as a man and the audience he addressed. Through Luke's eyes, you gain a better understanding and perspective of his writings. In *The New Testament in Antiquities* by Gary M. Burge and Gene L. Green, the authors discuss the relationship between The Gospel of Luke and the Book of Acts as a "two-volume" set with many overlapping themes.

Luke's main emphasis revolves around salvation, which he deems is for both Jews and Gentiles. Most scholars believe Luke was written in Rome between AD 60 and 61. Most also agree that he was the author of this book. Luke was a cultured, organized writer, also known as the beloved physician, whose sources come from eyewitnesses and multiple servants.[2] Luke wrote much of this gospel about individuals who are either in need or who conduct themselves through God's Spirit. This gospel reoccurs in some of Luke's most famous stories, for example, the great fish caught on the Lake of Gennesaret, the parable of the good Samaritan, Jesus and the robbers as they were dying on their crosses. Writing his gospel from Rome, readers of Luke should know that many believe Luke was an early gentile convert to Christianity. Allison Trites in *Who's Who in the Bible* states " [Luke] has been considered 'the beloved physician' (Col. 4:14), and some medical schools celebrate him in St Luke's Day services."[3] Luke, known for his role as a historian and literary artist, infused spiritual songs and praises into his writings. His emphasis on joy and stress on prayer, particularly praying over major decisions, are notable aspects of his work. Luke's interest in the Holy Spirit is evident throughout his writings in Luke and Acts, where the Holy Spirit is featured prominently. Furthermore, Luke had a strong conviction of evangelism, believing that the message of Jesus Christ was meant for all people.[4] Luke was a constant companion to Paul during his second, third, and final missionary journeys, including the unrecorded fourth journey mentioned in Acts. His travels took him from Troas in Asia Minor to Philippi in Greece along the Aegean route. Later, he joined Paul on the journey from Caesarea in Judea to Rome, standing by him faithfully throughout his captivity. Unlike Matthew and John, Luke's writing demonstrates a more favorable attitude towards Roman authorities, maybe because he was the only Gentile writer in the entire New Testament. Luke wrote this gospel to Theophilus, a lover of God, to show him the reality of Jesus Christ.

From the 1st century to this present age, anyone can receive Jesus. Many of the intended audience in early Christianity (Jews and Gentiles) were ready to learn truths about relating to people—including how to love their enemies.

Although there is debate on the literary genre of Luke, it combines history and biography. Luke's objective in authoring this book comes first when he unveils his purpose—emphasizing the "fulfillment of God's plan." The writing style is simple to understand, and his logical organization becomes evident as one reads from Jesus' birth to Jesus' crucifixion, resurrection, and ascension, always emphasizing salvation in every personal situation he finds himself in, such as in Luke 17:19 and Luke 7:49-50. The casual reader may not notice that in the latter part of the book, Luke shifts from third person to first person. This shift is known as the "we" section of the book. Many scholars believe this gospel could have been penned when Luke met Paul.

Luke, an investigative and orderly writer, created an easy-to-follow line of thinking. This continuity is seen in Luke 6:27-38 when he goes from loving one's enemies to doing good to those who hate you. Luke informs people how Jesus wants them to act, from loving enemies to not judging others. These verses involve how to treat people, including those who are an enemy.

The Beatitudes, a basis for the blessings and woes of living, precede this section and create a natural flow into how to act toward others. The verses following Luke 6:27-28 are a beautiful display of Jesus' illustrating how one should live through a parable along with statements and questions teaching believers how to live, for example, understanding that a pupil is not above their teachers; a good man out of good treasure brings what is good. As you ponder how to treat your enemies, you should consider their heart and desire to follow the principles outlined in the Bible.

More Content

Luke's *Sermon on the Plain* and Matthew's *Sermon on the Mount* are similar. In each sermon, Luke 6:27-38 and Matthew 5:43-48, one verse has been debated and examined over the years.

This debate revolves around the command to love one another and how loving neighbors and enemies should be conducted. William Barclay's *Gospel of Luke* states that while both verses extract from a text that starts with a series of beatitudes, there are differences between the versions of Matthew and Luke, but this one thing is clear—they are a series of "bombshells" on how Jesus wants believers in him to act. Barclay notes these debated sermons use different vocabulary that is different from what a typical person of those days would say.[5]

The general population shows an interest in love, hate, and enemies. This is evident in what appears in grocery stores. Most checkout lines include publications enticing readers to understand why they hate each other, such as

- "My Neighbor, My Enemy" (New York Times)

- "Hate in America" (Time Magazine)

- "It's a Thin Line between Love and Hate"
  (Psychology Today)

- "And They Will Know We are Christians by our Hate"
  (The Christian Post)

- "The Secret to Loving Your Enemies"
  (Today's Christian Women)

Definitions from Strong's Concordance—Luke 26:27-38

A Concise Dictionary of the Words in the Greek Testament and the Hebrew Bible by James Strong helps interpret the Bible's teachings on love, hate, enemies, and doing good from Luke 6.

This thorough concordance displays words from Hebrew and Greek in alphabetical order, their references, and brief definitions.

- Love: to love (in a social or moral sense), Strong's No. 25.

- Enemies: an adversary, foe, Strong's No. 2190.

- Hate: to detest, (especially to persecute), Strong's No. 3404.

- Do good: in a good, better, or fair place; well, Strong's No. 2573.[6]

Merriam-Webster defines the *Golden Rule* as "the ethical principle of treating other people as oneself would prefer to be treated."[7] As Christ-followers delve into the so-called *Golden Rule* verses, it is helpful to fully understand what Luke 6:27-28 is saying as they are imperative in grasping verses 29-38, which follow. In Luke 6:27-28, there are some instructions for Christ-followers to abide by:

There has been debate on the actual meaning of what "love one's enemy" means. The word here means the agape kind of love, distinguishing it from passionate love and love for only those who love them back! Barclay describes this kind of love as "an active feeling of benevolence toward the other person; it means that no matter what that person does to us we will never allow ourselves to desire anything but his highest good, and we will deliberately and of set purpose go out of our way to be good and kind to him."[8] Enemies today are viewed as people who want to hurt or betray—they may even gossip or tell lies about us as believers, and with the power of the Holy Spirit, one can trust in God's ability for humankind to love with this agape kind of love.

Humans are innately inclined to hate their enemies because of our sinful nature, which originated in the story of Adam and Eve. Despite this, Jesus continues to give more instructions on how to treat enemies in Luke 6:29-30 when reclining at the table with tax collectors. Jesus tells us, "whoever hits you on the cheek, offer him the other cheek, and whoever takes away your coat, do not withhold your shirt from him either." Jesus does not want us to pick and choose who we are to love, even if there is physical violence—in this case, the turning the other cheek reference. Leon Morris, an Anglican Australian New Testament scholar and theologian says that *cheek* is *siagon*, "a punch to the side of the jaw rather than a light slap on the face."[9] Many people might instinctively wish to retaliate, but Jesus advises believers to turn the other cheek and receive similar treatment again. Accordingly, it's our internal character and attitude that God is truly interested in, as he desires us to bring glory to him in all we do.

In this illustration and the example where Jesus tells of not withholding one's shirt if others need it, verse 30 says to give to everyone who asks and not demand it back. The ethics behind these two verses revolve around the ability to do good—TO EVERYONE! Regarding accepting a strike from an enemy, we need wisdom to discern when to be forgiving and when to stand up for what is right. No matter what we choose, Christian love should always be accompanied by discernment.

It is a complex concept to understand that we are to love everyone and give to everyone regardless of how we feel. But, in Luke 6:31, Jesus tells us that we are to treat others how we want to be treated. But how can *hurt* brothers and sisters treat others with love and kindness? It is impossible without the Holy Spirit helping Christians to show Christ's humility.

Robert H. Gundry shares how Jesus mingled and socialized with many people. As in ancient times, people mingle and socialize with all types of people today. Wherever Christians are and whatever people they encounter, Jesus tells us to treat each other with the same kind of treatment one wishes to receive.[8]

The Book of Romans says,

> *Be devoted to one another in brotherly love; give preference to one another in honor." Regarding a more inward way to act (Romans 12:10).*

The Book of Philippians says,

> *Do nothing from selfishness or empty conceit, but with humility of mind, let each of you regard one another as more important than himself (Philippians 2:3).*

It takes God's Holy Spirit to love the way Jesus did. Jesus did not want or demand credit for his works; he followed the Lord's path established for him in humility and with integrity. In Luke 6:32-4, one question Jesus asks in all three verses is "What credit is that to you?"

Many serve to obtain accolades for their service to the Lord. Christ is more concerned with the character of our hearts than he is with people receiving congratulations, fist bumps, or flattery for service. These accolades are in the following verses.

> *And if you love those who love you, what credit is that to you? For even sinners love those who love them. And if you do good to those who do good to you, what credit is that to you? For even sinners do the same. And if you lend [with interest] to those from whom you expect to receive, what credit is that to you? Even sinners lend to sinners, in order to receive back the same amount (Luke 6:32-4).*

First, loving a mother, father, son, or daughter does not take much. Second, it does not take much to love those who love us. And last, it only takes a little to lend to those who will pay us back. But, from Jesus' perspective, it is better to love one's neighbor, those who hate, and help others without knowing if they will repay a loan. If one only does their works and service to be seen, they are doing nothing more than a sinner would do. David Guzik mentions that we will have enemies, yet we are to respond to them in love, trusting that God will protect our cause and destroy our enemies in the best way possible, by transforming them into our friends.

As Luke 6 progresses, Luke tells us in verses 35 and 36 that as Christians, we are to love enemies and be merciful toward them. Regarding loving neighbors, much is written about how to resolve hate. We are to use conflict resolution techniques, kill someone with kindness, come to a healthy compromise, and create boundaries between each other.

The Bible wants people to initiate love toward enemies, first with a clean heart, through our own action stories. In Psalm 51:10, King David addresses God's desire for a clean heart. Believers in Christ should start by cleansing themselves as David did in the referenced psalm. "Create in me a clean heart, O God, and renew a steadfast spirit within me."

After loving someone with a clean heart, Christians are better equipped to show mercy to others. Author Andrew Herbert mentions one can extend mercy to others only when they have received sympathy, compassion, and forgiveness themselves, but "we do not have what it takes, but Jesus does, so we come to Him in brokenness and humility, hungering to be filled with what only He can give."

Not judging and giving to others concludes Luke 6:37-38. The Bible is ready to address judging others. In verse 37, Jesus clarifies what believers will gain. Christians should not judge or condemn others, believing they will gain when they follow his instructions. Leon Morris says the verse is unclear on whether it means gain, in this present judgment or the future judgment of God. He states, "If we are harsh with our judgments on other people, we generally find that they return the compliment and we ourselves are widely rewarded."

Application

When Christ and his Holy Spirit work significantly to where individuals understand the need to forgive and love our enemies, the fruit of the spirit of *love* becomes evident by giving of oneself. Because the Lord has given of himself, those who have turned their life over to Christ through the forgiveness of sin and repentance can love their enemies, thus reflecting Jesus Christ.

Luke 6:27 tells believers to love enemies. The Bible commands individuals to do that, but it is not easy. As ambassadors of the Lord, the desire to love like Jesus is there, but when one is offended, hurt, gossiped about, and betrayed, the human heart does not think of kindness as one's first choice of action. Learning to love and not to hate is a process. Sometimes, it is slow and lengthy, but the process of becoming more like Christ must commence in obedience to the Lord's command.

When facing hate, the following points will help people of all ages acknowledge their hate and move toward love.

Pray, Repent, and Forgive

Forgiveness is a powerful tool that can help us heal and move forward from difficult situations. It is not always easy to forgive, but it is important to remember that forgiveness is not just for the other person, it is also for our own well-being. In order to fully forgive, it is necessary to take certain steps such as asking God to address any issues, forgiving oneself and others, praying with passion, petitioning with passion, pleading for forgiveness, praying for oneself, pursuing an attitude change, repenting if needed, and showing concern and praying for the offender. By taking these steps, we can open ourselves up to a brighter future free from the weight of anger and resentment.

Trust

Trusting in God is a game-changer when it comes to facing life's challenges. It gives us a powerful sense of security and comfort, knowing we are not alone in our struggles. We can approach challenging situations confidently and optimistically by counting on God for a resolution. Additionally, trusting the Holy Spirit for understanding helps us gain valuable insights into any incidents or angst that we may be experiencing. It allows us to navigate the ups and downs of life with grace and resilience. So, start trusting in God today to live a life free from worry and fear. You won't regret it!

Action

As Christ-followers, we are called to love and forgive others, even when it's difficult. When trust is broken, knowing how to move forward can be challenging. Here are five actions we can take to manage such situations. (1) Empathize with the person who caused the problem by putting ourselves in their shoes. (2) Read verses related to love, hate, bitterness, cruelty, offenses, and how to behave in such situations. (3) Consider the possibility that God may use this incident for a greater good, (4) Be open to the idea that establishing boundaries might be necessary, and (5) Consider that moving on may be the best solution, as guided by God. By taking these steps, we can honor God and show love to others, even in difficult situations. Remember, forgiveness and reconciliation are at the heart of our faith, and trusting in God's plan can help us navigate even the toughest of circumstances.

Returning to the 2018 accident in Dallas, Texas, where Amber Guyger fatally killed Botham Jean, an innocent man, as he sat in his apartment eating ice cream. Guyger was sentenced to a ten-year sentence. On the witness stand during sentencing, Brandt Jean, the victim's eighteen-year-old brother, turned to Guyger, and said, "I know if you go to God and ask him, he will forgive you." Botham's family had every right to hate Guyger. However, in an act of kindness, the victim's brother Brandt continued to speak directly to Guyger. He said, 'I love you like anyone else,' and later hugged her in the courtroom before being led to her ten-year prison sentence by the bailiff. That is loving one's enemy in action![11]

The conclusion reached in Luke 6:27-38 is that God commands believers to love their enemies by following and obeying him.

Be Unstoppable—Go the Distance with God,

A new commandment I give to you, that you love one another, even as I have loved you, that you also love one another. By this all men will know that you are My disciples, if you have love for one another.
John 13:34-35

CHAPTER 42

MANAGING STRESS

> *Jesus did not promise to change the circumstances around us.*
> *He promised great peace and pure joy to those*
> *who would learn to believe that God actually controls all things.*
>
> Corrie Ten Boom

Understanding Stress and Its Effects

In our fast-paced and ever-demanding world, it's all too easy to be swept away by stress and anxiety. The weight of work, relationships, and various commitments can feel like a heavy burden, making emotional meltdowns or what some refer to as nervous breakdowns all too common. These moments can be profoundly challenging, often pushing us to our limits. Although each person's experience with emotional breakdowns is distinct, it's not unusual to feel a sense of despair when we find ourselves in the thick of it. Whether we're sobbing uncontrollably, turning to food for comfort, or losing our appetite altogether, fixating on negative thoughts, or retreating from the world, it is crucial to recognize that these feelings are valid and part of the human experience.

Emotional breakdowns typically occur when stress becomes overwhelming, leaving us at a loss for how to cope. We reach a tipping point. Individuals may display a variety of symptoms, as different stressors can lead to emotional turmoil, health issues, and a sense of spiritual disarray. Once we hit our breaking point, we might be teetering on the edge of an emotional breakdown.

Definition of Stress

Merriam-Webster's Thesaurus lists various descriptors for stress, from being burned-out, which is "depleted in strength, energy, or freshness."[1]

Emotional and Physical Stressors

In conducting an unsystematic Internet search to identify situations that lead to emotional stress, it appears that feeling overwhelmed is a frequent response when individuals encounter multiple stressors. It's a delicate balance, managing the emotional toll of various circumstances. Whether it's dealing with an unexpected pregnancy, battling post-traumatic stress disorder, managing obsessive-compulsive disorder, or coping with the aftermath of sexual abuse, each situation carries its weight. The fear of dementia, distress over family decisions, or the anguish of a fractured relationship can all compound the burden. Additionally, struggling with employment, questioning one's faith, or the responsibility of caregiving can further exacerbate stress levels. Mistakes at work, legal concerns, or the upheaval of divorce only add to the strain. In such moments, it's crucial to acknowledge the depth of these struggles and seek support where needed, recognizing that no one should navigate these challenges alone.

The *Reader's Digest Guide to Medical Cures and Treatments* highlights various psychological and medical conditions that can be exacerbated by worsening stress. These include alcoholism, angina and other forms of heart disease, asthma and allergies, backache and other pain syndromes, and chronic fatigue syndrome. Additionally, stress can contribute to diabetes, eating disorders, and headaches, both migraine and tension. It may also lead to high blood pressure, irritable bowel syndrome and other intestinal disorders, lupus and other autoimmune disorders, menstrual irregularities, obesity, rheumatoid arthritis, sexual dysfunction, ulcers, and more.[2]

If you encounter any of these stressors, please talk to a medical doctor, as medication might be an option to consider. However, only after a physical exam can a physician properly rule out a physical conclusion to address stress.[2]

Many times, emotional stress is accompanied by physical stressors. Stress affects our moods in the form of anxiety, restlessness, lack of motivation or focus, feeling overwhelmed, irritability or anger, sadness, or depression. Our behavior fluctuates depending on our stress as well. The most common effects are overeating or undereating, angry outbursts, drug or alcohol use, social withdrawal, or exercising less often. Stress comes about when we feel overloaded or the pressure to continue at our current pace seems overwhelming.

Emotional Breakdown Testimonies

Twice in my life, I have experienced what I would call an emotional (nervous breakdown), one relational and the other relating to caregiving stress.

In my early twenties, I experienced a profound emotional struggle reminiscent of broken heart syndrome, which left me with a persistent sense of heartache, stress, and anxiety. During this difficult period, I immersed myself in the Bible daily and clung tightly to verses that spoke of peace, healing, and hope. I felt a strong sense of God's presence, which empowered me to face my challenges head-on. Although my instinct urged me to remain in Fort Worth for the stability of a guaranteed job and the comfort of familiar surroundings, I felt a compelling pull to leave that life behind and move to Houston. I believed this change might provide peace, closure, and normalcy, which I desperately sought. As part of my journey, I read the entire Bible for the first time, yearning for the Lord's instruction. When I finished, a verse from Ecclesiastes 11:5 stood out to me, offering the confirmation I needed. It encouraged me to embrace the unknown and step out in faith, trusting in God's plan for my future, although that meant leaving some good friends behind.

> *Just as you do not know the path of the wind, and how bones are formed in the womb of the pregnant woman, so you do not know the activity of God who makes everything (Ecclesiastes 11:5).*

Ecclesiastes 11:5 became my life verse, a passage that holds special significance and offers me guidance and direction. I can't fully explain how God used that verse to confirm my move to Houston; it was as though the Holy Spirit revealed to me that I needed to relocate. I had been praying for wisdom, and it was time to step out in obedience, even though I didn't understand this mysterious leading and was greatly fearful of the uncertain future ahead. Leaving behind my heart's desire for ministry in Fort Worth was painful. However, in God's graciousness, he allowed me to attend a seminary extension in Houston. Then, as mentioned earlier, during retirement, I completed a master's degree in Theological Studies from Dallas Baptist University. Yes, over forty-eight years later, the Lord allowed me to complete my life-long dream.

My desire for ministry, which some label "a calling," has been the rudder that has directed my entire life. I learned that you do not need a formal degree to follow and obey God. This was a priceless lesson from the Lord, and he made it clear to me as soon as I began my new life in Houston. Since 1976, I've experienced a fulfilling life in the ministry, faithfully serving him through various ups and downs. A year after relocating to Houston, I met my husband, and we married a year later. I am grateful to have learned that God always knows what he is doing, and I am glad I realized this at a young age!

Forty-three years later, my husband and I closed up our home and lived with my mother in her home. Things were great for about two and a half years, but I gradually went downhill. Toward the end of four years of being a caregiver, I was fainting and having panic attacks. Then, the week before my mother passed away, I had a full, unexpected emotional breakdown. I returned to our own home. I could not get out of bed for about four or five days. I returned to Mom's home a few days before she passed on. The emotional stress of caregiving finally took hold of me. From a spiritual viewpoint, many may look at people in these situations as affecting only those who are weak in faith. I would argue that point. Knowing that God has a purpose for everything in our lives, I knew he could use all my experiences for good, because he loves us; yes, he truly does! And since that time, I have been able to teach three classes on caregiving at various churches.

God uses those in medical, counseling, and pastoral positions to help caregivers. But, learn from me, because I DIDN'T. Nevertheless, I will never regret the years caring for my mom, although it was difficult at times. Of course, I had my husband right by my side helping me physically and emotionally.

A Practical Step to Handle Stress

By removing a few stressors, individuals can rebound somewhat from the emotional stress they are carrying and rise above challenges, but it often takes time. Unfortunately, others may not snap back even when their load lightens. Timely medical help may even necessitate an urgent doctor visit or emergency room visit. Never ignore your emotional well-being. It could be the difference between life and death. Being a Christ-follower does not shield us from all the rises and falls we encounter in life. Life happens.

Trusting God During Difficult Times

Life can be unpredictable. I remember several difficult moments our family has faced: receiving an early morning phone call that my husband had been in a serious accident in the Netherlands, our youngest son being thrown to the ground by the police with a loaded gun pointed at his head due to a case of mistaken identity; job losses; caregiving responsibilities; the death of our parents; our home being completely flooded; various illnesses, and more. While my stresses may not be the same as yours, as believers, our ultimate source of strength remains the same. Our source is always God, our Father. He provides his words, people, and the Holy Spirit to help us. When times are hard, or troubles engulf you, allow the Lord to guide you. We may have difficulty praying in these emotional times, but God always provides. Many times, he works with other people or professionals. If you need to talk or receive counseling, choose someone you trust and share your difficulties with them.

When Jesus faced the most challenging time, he wanted his friends nearby. Even Jesus did not try to face his most difficult moment alone, and neither should we. Jesus came with them to Gethsemane and said to his disciples, "Sit here while I go over there and pray." And he took Peter and the two sons of Zebedee [James and John] with him and began to be grieved and distressed. Then he said to them, "My soul is deeply grieved, to the point of death; remain here and keep watch with me." And he went a little beyond them and fell on His face and prayed, saying, "My Father, if it is possible, let this cup pass from Me; yet not as I will, but as You will" (Matt. 26:36-39).

How to Handle Stress

Managing stress can be a multifaceted approach, and while physical techniques are important, it's also beneficial to consider the spiritual side of dealing with stress. In "10 Tips to Manage Your Stress," WebMD offers valuable suggestions such as exercising, relaxing your muscles, practicing deep breathing, eating well, slowing down, taking breaks, making time for hobbies, discussing problems with others, being gentle with yourself, and identifying and eliminating triggers.[3] These tips provide a solid foundation for managing stress, but they certainly aren't the only methods available. Incorporating spiritual practices like prayer, fasting, Bible reading, worship, and more may further enhance one's ability to cope with stress.

Role of Faith

Stress affects our physical and emotional life. But our spiritual dimension is often overlooked. It's easy for some to say we lack faith when we experience stress or anxiety. But that is not necessarily the case. It could be that we are tired, sick, or unable to adequately balance our work/home life adequately. Our situation may seem chaotic, and no solution seems possible. However, as Christians, our faith is an anchor that holds everything together during challenging and stressful times. We must lean on the strong arms of Jesus to get us through, alongside medical guidance and spiritual practices like prayer, meditation, and seeking solace, which provide profound comfort and strength in Bible verses. As Christians, we are not immune to marital, family, personal, health, job, technology, or just "living in the world" stress. But, whenever and however trouble and stress occur, it is not pleasant. It may cause us to erupt at someone we love or shout at our boss. We may desire to close ourselves up in a dark room and sleep all day and night. We might over-medicate or under-medicate ourselves. We might consider suicide, or we might get professional help. Nevertheless, know that our mighty God loves us with a love that is incomparable to any other love we will experience. He's got us!

Cultivating a Biblical Framework

In times of stress, turning to your faith for support is essential. Begin each day by praying, meditating, and connecting with God. Call upon the Holy Spirit to guide and comfort you through difficult times. Take solace in the words of the Bible, seeking out verses that bring calmness to your fears and anxieties. Trust in the wisdom in the Bible, even when it feels challenging. Cultivate an attitude of gratitude, acknowledging the blessings that God has already bestowed upon you. Surround yourself with fellow Christ-followers by actively participating in church and fellowship. Allow Christian music to uplift and inspire you. If you haven't already done so, consider opening your heart to Jesus Christ, confessing your sins, and accepting him as your Lord and Savior. You will find strength, peace, and reassurance through these practices in your faith journey.

I recently took an online test on Facebook titled "What Song Will Be Played at Your Funeral?" and was surprised (or should I say embarrassed) when the site suggested "My Way" as my funeral song. "My Way" was written by Paul Anka and popularized by Frank Sinatra. The song's theme is about a man who is close to the end of his life. He claims that he has lived his life on his own terms and has few regrets. However, when faced with losses and failures, he still faced them his way.

While I don't take stock in online tests, I wasn't particularly pleased "My Way" was my chosen funeral song. As I go through life, I want God's way as I face stresses, challenges, and hard circumstances as best as possible.

I once visited the cemetery where my paternal grandparents were laid to rest. I glanced over to the left of my grandparents' graves and noticed a marker that proclaimed, "I Did It My Way." Rather than looking at life through our human eyes, God's delight comes when we look at our God-given life through his eyes. The song "Thy Way, Not Mine, O LORD," portrays a healthy example of how to live our lives depending on him.

THY WAY, NOT MINE, O LORD

By Horatius Bonar

(1808-1889)

Thy way, not mine, O Lord,
However dark it be!
Lead me by Thine own hand,
Choose out the path for me.
Smooth let it be or rough,
It will be still at best;
Winding or straight, it matters not,
Right onward to Thy rest.
I dare not choose my lot;
I would not, if I might;
Choose Thou for me, My God;
So I shall walk aright.
The kingdom that I seek
Is Thine: so let the way
That leads to it be Thine,
Else I must surely stray.
Take Thou my cup, and it
With joy or sorrow fill,
As best to Thee may seem;
Choose Thou my good and ill.
Choose Thou for me my friends,
My sickness or my health;
Choose Thou my cares for me,
My poverty or wealth.
Not mine, not mine the choice
In things both great or small;
Be Thou my guide, my strength,
My wisdom, and my all.[4]

As we encounter stress in our lives, through our body, mood, behavior, and spirit, I pray that we will face life "God's way"— never forgetting the spiritual component of getting well. If we don't. Someone might put, "They Did It Their Way" as our epitaph!

How to Help Ourselves

Bible Principle 1: Get Rid of Anger

> My dear brothers and sisters, take note of this: Everyone should be quick to listen, slow to speak and slow to become angry (James 1:19 NIV).

Bible Principle 2: Reduce Your Load

> In everything I did, I showed you that by this kind of hard work, we must help the weak, remembering the words the Lord Jesus himself said: 'It is more blessed to give than to receive.' (Acts 20:35 NIV).

How to Help Others

Bible Principle 1: Encourage Others

> *Therefore encourage one another and build each other up, just as in fact you are doing (1 Thessalonians 5:11 NIV).*

Bible Principle 2: Provide Hope to Others

> *'For I know the plans that I have for you,' declares the LORD , 'plans for welfare and not for calamity to give you a future and a hope' (Jeremiah 29:11 NIV).*

Principle 3: Intervene if Needed and Be Prepared if an Emergency Occurs

> *But Phinehas stood up and intervened, and the plague was checked (Psalm 106:30 NIV).*

Principle 4: Gossip Betrays

> *A gossip betrays a confidence; so avoid anyone who talks too much (Proverbs 20:19 NIV).*

As we conclude this chapter, it is imperative to remember that faith doesn't shield us from stress and challenges, but God provides support through the guidance and protection of his Holy Spirit, Jesus, and his servants in tough times. Relying on him and seeking support from trusted individuals gives us the opportunity for joy and hope.

Be Unstoppable—Go the Distance with God,

It is the LORD who goes before you; He will be with you.
He will not fail you or abandon you. Do not fear or be dismayed
Deuteronomy 31:8

Trust in Him at all times, O People; Pour out your heart before Him;
God is a refuge for us
Psalm 62:8

CHAPTER 43

TESTS AND TRIALS

The Lord sometimes allows sorrow and pain and loss and tribulation to come but He wants us to know, "This is good for you, and I'm thinking of your profit."

A. W. Tozer

L ife often presents challenges that aren't visible to others, causing internal turmoil. You look remarkable to others, but privately, you feel threats, encounter significant problems, or experience suffering that people can't see. These are what the Bible calls tests and trials. When people start seeing through us, it's tough. We don't want to feel weak in front of other people. We don't like them to visit the difficulties we might face, the threats we might be encountering, or the internal unrest we are going through. However, we know they exist. While significant trials and tests can devastate us, so can the small tests and trials we might encounter. These can generate havoc in your life, mainly if one follows another and another.

My Test and Trial

Once, my blog vanished, and "unauthorized content" was sent to subscribers. I know it seems like a small trial, but to me it was huge. Emails were sent to my blog subscribers, which I did not send. And they were not aligned with my Christian standards at all. I panicked—fearing that some obscene images or articles might appear on my site sent by an intruder. Despite attempts to fix it, the damage was severe — hackers had infiltrated my site. My emotions and concerns went ballistic. Questions ran through my mind, such as "What if people thought I wrote such disgusting things? What if the blogs being sent out would get worse? Is my reputation going to be ruined or has it been ruined already?" With a lot of work, and of course money, the hack was resolved, but not soon enough for me. While this is an example of a minor trial, many people encounter huge trials such as the death of a child, spouse, or a life-threatening illness.

What trials in your life have shaped your relationship with the Lord?

Our Source is God

In both the small and the huge trials, we should look to God as our source. In our lives, personal pressures and problems consume our thoughts, and nobody but us know they are there. Our thoughts become intrusive. We search our trusted websites or self-help books to help to no avail. When we face inner struggles, God should be our first resort. He understands our inner battles and guides us until his purpose reveals itself. Too often, we first contact our friends, pastors, and counselors before seeking God and discussing our situations and concerns with him. But we keep our thoughts and ruminations to ourselves to build up and build up until personal damage becomes unbearable—physically, emotionally, and spiritually. I am the worst at sharing my struggles or concerns with others. I keep my trials, struggles, and thoughts bottled up inside myself, only sharing with the Lord, but I know at some point it may become necessary to share with others for release and for prayer. We are all human and not perfect, and there are always areas we can work on and improve on. So, what should we do? We must become resilient, persevere through our tests and trials, and remember to sit before our heavenly Father.

Sit before the Heavenly Father

The Bible teaches us that we will face struggles and trials. Being a Christian does not eliminate the challenges of living in a fallen world. Before seeking help from friends, family, the Internet, or books, we should sit before the Lord, rest in his presence, and ask him to manage our stress level, whether it originates due to threats, problems, struggles, intrusive thoughts, or more.

The Bible says,

> *Consider it all joy, my brethren, when you encounter various trials, knowing that the testing of your faith produces endurance. And let endurance have its perfect result, so that you may be perfect and complete, lacking in nothing. But if any of you lacks wisdom, let him ask of God, who gives to all generously and without reproach, and it will be given to him (James 1:2-5).*

When we are under pressure, God sometimes answers quickly, but we are frequently left waiting, yearning, and seeking his response for even years. As we wait, let us grow in our abundant love for our Lord and Savior. Live in joy and service until the time comes when we have "been approved" for our dedication and undefiled obedience, whether in this life or the next. It is not easy, but we will be blessed by persevering.

> *Blessed is a man who perseveres under trial; for once he has been approved, he will receive the crown of life which the Lord has promised to those who love Him (James 1:12).*

How to Handle Tests and Trials

Recognize that tests and trials are inevitable and come to all people. Stand firm no matter how long they persists, knowing that the Crown of Life (a symbolic reward referring to eternal life and blessings given for one's faithfulness in enduring our trials). This Crown of Life is given to Christ-followers when we have stood the tests, and our trials are over. When we are in the midst of a storm, no matter how big or small, seek God's guidance and wisdom and trust, because he knows what he is doing. He again sees the big picture. And as those you love experience trials, be patient with them. Everybody has different tolerance levels, and it takes some people longer to overcome what life has thrown upon them. As we seek the Lord and follow the principles and teachings found in the Bible, we should also recognize that the tests and trials creating stress are opportunities to honor the Lord. When we face difficult circumstances and allow them to strengthen our faith, we will grow stronger. This growth will be evident in our lives.

If you have traveled through this book with me, and don't have a Bible, please purchase one as soon as possible. Look for a version that fits you. Decide what size font you need. Do you want the words of Jesus in red print? What size do you require? Check out how heavy it is? Why? Because your Bible will become your best friend and instrumental in a life where tests and trials abound.

Hope

Embracing hope through our storms helps us to keep our heads above water. In *Hope: The Anchor of Your Soul*, June Hunt describes what calming our storms brings.

God's hope . . .

- Provides you with joy in living.

Rejoice in our confident hope. Be patient in trouble, and keep on praying (Romans 12:12 NLT).

- Generates faith and love in you.

For we have heard of your faith in Christ Jesus and your love for all of God's people, which come from your confident hope of what God has reserved for you in heaven. You have had this expectation ever since you first heard the truth of the Good News (Colossians 1:4-5 NLT).

- Causes you to live a pure life.

And all who have this eager expectation will keep themselves pure, just as he is pure.(1 John 3:3 NLT).

- Inspires you to persevere with endurance.

As we pray to our God and Father about you, we think of your faithful work, your loving deeds, and the enduring hope you have because of our Lord Jesus Christ (1 Thessalonians 1:3 NLT).

- Uplifts your downcast soul.

Why am I discouraged? Why is my heart so sad? I will put my hope in God! I will praise him again—my Savior and my God (Psalm 42:5 NLT).

- Causes you to praise God.

But I will keep on hoping for your help; I will praise you more and more (Psalm 71:14 NLT).

- Anchors your soul.

This hope is a strong and trustworthy anchor for our souls. It leads us through the curtain into God's inner sanctuary (Hebrews 6:19 NLT).

- Generates boldness in you.

Since this new way gives us such confidence, we can be very bold (2 Corinthians 3:12 NLT).

- Develops your patience.

But if we look forward to something we don't yet have, we must wait patiently and confidently (Romans 8:25 NLT).

- Gives you reason to rejoice.

Because of our faith, Christ has brought us into this place of undeserved privilege where we now stand, and we confidently and joyfully look forward to sharing God's glory (Romans 5:2 NLT).

- Establishes your security and safety.

Having hope will give you courage. You will be protected and will rest in safety (Job 11:18 NLT).

- Guarantees your eternal life.[1]

… he saved us, not because of the righteous things we had done, but because of his mercy. He washed away our sins, giving us a new birth and new life through the Holy Spirit. He generously poured out the Spirit upon us through Jesus Christ our Savior. Because of his grace he made us right in his sight and gave us confidence that we will inherit eternal life (Titus 3:5-7 NLT).

Just as it took time and money to fix my blog, align with the Lord during stressful times, cry out to the Lord, and let him walk with you through your tests and trials. He will rescue you as you continue praying for hope and relief. He is a mighty God whose love for us is stronger—way stronger—than our love for him.

Be Unstoppable—Go the Distance with God,

The righteous cry out, and the Lord hears
And rescues them from all their troubles.
The Lord is near to the brokenhearted
And saves those who are [a]crushed in spirit.
The afflictions of the righteous are many,
But the Lord rescues him from them all.
Psalm 34:17-19

CHAPTER 44

NAVIGATING SUICIDE

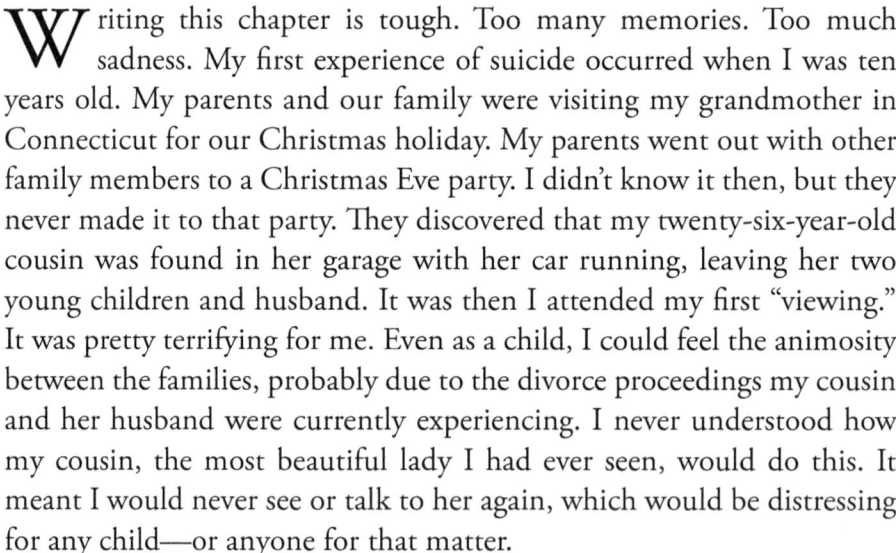

If you're grappling with suicidal thoughts, know you're not alone.
God's intention for you is life, not death.

Sound of Heaven

Writing this chapter is tough. Too many memories. Too much sadness. My first experience of suicide occurred when I was ten years old. My parents and our family were visiting my grandmother in Connecticut for our Christmas holiday. My parents went out with other family members to a Christmas Eve party. I didn't know it then, but they never made it to that party. They discovered that my twenty-six-year-old cousin was found in her garage with her car running, leaving her two young children and husband. It was then I attended my first "viewing." It was pretty terrifying for me. Even as a child, I could feel the animosity between the families, probably due to the divorce proceedings my cousin and her husband were currently experiencing. I never understood how my cousin, the most beautiful lady I had ever seen, would do this. It meant I would never see or talk to her again, which would be distressing for any child—or anyone for that matter.

If suicide has touched your family or friends, I am sure you can relate to my experience in some way or another. Suicide is hard to explain or accept. My children have lost their friends due to this unfortunate occurrence, and they are left with the age-old question, "What could I have done to prevent this?"

A few years ago, I attended an end-of-life service of a young adult man who committed suicide. He was one of our youngest son's best friends in high school. With his academic achievements, including a doctorate degree from an Ivy League college, his future looked promising. However, his suicide left many bewildered, grieving, and shocked, including his wife, parents, and friends.

When greeting this man's parents at his service, I experienced something I will never forget—the big, long hug from a desperate mom, the deep cry of a troubled yet still shell-shocked mother, and the complete agony of his father. It is the father's furrowed face that is etched in my mind—for no other reason but to recall how awful suicide affects those involved. As I looked into this father's face, his eyes penetrated mine. I've never seen such discouragement, hopelessness, and despair before in my entire life. Although his eyes were empty, his countenance was reaching out for me to tell him that being in that funeral home pew was just a bad dream and that what had just happened didn't happen. But I couldn't, and neither could anyone else.

Today, similar struggles persist, from the loss of a job, unemployment, grades, death of a family member or someone close, divorce, rape, injury, being neglected, having trouble with the law, alcoholism, not getting into the college of choice, pressure to be someone you aren't, moral distress, or comparing your situation to others. These can all be catalysts that could lead to thoughts of suicide. Recognizing the warning signs and reaching out for help can make a difference. If you identify any of these examples in your life or in the faces of those you know, please get help for yourself or them. Don't wait. It may be too late. Strive to be vigilant and compassionate, extending a helping hand to those in need so that the tragedy of suicide may be spared from those who are left behind in despair.

The ripple effects of suicide extend far beyond the individual, impacting even those who only hear about the tragedy. The haunting question of "why" often lingers in the minds of loved ones, accompanied by a wave of regret and countless what-ifs. After a suicide death occurs, an array of questions persists: What could I have done to prevent this senseless act? Did I inadvertently make them feel unappreciated? Why didn't they ask for help? Where was the divine intervention? How could I have missed the signs? Should I have maintained closer contact with my friend or relative? As the grieving process unfolds, individuals grapple with how to cope and move forward. While thoughts associated with the loss can linger for a lifetime, being a survivor of someone's suicide can be unbearable. So, I delved into the stories of suicides in the Bible, uncovering seven individuals who succumbed to despair, regret, and various struggles.

Seven Suicides Mentioned in the Bible

1. Regret: Judas Iscariot Hanged himself.

Judas was one of Jesus' twelve disciples. He was the treasurer of the disciples, responsible for their funds and distributing them as needed. He betrayed Jesus by leading Jewish officials to him to receive thirty silver coins. Once he discovered that the Jews were going to kill Jesus, he brought the money back to the Jewish officials and threw it on the temple floor. Many say Judas' motivation was greed. No matter his true motivation, it was apparent he regretted his action. Not knowing how to handle that regret and remorse resulted in him hanging himself.

> *And throwing down the pieces of silver into the temple, he departed, and he went and hanged himself (Matthew 27:5).*

Some examples of present-day regret might be not having enough confidence in oneself, regretting one's chosen occupation, breakup of a relationship, or a loved one passing on.

2. Humiliation: Abimelech, Son of Gideon, ordered his Armor-Bearer to Kill him.

Abimelech ruled Israel for three years. Some say he should not be counted as a king because God did not anoint him. During his reign, he destroyed the city of Shechem. After that, he attacked the city of Thebes. During that siege, a woman dropped a millstone on his head, wounding him. He was embarrassed that he would be known as being killed by a woman, so he asked his armor-bearer to kill him. And the armor-bearer did.

> *He quickly called his armor-bearer and said to him, "Draw your sword and kill me, or they'll say about me, 'A woman killed him.'" So, his armor-bearer thrust him through, and he died (Judges 9:54 HCS),*

Today, if one is humiliated by friends, family members, or co-workers, experiences depression, has low self-confidence, experiences embarrassment due to abuse, faces mental illness, or experiences feelings of hopelessness or shame, suicide may occur.

3. Bullying: Samson Caused a Disaster and Killed himself Along with Others.

Samson was a judge of the Dan tribe. Jewish leaders chose him before Israel decided to have Kings. Due to being a Nazarite, his life was dedicated to God. He was known for his Herculean strength. He is most famous for his Philistine wife, Delilah, who continually betrayed and humiliated him. She eventually shaved Samson's hair off, and the Philistines captured him, gouged out his eyes, and placed him in prison. He was called out of prison and made fun of. Tied to pillars, he pulled down the entire temple. The temple collapsed, destroying both his life and the lives of many others.

> Samson said, *"Let me die with the Philistines." He pushed with all his might, and the temple fell on the leaders and all the people in it. And the dead he killed at his death were more than those he had killed in his life* (Judges 16:30 HCS).

When friends or foes make fun of each other or are laughed at, bullied, or nagged regarding their perceived weaknesses, such as their appearance or intelligence, keep a close eye on them.

4. Fear: King Saul fell on his sword.

The Philistines fought against Israel, and Israel's men fled from them. Many were killed on Mount Gilboa. The Philistines overtook Saul and his sons and killed his sons, Jonathan, Abinadab, and Malchishua. When the battle intensified against Saul, the archers caught up with him and severely wounded him. Then Saul said the following to his armor-bearer,

> *Draw your sword and run me through with it, or these uncircumcised men will come and run me through and torture me. But his armor-bearer would not do it because he was terrified. Then Saul took his sword and fell on it* (1 Samuel 31:1-4 CSB).

Good examples of present-day fear might be the desire to be free of pain, terminal illnesses, fear of being mocked, fear of possible abuse, actual verbal abuse, actual physical abuse, sexual ridicule, mocked for being poor or handicapped, or fear of mistreatment.

5. **Witnessing Violence or Death: Saul's Armor-Bearer Fell on his Sword.**

The purpose of an armor bearer in the Bible was to be by their king's side during dangerous times. Kings chose armor-bearers because they were known as courageous people. Possibly, Saul's armor-bearer could not deal with the guilt of disobeying King Saul's command to kill him, or maybe he couldn't accept that he just witnessed the violent death of someone else – King Saul.

> *When his armor-bearer saw that Saul was dead, he also fell on his own sword and died with him (*1 Samuel 31:5 *CSB).*

Witnessing violence or death, having PTSD, witnessing abuse (domestic or otherwise), being traumatized by witnessing natural disasters, being devastated by seeing another's suicide, guilt, or terrorism could all be indicators of someone who might contemplate suicide.

6. **Powerlessness: Ahithopel Planned his Suicide, Put his House in Order, and Hanged himself.**

Ahithopel was King David's counselor. But, at one point, he deserted King David and went to serve King David's son Absolom. Hushai was known as Absalom's friend and trusted counselor. Absalom valued Hushai's counseling skills more than Ahithophel's. That disturbed Ahithophel, so he went home to Giloh, put his house in order, and then hanged himself.

> *When Ahithophel realized that his advice had not been followed,*
> *he saddled his donkey and set out for his house in his hometown.*
> *He set his affairs in order and hanged himself. So he died and was*
> *buried in his father's tomb (*2 Samuel 17:23 *CSB).*

Some people may contemplate suicide if they are insulted, feel unworthy or, non-essential, jealous of others' success, experiencing elder abuse, being talked about behind their back, being disrespected, or unable to break a drug habit.

7. Distress-Zimri Killed himself and Others by Fire.

Zimri was a chariot commander. He murdered King Elah and all his family in Tirzah. He succeeded King Elah as king, but only for seven days, the army elected Omri as king instead of him. He wanted power and was distressed that the military would besiege Tirzah. He was unable to cope with the besiege of Tirzah and the loss of position, so he set the palace on fire, killing himself along with many others.

> When Zimri saw that the city was captured, he entered the citadel of the royal palace and burned down the royal palace over himself. He died because of his sin he committed by doing what was evil in the Lord's sight and by following the example of Jeroboam and the sin he caused Israel to commit (1 Kings 16:18).

Each of these stories offer insights into the complex factors that can lead someone to contemplate suicide, from deep regret to overwhelming distress.

One night, I watched *"Remembering Anthony Bourdain"*—CNN's television show honoring Anthony Bourdain. Known as a good-looking, talented man, author of many books, a culinary genius, and a travel documentarian, Bourdain was discovered unresponsive in his French Kaysersberg hotel room, having hung himself. His "claim to fame" included his trips worldwide, documenting the cuisine, politics, people, and cultures in his *"Parts Unknown"* show for CNN.[1] As I watched the show, I was drawn to our similarities.

Resonating our likenesses, I write them below in the present tense as I don't want to admit that a man I had so much in common with committed suicide. Both Bourdain and I share a passion for writing, though I consider myself a novice while he was a seasoned journalist. Our interests also intersect in social issues; I majored in sociology, and he had a deep appreciation for sociological themes, including culture, customs, and global perspectives. We both love the stunning North Atlantic coastline and enjoy engaging with others by asking questions to understand what makes them tick. We were both born in New York City and came from a Catholic/Jewish background, we both attended reputable colleges— Baylor for me and Vassar for him, although he left after two years to pursue his education at The Culinary Institute of America. Our mutual enthusiasm for learning defines us as lifelong learners, constantly seeking new knowledge and experiences throughout our lives.

On Bourdain's arm is a tattoo inscribed with the sentence, "I am certain of nothing." As I ponder his life, achievements, and personality, I believe God could have significantly used him. I'm not one to judge whether God's grace was a part of his life, but his fruit was probably evident that he rarely thought of God or God's provision. He battled demons on and off his entire life: drinking, drugs, profanity, sex, and more. Bourdain's death by suicide creates a "bitter pill to swallow" when we realize that just a word, a touch, or an encouragement may have swayed his decision. Tragically, many people are left with that very form of regret when a loved one chooses to end their life. What would Bourdain's life have been if he had believed that our triune God loved him unconditionally? What was the foundation of Bourdain's strength? What demons and strongholds did he possess? Only God knows the answers to those questions. But I bet he could have been an outstanding Christ-follower.

If you are contemplating suicide, "PLEASE DON'T!" Call a friend, family member, pastor, or anyone, and convey your thoughts. Remember, there is no turning back from suicide.

It's important to remember that we can all play a role in suicide prevention. The 988 Lifeline is available 24/7 to provide free and confidential support to anyone in distress. Whether you are seeking resources for yourself or a loved one, Lifeline offers crisis prevention and intervention services that can help. By reaching out to the Lifeline, you can proactively improve your mental health and well-being. Lifeline's best practices are designed to ensure that everyone who contacts them receives the care and support they need to overcome their difficulties.[2] Another alternative is to Text HOME to 741741 to talk to a trained crisis counselor via Crisis Text Line, a non-profit organization providing free, confidential, 24/7 support.

Be Unstoppable—Go the Distance with God,

Do not fear, for I am with you; Do not anxiously look about you, for I am your God. I will strengthen you, surely, I will help you, Surely I will uphold you with My righteous right hand.
Isaiah 41:10

I called on Your name, O LORD,
Out of the lowest pit.
You have heard my voice,
"Do not hide Your ear
From my cry for help."
You drew near when I called on You;
You said, "Do not fear!"
Lamentations 3:55-57

CHAPTER 45

COPING WITH GRIEF: MINNIE'S STORY

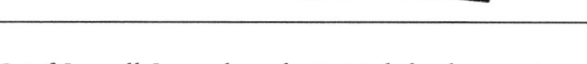

Grief [usually] involves the initial shock, emotional release, loneliness, depression, guilt, anger, hostility, inertia, a gradual return to hope, and the return to reality and normality.

Billy Graham

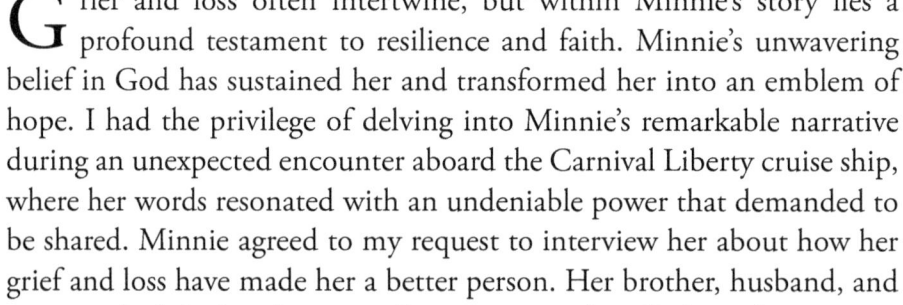

Grief and loss often intertwine, but within Minnie's story lies a profound testament to resilience and faith. Minnie's unwavering belief in God has sustained her and transformed her into an emblem of hope. I had the privilege of delving into Minnie's remarkable narrative during an unexpected encounter aboard the Carnival Liberty cruise ship, where her words resonated with an undeniable power that demanded to be shared. Minnie agreed to my request to interview her about how her grief and loss have made her a better person. Her brother, husband, and two sons had died at the time of my interview, but God was her support before, during, and after her losses.

Once Minnie agreed to an interview, I hurried back to my cabin and swiftly penned out my interview questions. This was only my second "journalistic interview." My first interview attempt transpired with Phyliss Schlafly, an American attorney, conservative activist, author, and anti-feminist spokesman for the national conservative movement. So, I had a little experience, but not much!

Life in a Nutshell

Q: Minnie, I appreciate the opportunity to ask you some tough and candid questions about your life. In this interview, I aim to pull out some insights so others may benefit from your life experiences regarding healing, death, grief, sorrow, and the ability to move on. Please tell me a summary of your life.

A: I married at a young age in 1962. After having three boys, Jimbo, Kurt, and Paul, I became a single mother through divorce. My first husband and I were unequally yoked in the things of God, so I knew that if I ever remarried, I would only marry a firm believer. I wanted to seek God again but I didn't know how to. After some time being a single mom and growing in the Lord, I married my second husband, Morgan. We became parents to two lovely daughters, Melody and Robin. My brother died at the age of 40 in 1986. My son Kurt passed away at the age of 24 from a tragic motorcycle accident in 1990. My husband, Morgan, passed away in 2013. My son Jimbo passed away at the age of 51 from alcoholism in 2014. I became a believer at 10 and was baptized at Nederland Hillcrest Baptist Church. I have always had a heart for God, even though I haven't always walked close to him. As a child, I put a map on my bed and I prayed for the nations. I am 72 years old now.

Q: In 1986, you prayed for your brother's healing. In 1991, you prayed for your husband's healing. Your brother was not healed, but your husband was healed. Any insights?

A: In 1986, when my brother was gravely ill, Morgan and I prayed so much for his healing. In the hospital, I was paralyzed with fear. I was so scared and afraid. Now, I know that it was [spiritual] warfare – a fight of faith. God was unstoppable, trying to teach me to walk by faith. I was disappointed because I was learning my new walk with God, and I didn't know why my prayers of faith did not work for my brother. And he died. Then, in 1991, my husband was diagnosed with Mesothelioma, which is a rare form of cancer directly related to asbestos exposure. Mayo Clinic says, "Mesothelioma is an aggressive and deadly form of cancer. Mesothelioma treatments are available, but for many people with Mesothelioma, a cure is not possible."[1] At the time, I knew I served a powerful God and that he could do anything. One day, as I laid beside my husband during his illness, I thought I was smothering to death. But I went into another room and fell to my knees knowing that God wanted to talk to me, I asked, "Are you going to require my husband's life to do this?" God responded, "No, I am going to make you a woman of faith over this." This is when my faith journey began. Many people prayed for my husband during this illness. And Morgan was completely healed. He lived twenty-two years after his diagnosis. His medical case is documented at M.D. Anderson Hospital in Houston, Texas. The doctor said that he only knew of two other survivors of Mesothelioma, and they were not in the United States. But, with every loss I have had, I have become stronger and stronger.

Q: Tell me about the deaths of your sons Jimbo and Kurt.

A: Jimbo passed away from alcoholism in 2014. I took care of him for the last year of his life and watched his condition weaken until he passed. In 1990, Kurt died in a motorcycle accident when he was twenty-four years old. He was also struggling with alcoholism at the time.

Q: When your husband and son Jimbo died, you had time to prepare for their deaths, but when your son Kurt died unexpectedly in the motorcycle accident, was it a different experience?

A. Very much so. But I didn't have any regrets. I had many sweet talks with Kurt before he passed away. He shared an experience he had with God. He said he was in the front yard, and a plant had a hot flame flaring up from the gas. God told him, "Kurt, if you don't change your ways, this is what is waiting for you." He had another experience seeing the stars, the moon, and the clear skies. The Lord said, "This is what is waiting for you if you come back to me." Then, one night, Kurt called late at night, and he cried, and we spent time talking together. So, I didn't have any regrets.

Q: You had mentioned to me that your sons and husband were prepared for life after death. What do you mean?

A: They all had a personal relationship with Jesus. They knew him, and I know they are in Heaven.

Q: In Jonah 4:6, Jonah mentions, "It is better for me to die than to live." Did you ever feel that way?

A: Not like Jonah did. I was not in defeat or despair because God gave me glimpses of the other side [Heaven]. I realized that it is better to be in the presence of God. I never wanted to die due to my losses.

Q: Out of all your life experiences, what was the most challenging situation you have ever faced?

It was when Jimbo was sixteen, and Kurt was fourteen. They both wanted to go and live with their father. It was the first real heartbreak of my life. They were stripped from my arms. They both wanted to go where they could drink and have no restrictions. Jimbo was only gone a year because he could not live the Christian life at Daddy's house. But Kurt never came home.

Q: Any other heart-breaking experiences?

A: What broke my heart more than death was seeing the struggles my sons went through with their alcohol addiction. Jimbo would go off for months, and my mind thought the worst. But I know where they are; God has confirmed that for me.

Q: How has grief and loss affected you?

A: It has made me a better person. It has helped me to know how real God is. He is faithful to his Word. He has made me stronger. There is nothing he will not sustain me in.

Q: Did you ever ask God, "Why me?"

A: No. Never.

Q: It appears your sorrows were greatly multiplied more than others. Why do you think that happened to you?

A: He's been preparing and using me to help others during their dark times. I encourage others and help them see that what they are going through is not the end. God does not view death the way we do. He wants us to see death through His eyes. I don't view death as the end.

Q: What was your prayer life like during these times?

A: After each loss, I experienced grief differently. I gained more insight into prayer and how God works with each loss. I experienced times of fear when Kurt was in a coma before his passing. I could not pray. Words would not come. I just said the name of "Jesus" over and over. When I was in the hospital with Kurt in 1990, his nurse whispered in my ear and told me to keep praying. She said, "When you aren't here with him, I am praying for him." After Kurt passed away, I could not cry. My mom brought me into the hospital bathroom and said, "It's okay to cry." But I couldn't. I cared for everyone at the time, and I felt God was carrying me in his arms. I found my release after the funeral, and I grieved properly.

Q: What does "time is short" mean to you?

A: It means we are allotted so much time. We must make the most of every day. We should see God's work in all we do. His handiwork is everywhere. In Ephesians, it says,

> *Therefore be careful how you walk, not as unwise men but as wise, making the most of your time, because the days are evil. So then do not be foolish but understand what the will of the Lord is (Ephesians 5:15-17).*

Q: In 1991, you were impressed that God wanted you to be a "Woman of Faith." Can you explain that?

A: When I pray for people, I feel the power of God. I love to read the gospels and the life of Jesus. Jesus says in the Scriptures that he has given us power and authority to preach the gospel. I'm not a preacher, but we can teach daily. We can see people recover when we lay hands on the sick through the power Jesus gave us. If a child of God does not know about this power and authority, they may live far beneath what God's purpose is for them.

Q: As you look forward, do you have any goals?

A: Yes, I want to go to Africa. I want to touch as many lives as possible. I want them to be saved, healed, and delivered.

Q: If you could share one tidbit of wisdom with young women, what would it be?

A: I would tell young women to let God be the center of their lives. The cry of my heart is that they must pass his name on to the next generation. The greatest gift for children is to pass on a godly heritage to them. Parents must guide their children by example. If passing on God stops with us, we will have a lost generation. Another thing I see is people speaking death over their children by talking negatively about them. We must speak about life and good things over our children.

Q: Do you have a favorite Bible verse or passage after all the grief and loss you have been through?

A: Yes, it is Psalm 91. I encourage those reading this psalm to substitute their name in this chapter to make it more personal and meaningful to them.

My God, in whom I trust!
For it is He who delivers you from the snare of the trapper,
And from the deadly pestilence.
He will cover you with his pinions,
And under his wings you may find refuge;
His faithfulness is a shield and bulwark.
You will be afraid of the terror by night,
Or the arrow that flies by day
Or the pestilence that stalks in darkness,
Or of the destruction that lays waste at noon.
A thousand may fall at your side,
And ten thousand at your right hand;
But it will not approach you.
You will only look on with your eyes,
And see the recompense of the wicked.
For you have made the LORD. My refuge,
Even the Most High, your dwelling place.
No evil will befall you,
Nor will any plague come near your tent.
For he will give His angels charge concerning you,
To guard you in all your ways.
They will bear you up in their hands,
Lest you strike your foot against a stone.
You will tread upon the lion and the cobra,
The young lion and the serpent you will trample down.
Because he has loved Me, therefore I will deliver him;
I will set him securely on high, because he has known My name.

He will call upon Me, and I will answer him;
I will be with him in trouble;
I will rescue him, and honor him.
With long life I will satisfy him,
and let him behold My salvation.
Psalm 91

Q: Any last thoughts?

A: I want people to know Jesus as I know him. I don't want people to live for themselves. I want my life to count for him. I don't want to waste my life. Many people are throwing their lives away and living for the NOW. There is so much more, and we must go deeper with God.

Me: Minnie, thank you so much for sharing the love of Jesus with me. Through teary eyes, you shared your heart and soul. You are special.

Meeting Minnie was a divine appointment. Never in my wildest dream did I think I would meet a lady like Minnie on my one-and-only cruise! The Holy Spirit drew us together as we stood in the breakfast line one morning, only to meet again in the afternoon for the interview. This interview portrayed the life of a true Christ-follower, and I was blessed to be a participant. God will provide these kinds of opportunities to all fellow believers. When the Holy Spirit nudge occurs, follow the Spirit and see what an amazing God we serve.

Update: Minnie has since remarried and lives happily in Nederland, Texas, still serving her Lord and Savior.

Be Unstoppable—Go the Distance with God,

More than that, I count all things to be loss in view of the surpassing value of knowing Christ Jesus my Lord, for whom I have suffered the loss of all things, and count them but rubbish in order that I may gain Christ.
Philippians 3:8

CHAPTER 46

EMBRACING THE INEVITABLE

Your priorities must be God first,
God second, and God third,
until your life is continually face to face with God.

Oswald Chambers

Passing On

Death is an inevitable part of life, and each person's journey through it is unique. While grieving the loss of a loved one, practical matters often demand immediate attention, leaving little time for emotional processing. Most are left with no protocols for issues that need addressing, such as funeral arrangements, obituaries, notifications, and more. When mothers recall and retell their child's delivery experiences, you will not hear the same run-of-the-mill story. Each woman possesses a different and unique perception of birthing. It is the same with the dying process. Every person uniquely experiences death. And even when reading obituaries, we read diverse stories about a person's life. But one thing is for sure: We will all die! Death is a part of life.

My Friend, Felistus: Life, God, Cancer, and Death

There is an appointed time for everything. And there is a time for every event under heaven—A time to give birth and a time to die; A time to plant and a time to uproot what is planted (Ecclesiastes 3:1-2).

My friend Felistus' life served as a testament to the power of prayer and the impact of prayer and unconditional love. Despite her struggle with breast cancer, she consistently poured love and compassion onto others, leaving a lasting legacy of faith and resilience. We don't expect a single mom with four children to face a diagnosis of Stage 4 cancer that had metastasized to her brain, bones, liver, and stomach. She fought a valiant fight to survive. She did not want to leave her children. She was only in her early forties when she was diagnosed.

We all know someone who either has or had cancer; thus, this disease affects us all. I was honored to be chosen to speak the eulogy at Felistus' funeral service at our church—she was my friend who passed away way before her time. The following are the words I spoke at Felistus' funeral service, honoring a life lived well.

My Eulogy Honoring My Friend, Felistus

Thank you all for coming to Felistus' service. My name is Patti Greene and Felistus and I were extremely close friends. Today, I have two "notes" to share with you—one from me and one from Felistus.

But first, I would like to share my memories of a lovely lady. Felistus was a praying woman. She told me how scared she was when she moved from Zambia to Congo, from the Congo to the United States. But she said her parents always told her to PRAY, PRAY, PRAY. When she wasn't attending church, her mom said, "Felistus, you were raised in church – you need to take the children to church." Her mom gave her the idea to go to the closest church— that was this church, my church! One day, she told me she remembers our pastor saying, "You don't have to feel lonely!"

The following Sunday, Felistus attended the same Bible study class I did. She claimed she used to be shy, but she prayed one Saturday night, "God, who can I talk to?" After class, I approached Felistus and said, "Do you have anything special I can pray for you?" Those simple words were the catalyst for our deep friendship. In addition to Bible study, Felistus became an active participant in our Saturday morning fellowship luncheon, which was held once a month.

The happiest I had ever seen Felistus was in May 2013. Our Saturday group threw her a surprise thirty-ninth birthday party. And believe me, she was shocked. We had balloons, cards, presents, and birthday cake. We sang "Happy Birthday" to her. She was so overwhelmed with love that her joy went from laughter to tears. It was the first birthday party she had ever had. At this party, Felistus shared her life with us. The Holy Spirit filled the home and all of our hearts. While she was blessed, everyone who attended her birthday party left more filled and inspired than she was. She shared how her mom sold tomatoes to help her attend a school where she could learn English. She talked about the beautiful furniture her dad, a carpenter, made. In Felistus' own words, she said the following about her parents and her life in Zambia. "My parents raised all of their children to believe in God. My mum taught us that God is the only one you can depend on in life. My dad taught us how to pray for our food and for our sicknesses. My parents raised us well. In Zambia, where most of the people they knew died of AIDS, we had parents that took good care of us. We grew up in bad neighborhoods, but my parents were strict. They were always asking us if we prayed for this or prayed for that."

Felistus loved Skyping, a form of online connecting with people. She loved Skyping with her family in Africa. She used to tell me how her dad was quiet, but sometimes she would share something with them, and they would get so excited, praising God and dancing around. Once, Felistus was at my house, and I told her I prayed often for her. She said, "You do?" Then, I showed her in my prayer journal how I prayed for her every day. In a sneaky Felistus kind of way, she tried to read the lines in my "personal journal." She wanted to know exactly what I was praying for her.

Before she was diagnosed with cancer, I prayed for her peace, for hope, for a place to live, for a job, for a car wreck she was in, for her oldest son to get a job, for her children, and more. John and I's lives became intertwined with the family.

I have been blessed by knowing Felistus and her family and walking through every stage of her cancer with her. She taught me *how to love unconditionally, she taught me always to be faithful; she taught me so much about the African culture, so when I moved to Nigeria eighteen months later, I felt ready to face the challenge. But one thing Felistus didn't get around to teaching me—and she kept promising me she would—was how to tie those African scarves around my head. So, the first thing I will do when I see her in heaven is to get her to show me that.*

In May 2014, Felistus requested that I write her words down for her and keep it. Today, I would like to share those words with you, spoken five months before her passing.

Felistus' Words

In August 2013, I was diagnosed with breast cancer. God is my help through all this. He has helped me with this sickness. People I don't even know are standing in prayer for me. The doctors are standing with me, too. My parents always taught me that God is always able, and I believe that. My encouragement to you is this: whatever is going on in your life, remember, as my mom has always told me, that "God will always have his angels around you, taking your hand, and Jesus will deliver you in due time" (Matthew 4:6).

John and I were with Felistus through every stage of her cancer—before her diagnosis, during her diagnosis and treatment, and until her memorial service. Her life was entrenched in ours. We were with her when she died. We were the ones who told her children she had passed on.

Encountering Death

A story about death may be a strange way to conclude this book, but I want you to see that we are all here on earth for a specific purpose. Each of us has a different assignment for the Lord until our final day comes. Let's be people of love and compassion until then. He will show us why we are here if we allow him to be the Lord of our lives.

Losing our loved ones is one of the hardest things we have to deal with in life. It's never easy to say goodbye to someone we deeply love and care about, but it's important to remember that God knew when our loved ones would be born and when they would pass on. We can find comfort in knowing that our lives are in his hands and that he has known our journey from the beginning to end. Although it is tough, we must face the reality that our time on earth is limited; thus, we should make the most of it.

I hope John and our children, along with yours, will always remember us as those who loved them profoundly and truly wanted the very best for their lives. I cherish the memories we've created as a family, like the times I draped tablecloths over our console TV to shield them from the less-than-stellar shows. Those little moments, filled with laughter and love, are what I hope they hold dear. I also want them to remember that our family was deeply rooted in faith. We spent countless hours at church, mingling with believers of all ages and backgrounds, and learning about God, Jesus, and the Holy Spirit together. My greatest wish is for them to carry these memories in their hearts and continue to serve the Lord with the unwavering strength of the Holy Spirit. May they always find comfort and inspiration in our shared experiences, knowing that love and faith bind us forever.

When our time comes, I hope our children and yours will find comfort knowing that a person's natural home is in Heaven and that the Lord will be there waiting for them because they have been raised to accept Christ as their Lord and Savior. Until then, cherish every moment with your God and continue to instill the values and beliefs that have shaped your life until we experience Jesus Christ face-toface.[1]

Be Unstoppable—Go the Distance with God,

For God so loved the world, that He gave His only begotten Son,
that whoever believes in Him should not perish, but have eternal life.
John 3:16

EPILOGUE

As stated in the introduction of *Unstoppable: Go the Distance with God*, my greatest hope in writing this book—both for your children and mine—was to illuminate the path to understanding our God-given purpose and to instill the strength to endure life's many challenges.

As you continue your journey, may you remain steadfast in your commitment to go the distance with God, persevering in faith until the Lord calls you home. Let Scripture and prayer be your compass, guiding you toward a life rooted in his unwavering love. Speak with him, walk with him, and then share his truth with others. Pass this wisdom on to your children—not just in spoken words, but in the legacy you leave behind, through letters, recordings, reflections, and even this book.

Fight the good fight. Stay the course. Keep the faith. And through it all, never forget—you are immeasurably loved and unstoppable.

ENDNOTES

Introduction

[1] *Elementary Bible Truths Handbook.* Bob Jones University Press. 1981.

Section 1 Bible and Biblical Characters

Chapter 1

[1] "Bible, Ignorance of," Wycliffe Handbook of Preaching and Preachers, Chicago: Moody, 1984, 213. SermonIllustrations.com.

Chapter 2

[1] *Understanding the Bible Guinness World Record,* "Best-Selling Book," https://www.guinnessworldrecords.com/world-records/best-selling-book-of-non-fiction (accessed March 10, 2024).

[2] Gary Michuta, *The Pilgrims' Regress: The Geneva Bible and The Apocrypha* http://www.handsonapologetics.com/Geneva_Bible.htm (accessed March 10, 2024).

[3] David Briggs, "Who Reads the Bible—and Why," Ahead of the Trend, 7 March 2014. https://www.huffingtonpost.com/david-briggs/who-reads-the-bibleand_b_4919444.html (accessed 18 March 2019).

[4] Adrian Roger, "How to Make the Bible Come Alive," *Love Worth Finding. OnePlace.* https://www.oneplace.com/ministries/love-worth-finding/read/articles/how-to-make-your-bible-come-alive-15522.html (accessed 18-18-2019).

[5] "Is Faith in God a Crutch?". https://www.gotquestions.org/faith-God-crutch.html (accessed 8 March 2019).

[6] "Bernard Ramm," Wikipedia, https://en.wikipedia.org/wiki/Bernard_Ramm (accessed 17 March 2019).

Chapter 3

[1] Various magazines.

[2] Touch of Class, Touchofclass.com

Chapter 4

[1] Caleb Bell, "Poll: Americans love the Bible but don't read it much," *Religion News*, April 4, 2013, December 27, 2015, https://religionnews.com/2013/04/04/poll-americans-love-the-bible-but-dont-read-it-much.

Chapter 6

[1] John Bunn, "Ezekie," *The Broadman Bible Commentary, No. 6* (Nashville: Broadman Press, 1971), 223-371.

[2] Tony Evans, *Book of Illustrations: Stories, Quotes, and Anecdote* (Chicago: Moody, 2009), 279-280.

[3] John Pollock, "Victory in 30 Seconds: How Castrated Hogs, Baseball, and Other Analogies Shape U.S. Elections," *Washington Monthly.* November 6, 2014, https://washingtonmonthly.com/2014/11/06/victory-in-30-seconds-how-castrated-hogs-baseball-and-other-analogies-shape-u-s-elections/ (accessed June 1, 2024).

Chapter 7

[1] Exploring Spiritual Gifts. "What's a Spiritual Gift? – Arriving at a Biblical Definition," *Ministry Tools Resource Center*, https://mintools.com/spiritual-gifts-definition.htm. (accessed March 12, 2023).

[2] "Pneuma," *New Testament Greek Lexicon,* www.biblestudytools.com/Lexicons/Greek/nas/pneuma.html (accessed Oct. 13, 2022).

[3] Richard L. Pratt, "I & II Corinthians," vol. 7, Holman New Testament Commentary. (Nashville: Broadman & Holman Publishers, 2000).

4 Brannon Deibert, "What are the Seven Gifts of the Holy Spirit?" www.christianity.com (accessed Sept 4, 2022).

5 Melissa Henderson, "A Comprehensive Spiritual Gifts List to Discover Your Gifts and Callin," *Bible Study Tools*, https://www.biblestudytools.com/bible-study/topical-studies/a-comprehensive-spiritualgifts-list-to-discover-your-gifts-and-calling.html.

6 Billy Graham, *The Holy Spirit: Activating GOD'S Power in Your Life* (Waco: Word Books, 1978), 134.

7 Brand, Chad, "Spiritual Gifts," Holman Illustrated Bible Dictionary (Nashville: Holman Reference, 2009), 759.

8 Brian DeVries, "Spiritual Gifts for Biblical Church Development: The Holy Spirit Working through Believers to Build Up the Body of Christ," *Puritan Reformed Journal*, DBU Library, (accessed Sept. 24, 2022). [See Spiritual Gifts for Biblical Church Growth by DeVries also]

9 Thomas R. Schreiner, "It All Depends upon Prophecy: A Brief Case for Nuanced Cessationalism," *Gospel Coalition*, Themelios 44, no.2019, https://www.thegospelcoalition.org/themelios/article/it-all-depends-upon-prophecy-a-brief-case-for-nuanced-cessationism.

10 Douglas C. Weaver, *Baptists and the Holy Spirit: The Contested History with Holiness-Pentecostal Charismatic Movements* (Waco: Baylor University Press, 2019).

11 Brand. "Spiritual Gifts." 1584-1585.

12 Charles Stanley, "Your Life is Your Time." *In Touch Ministries with Charles Stanley.* Oct. 17, 2022, www.crosswalk.com/devotionals/in-touch.

Chapter 9

1 A.W. Tozer, *Three Spiritual Classics in One Volume, The Knowledge of the Holy, The Pursuit of God, God's Pursuit of Man* (Chicago: Moody, 2006).

2 ——107.

3 ——298.

[4] ——411-412.

[5] ——Delighting in God, (Minneapolis: Bethany, 2015), 74-75.

[6] ——*The Crucified Life: How to Live Out a Deeper Christian Experience (Bloomington*: Bethany, 2001), 177.

[7] ——*A Cloud by Day, A Fire by Night: Finding and Following God's Will for You,* (Minneapolis: Bethany, 2021), 17.

Chapter 10

[1] First Published in The Baptist Standard under the title, *Four things help us find God's call in our lives.* Minor changes have been made to this chapter.

Chapter 11

[1] Patti Greene, Black, Eric, ed., "Voices: Four things help us to find God's Call in our lives." Baptist Standard: Connecting God's story and God's people, First published in *The Baptist Standard* on April 11, 2023. Chapter section in this book has been renamed to Discovering God's Call. https://www.baptiststandard.com/opinion/voices/four-things-help-us-find-gods-call-in-our-lives.

[2] Mark Hiehle, "God Uses Ordinary People," *Amos: The Life of an Ordinary Man*, January 2010, http://atcmag.com (accessed 2 January. 2016).

[3] Mike Huckabee, January 2, 2016, www.brainquote.com.

Chapter 12

[1] Gordon Fee and Douglas Stuart, *How to Read the Bible for All Its Worth.* (Grand Rapids: Zondervan Academic, 2014), 154.

[2] *The Baptist Standard* published a condensed version of this section under the title, God Uses Ordinary People on July 18, 2023. My title is Amos: The Life of an Ordinary Man. https://www.baptiststandard.com/opinion/voices/god-uses-ordinary-people./

Section 2 The Power of Prayer and Biblical Characters

Chapter 13

[1] Patti Greene, *Answer Me: Developing a Heart for Prayer.* Bloomington: (Westbow Press, 2017), 17.

Chapter 14

[1] Patti Greene, Eric Black, ed., Voices: The Power and Importance of Prayer, *The Baptist Standard*, 2-February 13, 2024, Voices: The power and importance of prayer, baptiststandard.com.

Chapter 15

[1] Warren Wiersbe, *The Bible Exposition Commentary: Old Testament, The Prophets, Isaiah—Malachi*, vol.4, (Cook: Colorado Springs, 2002), 10.

[2] Patti Greene, *Answer Me. Developing a Heart for Prayer* (Bloomington: Westbow Press, 2017), 5.

Chapter 16

[1] Source Unknown.

Chapter 17

[1] Cypress Bible Church, "Praying for Your Children," Flyer. [1983], https://www.cypressbible.org.

Chapter 18

[1] "Habakkuk: A Model of Prayer and Worship Books of the Bible," *At a Glance, "Teach Sunday School*, n.p. : n.d., marykate@teachsundayschool.com (accessed March 2019).

Chapter 19

[1] Warren Wiersbe, *Real Worship: Playground, Battleground, or Holy Ground?* 2nd ed., (Grand Rapids: Baker Books, 2004), 82.

Chapter 20

[1] Charles, H.B., *On Preaching: Personal & Pastoral Insights for the Preparation & Practice of Preaching* (Chicago: Moody, 2014).

[2] ——*On Preaching: Personal & Pastoral Insights for the Preparation & Practice of Preaching* (Chicago: Moody, 2014).

Chapter 21

[1] Cynthia Rylant and Stephen Gammell, *The Relatives Came* (New York City: Aladdin, 1993).

[2] "[Barna] State of the Bible: USA 2023", Chicago: American Bible Society, 2023. https://sotb.research.bible.

Chapter 22

[1] Richard Stefanacci, Overview of Aging, *Merck Manual Consumer Version*. April 2024, https://www.merckmanuals.com/home/older-people-s-health-issues/the-aging-body/overview-of-aging.

[2] A.W. Tozer, Experiencing the Presence of God: Teachings from the Book of Hebrews, Minneapolis: Bethany House, 2010. Page 54 about preachers.

[3] *How to Experience New Life in Christ* Bookmark. Originally purchased on Amazon.com

[4] Patti Greene, Eric Black, ed., "Voices: Continuing to serve God while aging," *The Baptist Standard:* Connecting God's story and God's people, First published in the Baptist Standard on October 9, 2023. https://greenepastures.org/new-blog-continuing-to-serve-god-while-aging-by-patti-greene.

Section 3 Navigating the Path of Christian Living and Biblical Characters

Chapter 23

[1] *Elementary Bible Truths Handbook,* "Wisdom" (Greenville: Bob Jones University Press, 1981), 92.

[2] Adrian Rogers. "Daily Devotional: God's Point of View" https://www.lwf.org/daily-devotionals/gods-point-of-view October 16, 2022 (accessed March 11, 2023).

[3] Pelagie Doane, *A Small Child's Bible* (New York: Oxford University Press), 1945, 70, 86.

[4] Warren Wiersbe.

[5] Lance Benzel, "Former Colorado Springs mayoral candidate allegedly duped local man before baby abduction plot," *The Gazette*, Feb 18, 2020, Updated Feb 25, 2020, Gazette.com.

Chapter 24

[1] Gertrude Crampton, *Scuffy the Tugboat,* Racine: Golden Books, 2001.

[2] Patti Greene, Eric Black, ed., "Voices: Choose to Follow God's Path of Life," First published in *The Baptist Standard* on August 28, 2023, Chapter title is Choosing God's Path. https://www.baptiststandard.com/opinion/voices/choose-to-follow-gods-path-of-life. [Derek Kidner Quote].

[3] —— Voices: "Choose to Follow God's Path of Life."

Chapter 25

[1] Tony Evans, "Taking out the trash: Bring it to Jesus," Dallas: The Urban Alternative, 2022, https://tonyevans.org/taking-out-the-trash.

[2] Charles Haddon Spurgeon, August 12, "1888 Scripture: Joshua 1:10-11" from *Metropolitan Tabernacle Pulpit*, vol. 34, https://www.spurgeon.org/resource-library/sermons/crossing-the-jordan/#flipbook, (accessed 1-31-2023).

[3] Marissa Laliberte, "The Surprising Origin of Nike's 'Just Do It' Slogan," *Reader's Digest*, Updated Nov. 9, 2022, https://www.rd.com/article/nike-just-do-it-origin (accessed March 11, 2023).

[4] Richard S. Hess, *Joshua: An Introduction and Commentary*, vol. 6, Tyndale Old Testament Commentaries (Downers Grove: InterVarsity Press, 1996), 107-117.

[5] Charles Stanley, "The Path of Life," *In Touch Ministries*, January 3, 2023, https://www.intouch.org/read/daily-devotions/the-path-of-life.

Chapter 26

[1] Unknown, Vice-President for Peas Please. Stories for Preaching, (accessed January 16, 2004). http://storiesforpreaching.com,au/sermonillustrations/vic-president-of-peas-please.

[2] Adrian Rogers, 'The Problem of Pride," (accessed March 11, 2024, April 16, 2023. http://www.lwf.org/sermons/video/the-problem-with-pride-2223.

[3] Adrian Rogers, "The Peril of Pride: Love Worth Finding," *One Place,* 15 Feb 2011. https:www.oneplace.com/ministries/love-worth-finding/read/articles/the-peril-of pride-12738.html.

Chapter 27

[1] Vance Christie, "The Little Servant of an Illustrious Master," 2014. https://vancechristie.com/2014/09/06/little-servant-illustrious-master-hudson-taylor/

[2] Spurgeon, Charles Haddon, "Pride and Humility." *The Spurgeon Center for Biblical Preaching at Midwestern Seminary*, August 17, 1856, https://www.spurgeon.org/resource-library/sermons/pride-and-humility/#flipbook (accessed March 11, 2024).

Chapter 30

[1] Catherine Treyz, "Ohio Fugitive Who Sent Police a Selfie is Arrested," *CNN*, January 12, 2016, https://www.cnn.com/2016/01/12/us/ohio-fugitive-sends-selfie-to-police/index.html.

[2] Dee Leone. Text messages between Patti Greene and Dee Leone, 2024.

Chapter 32

[1] "Motive," Merriam-Webster Dictionary. http://www.Merriam-Webster Dictionary.com/dictionary/Motive

2 "Intention," Merriam-Webster Dictionary. http://www.Merriam-WebsterDictionary.com/dictionary/Intention

3 Joshua Kennon, "To Have a More Successful Life, Understand the Motivations and Motives of Yourself and the People Around You," (accessed 20 Oct 2018). http://JoshuaKeenan.com/motives-and-motivations-matter.

Chapter 33

1 Penman Tarisai, "The Wisdom of Purah: Gideon's Mentor," *Blog*, October 16, 2011, https://writersfield.wordpress.com/2011/10/16/the-wisdom-of-purah.

2 "Judges 7 Summary in 5-minutes", Accessed May 1, 2025, https://www.2belikechrist.com/articles/judges-7-summary-in-5-minutes.

Chapter 34

1 Bill Bright, *Ten Basic Stops toward Christian Maturity*, Arrowhead Springs: San Bernardino, 1968.

2 Jim Scott Orrick, "Sanctification," *Holman Illustrated Bible Dictionary*, revised and expanded (Nashville: B&H, 2015),1412-1413.

Section 4 Pioneering Leadership Principles and Biblical Characters

Chapter 36

1 "Barnabas," *Lexham Bible Dictionary*, *Logos Bible Software*, www.logos.com.

(accessed June 2, 2022).

2 Peter G. Northouse, *Leadership: Theory & Practice*, 9th ed. (Thousand Oaks: Sage,

3 C. Gene Wilkes, *Jesus on Leadership: Timeless Wisdom on Servant Leadership*, (Carol Stream: Tyndale, 1998), 11-12.

[4] Norman Blackaby and Gene Wilkes, *Character: The Pulse of a Disciple's Heart*, (Birmingham: New Hope, 2012), 166+.

[5] ——C. Gene Wilkes, Jesus on Leadership.

Chapter 37

[1] "Nehemiah: Who wrote the book?" The Bible-Teaching Ministry of Charles R. Swindoll, Insight for Living, June 2015, Insight.org.

[2] Stedman, Ray, "Nehemiah: Rebuilding the Walls," *Authentic Christianity*, June 21, 2015,

Accessed March 15, 2024. http:www.raystedman.org/old-testament/Nehemiah.

Chapter 38

[1] Richard, Losch, "Ahab." *All the People in the Bible: An A-Z Guide to the Saints, Scoundrels, And Other Characters in Scripture,* (Grand Rapids: Eerdmans, 2008), 20.

[2] Neil Thanedar, "15 Traits of a Terrible Leader," *Success Magazine*, https://www.success.com/15-traits-of-a-terrible-leader (accessed January 13, 2015).

[3] Jay Tolson, "Worst Presidents: Warren Harding (1921-1923)," *U.S. News and World Reports,* Feb 16, 2007, https://www.usnews.com/news/special-reports/the-worst-presidents/articles/2014/12/17/worst-presidents-warren-harding-1921-1923.

Section 5 Overcoming Spiritual Breaking Points

Chapter 39

[1] [Barna] *State of the Bible: USA 2023*, https://sotb.research.bible (Chicago: American Bible Society, 2023), 189-190.

[2] "Taming the Crisis at Lagos Airport Cargo Terminal," *This Day*, November 28, 2014, https://www.pressreader.com/nigeria/thisday/20141128/281646778455906

Chapter 40

[1] Mark Altrogge, "There Are No Accidents with God," [Originally taken from Tony *Evans' Book of Illustrations: Stories, Quotes, and Anecdotes from more than 30 years of preaching and public speaking,* September 14, 2015, https://churchleaders.com/pastors/pastor-articles/262020-no-accidents-god.html/2.

[2] "Top ? People Want to Ask God: Why allow pain and suffering in this world," *Christianity Today,* n.d., https://www.christiantoday.com.au/news/top-question-people-want-to-ask-god-why-allow-pain-and-suffering-in-this-world.html.

[3] Mary J. Yerkes, "When We Suffer: A Biblical Perspective on Chronic Pain and Illness," *Focus on the Family,* February 1, 2007. https://www.focusonthefamily.com/get-help/when-we-suffer-a-biblical-perspective-onchronic-pain-and-illness.

[4] David Wilkerson, *David Wilkerson's Quotes,* Brainy Quotes, https://www.brainyquote.com/quotes/david_wilkerson_296533 (accessed March 12, 2024).

[5] Elisabeth Elliott, "Quotes by Elisabeth Elliott," *Goodreads,* https://www.goodreads.com/quotes/1087066-i-am-not-a-theologian-or-a-scholar-but-i, (accessed March 12, 2024).

[6] Billy Graham, *The Billy Graham Christian Worker's Handbook: A Layman's Guide for Soul Winning and Personal Counseling* (Minneapolis: World Wide, 1984), 223.

Chapter 41

[1] Bill Hutchinson, "Extraordinary act of mercy: Brother of Botham Jean hugs and forgives Amber Guyger after 10-year sentence imposed," *ABC News,* October 2, 2019, https://abcnews.go.com/US/jury-deciding-sentence-police-officer-amber-guyger-wrong/story?id=66002182, (accessed March19, 2022).

[2] Gary M. Burge and Gene L. Green, *The New Testament in Antiquity: Survey of the New Testament,* 2nd ed. (Grand Rapids: Zondervan, 2020), 248.

[3] Allison Trites, "Luke," Paul D. Gardner, ed., *Who's Who in the Bible?* (Grand Rapids: Zondervan, 1995). 422.

[4] ——Luke. 422-428.

[5] William Barclay, ed., *The Gospel of Luke,* rev. ed. (Philadelphia: Westminster, 1975), 76.

[6] James Strong, *A Concise Dictionary of the Words in The Greek Testament and The Hebrew Testament: with their renderings in the Authorized English Version*, Logos Bible Software, (accessed March 24, 2024).

[7] "Golden Rule," *Merriam-Webster*, m-w.com (accessed 3-12-2024).

[8] William Barclay, ed., *The Gospel of Luke.*

[9] Leon Morris, Luke: An Introduction and Commentary, vol. 3, Tyndale New Testament Commentaries (Downers Grove, IL: InterVarsity Press, 1988), 149–152.

[10] Robert H. Gundry, *A Survey of the New Testament,* Grand Rapids: Zondervan, 1976.

[11] Bill Hutchinson, "Extraordinary act of mercy: Brother of Botham Jean hugs and forgives Amber Guyger after 10-year sentence imposed," *ABC News*, October 2, 2019, https://abcnews.go.com/US/jury-deciding-sentence-police-officer-amber-guyger-wrong/story?id=66002182, (accessed March19, 2022).

Chapter 42

[1] "Burned-out," *Merriam Webster's Thesaurus*, https://www.merriam-webster.com/thesaurus/burned-out (accessed 6-1-2024).

[2] *Guide to Medical Cures & Treatments*, Montreal: The Reader's Digest Association, 1996. 392.

[3] "10 Tips to Manage Stress," *WebMD Editorial Contributors*, April 29, 2023, https://www.webmd.com/balance/tips-to-control-stress.

[4] Bonar, Horatius. "Thy Way, Not Mine, O Lord."
Public Domain. Accessed March 12, 2024
https://hymnary.org

Chapter 43

[5] June Hunt, *Hope: The Anchor of Your Soul,* Hope for the Heart. Rose Publishing, 2025. 6-8.

Chapter 44

[6] "Remembering Anthony Bourdain," hosted by Christiane Amanpour, *A CNN Special Report,*2018, on CNN, April 6, 2022, reposted on YouTube, https://video.search.yahoo.com/search/video?fr=mcafee&p=cnn+and+%E2%80%9CRemembering+Anthony+Bourdain%E2%80%9D+what+day+was+it+on+tv&type=E210US885G91826#id=2&vid=ebe24bfa40b1b0403be9f01d5bb892a3&action=click.

[7] "Lifeline and 988," 988 Suicide and Crisis Lifeline, https://988lifeline.org (accessed March 13, 2024).

Chapter 45

[1] "Mesothelioma," *Mayo Clinic,* https://www.mayoclinic.org/diseases-conditions/mesothelioma/symptoms-causes/syc-20375022 (accessed March 13, 2024).

[2] Greene, Patti, "Coping with Grief and Loss," Minnie Patterson's Story, Interview by Greene, August 18, 2016. GreenePastures.org. Minnie Patterson granted permission to use this article by text on March 15, 2024.

Chapter 46

[1] Greene, Patti, "My friend Tamara: Life, God, Cancer, and Death," GreenePasturs.org. December 8, 2015, https://greenepastures.org/?s=tamara. The original name used in this article was a pen name. The subject's birth name is used in this article—Felistus.

Photo Credits

Author Photo: John Greene, Sr.

Cover: Canva

Chapter 1-5: Canva

BIBLIOGRAPHY

Altrogge, Mark. "There Are No Accidents with God." [Originally taken from Tony Evans' *Book of Illustrations: Stories, Quotes, and Anecdotes from more than 30 years of preaching and public speaking.* September 14, 2015. https://churchleaders.com/pastors/pastor-articles/262020-no-accidents-god.html/2.

Barclay, William, *The Gospel of Luke.* revised ed. Philadelphia: Westminster Press, 1975.

[Barna] "*State of the Bible: USA 2023.*" Chicago: *American Bible Society,* 2023. https://sotb.research.bible.

Barnabas. (2002). R. Brownrigg, *Who's Who in the New Testament.* Routledge (2nd ed.). Routledge. Credo Reference. http://library.dbu.edu:2048/login?url=https://search.credoreference.com/content/entry/routwwnt/barnabas0?institutionId=2659.

"Barnabas." in *Lexham Bible Dictionary. Logos Bible Software.* Accessed June 2, 2022. www.logos.com.

Bell, Caleb. "Poll: Americans love the Bible but don't read it much." *Religion New,* April 4, 2013. Web. December 27, 2015. https://religionnews.com/2013/04/04/poll-americans-love- the-bible-but-dont-read-it-much/

Benzel, Lance. "Former Colorado Springs mayoral candidate allegedly duped local man before baby abduction plot," *The Gazette.* Feb 18, 2020; Updated Feb 25, 2020. Gazette.com.

"Best-Selling Book." *Guinness World Records.* Accessed March 10, 2024. https://www.guinnessworldrecords.com/world-records/best-selling-book-of-non-fiction.

"Bible, Ignorance of." Wycliffe Handbook of Preaching and Preachers Chicago: Moody, 1984, SermonIllustrations.com.

Blackaby, Norman and Gene Wilkes, *Character: The Pulse of a Disciple's Heart*. Birmingham: New Hope, 2012.

Boner, Horatius. "Thy way, Not Mine, O Lord." Public Domain. Public Domain. Accessed March 12, 2024 https://hymnary.org.

Brand, Chad, "Spiritual Gifts." *Holman Illustrated Bible Dictionary*. Nashville: Holman Reference, 2009.

Bright, Bill. *Ten Basic Stops toward Christian Maturity*. Arrowhead Springs: San Bernardino, 1968.

Brooks, James. "Barnabas." *Holman Illustrated Bible Dictionary*, revised ed. by Chad Brand, Eric Mitchell, and Holman Reference Editorial Staff. Nashville: B&H Publishing, 2015.

Briggs, David. "Who Reads the Bible—and Why." *Ahead of the Trend*. 7 March 2014. Accessed 18 March 2019. https://www.huffingtonpost.com/david-briggs/who-reads-the-bibleand_b_4919444.html.

Bunn, John, "Ezekiel" *The Broadman Bible Commentary*, No. 6. Nashville: Broadman Press, 1971.

Burge, Gary M. and Gene L. Green. *The New Testament in Antiquity: Survey of the New Testament*, 2nd ed. Grand Rapids: Zondervan, 2020.

"Burned-out," *Webster's Thesaurus*. Accessed 6-1-2024. https://www.merriam-webster.com/thesaurus/burned-out.

Charles, H.B., *On Preaching: Personal & Pastoral Insights for the Preparation & Practice of Preaching*. Chicago: Moody, 2014.

Christie, Vance. "The Little Servant of an Illustrious Master," 2014. http://vancechristie.com.2014/09/06/little-servant-illustrious-master-hudson-taylor.

Crampton, Gertrude. *Scuffy the Tugboat* Racine: Golden Books, 2001.

Cross, Frank and Elizabeth Livingstone, ed. "Barnabas." *Oxford Dictionary of the Christian Church,* 3rd ed. Accessed June 2, 2022. https://wwwoxfordreference.com.library.dbu.edu/view/10.1093/acref/9780192802903.001.0001/acref-9780192802903.

Cypress Bible School, Flyer, 1983. https://www.cypresschristian.org.

Deibert, Brannon, "What are the Seven Gifts of the Holy Spirit?" Accessed Sept 4, 2022. www.christianity.com.

DeVries, Brian. "Spiritual Gifts for Biblical Church Development: The Holy Spirit Working through Believers to Build Up the Body of Christ." *Puritan Reformed Journal.* Accessed DBU Library, Sept. 24, 2022.

Doane, Pelagie, *A Small Child's Bible.* New York: Oxford University Press, 1945.

Elementary Bible Truths Handbook. Greenville: Bob Jones University Press, 1981.

Elliot, Elisabeth. "Quotes by Elisabeth Elliott." *Goodreads.* Accessed March 12, 2024. https://www.goodreads.com/quotes/1087066-i-am-not-a-theologian-or-a-scholar-but-i.

Evan, Tony. "Taking out the trash: Bring it to Jesus." Dallas: The Urban Alternative, 2022. https://tonyevans.org/taking-out-the-trash.

Fee, Gordon and Douglas Stuart, *How to Read the Bible for All Its Worth.* Grand Rapids: Zondervan Academic, 2014.

Graham, Billy, *The Billy Graham Christian Worker's Handbook: A Layman's Guide for Soul Winning and Personal Counseling.* Minneapolis: World-Wide, 1984

Graham, Billy, *The Holy Spirit: Activating GOD'S Power in Your Life.* Waco: Word Books, 1978.

Greene, Patti, *Answer Me: Developing a Heart for Prayer.* Bloomington: Westbow, 2017.

Greene, Patti. "Coping with Grief and Loss." Minnie Patterson's Story. Interview by Greene. August 18, 2016. GreenePastures.org.

Greene, Patti, Eric Black, ed., "Voices: Choose to Follow God's Path of Life." First published in the *Baptist Standard: Connecting God's story and God's people,* August 28, 2023. Chapter title is Choosing God's Path, https://www.baptiststandard.com/opinion/voices/choose-to-follow-gods-path-of-life. Permission given by Eric Black to use this article by email on March 15, 2024.

Greene, Patti. Eric Black, ed., "Voices: Continuing to Serve God while Aging." First published in the *Baptist Standard: Connecting God's story and God's people*, October 9, 2023. Chapter title is Continuing to Serve God While Aging, https://www.baptiststandard.com/opinion/voices/continuing-to-serve-god-while-aging. Permission given by Eric Black to use this article by email on March 15, 2024.

Greene, Patti. Eric Black, ed. "Voices: Four things help us to find God's Call in our lives." First published in the *Baptist Standard: Connecting God's story and God's people*, April 11, 2023. Chapter title is "Discovering God's Call," https://www.baptiststandard.com/opinion/voices/four-things-help-us-find-gods-call-in-our-lives. Permission given by Eric Black to use this article by email on March 15, 2024.

Greene, Patti. Eric Black, ed., "Voices: God uses Ordinary People. First published in the *Baptist Standard: Connecting God's story and God's people*," July 18, 2023. *The Baptist Standard* used a condensed version of the article used in this book. https://www.baptiststandard.com/opinion/voices/god-uses-ordinary-people. Permission given by Eric Black to use this article by email on March 15, 2024.

Greene, Patti. Eric Black, ed., "Voices: The Power and Importance of Prayer," First published in the *Baptist Standard: Connecting God's story and God's people*, February 13,2024. The chapter title is The Power and Importance of Prayer. https://www.baptiststandard.com/opinion/voices/the-power-and-importance-of-prayer. Permission given by Eric Black to use this article by email on March 15, 2024.

Greene, Patti. Taken from "My Friend Tamara: Life, God, Cancer, and Death. December 8, 2024. https://GreenePastures.org/?s=tamara.

Guide to Medical Cures & Treatments. Montreal: The Reader's Digest Association, 1996.

Gundry, Robert H, *A Survey of the New Testament.* Grand Rapids: Zondervan, 1976.

"Habakkuk." *Books of the Bible: At a Glance. Teach Sunday School.* Accessed March 2019. n.p.: n.d. marykate@teachsundayschool.com.

Henderson, Melissa. "A Comprehensive Spiritual Gifts List to Discover Your Gifts and Calling." *Bible Study Tools.* Accessed March 14, 2024. https://www.biblestudytools.com/bible-Study/topical-studies/a-comprehensive-spiritual gifts-list-to-discover-your-gifts-and-calling.html.

Hess, Richard S, *"Joshua: An Introduction and Commentary,"* vol. 6. *Tyndale Old Testament Commentaries.* Downers Grove: InterVarsity Press, 1996.

Hiehle, Mark, *God Uses Ordinary People.* "Amos: the Life of an Ordinary Man." http://atcmag.com. January 2010. Web. January 2 2016.

The Holy Bible: *English Standard Version containing the Old and New Testament.* Wheaton: Crossway, 2001.

How to Experience New Life in Christ Bookmark. Originally purchased on Amazon.com

Huckabee, Mike. Web. January 2, 2016. www.brainquote.com.

Hunt, June. *Hope: The Anchor of Your Soul.* Hope for the Heart. Black Mountain, ND: Rose Publishing, 2025.

Hutchinson, Bill, "Extraordinary act of mercy: Brother of Botham Jean hugs and forgives Amber Guyger after 10-year sentence imposed," *ABC News*, October 2, 2019. Accessed March 19, 2022). https://abcnews.go.com/US/jury-deciding-sentence-police-officer-amber-guyger-wrong/story?id=66002182.

"Is Faith in God a Crutch?" Accessed 8 March 2019. https://www.gotquestions.org/faith-God-crutch.html.

"Judges 7 Summary in - 5-minute.," Accessed May 1, 2025. https://www.2belikechrist.com/articles/judges-7-summary-in-5-minutes.

Kennon, Joshua. "To Have a More Successful Life, Understand the Motivations and Motives of Yourself and the People Around You."

Accessed 20 Oct 2018. http://JoshuaKeenan.com/motives-and-motivations-matter.

Laliberte, Marissa. "The Surprising Origin of Nike's 'Just Do It' Slogan." *Reader's Digest.* Accessed March 11, 2023. Updated Nov. 9, 2022. https://www.rd.com/article/nike-just-do-it-origin.

Leone, Dee. Text messages between Patti Greene and Dee Leone, 2024.

"Lifeline and 988, The." *988 Suicide and Crisis Lifeline,* Accessed March 13, 2024. https://988lifeline.org.

Losch, Richard, *All the People in the Bible: An A-Z Guide to the Saints, Scoundrels, And Other Characters in Scripture.* Grand Rapids: Eerdmans, 2008.

Merriam-Webster, "Golden Rule." Accessed March 12, 2024. m-w.com.

Merriam-Webster's Thesaurus. "Stressed." Accessed March 12, 2004. https://www.merriam webster.com/thesaurus/stressed.

"Mesothelioma." *Mayo Clinic.* Accessed March 13, 2024. http://www.mayoclinic.org/diseasesconditions/mesothelioma/symptoms-causes/syc-20375022.

Michuta, Gary. *The Pilgrims' Regress: The Geneva Bible and the "Apocrypha."* Accessed March 10, 2024. http://www.handsonapologetics.com/Geneva_Bible.htm.

Morris, Leon, *Luke: An Introduction and Commentary,* Vol. 3, *Tyndale New Testament Commentaries.* Downers Grove, IL: InterVarsity Press, 1988.

"Motive." *Merriam-Webster Dictionary.* Accessed 5-23-2004. http://www.merriam-webster.com/thesaurus/motive.

"Nehemiah: Who wrote the book?" The Bible-Teaching Ministry of Charles R. Swindoll. Insight for Living. June 2015. Insight.org.

Northouse, Peter G, *Leadership: Theory & Practice,* 9th ed. Thousand Oaks: Sage, 2022.

Orrick, Jim Scott, "Sanctification." *Holman Illustrated Bible Dictionary.* Revised and expanded.

Nashville: B&H, 2015. "Pneuma." *New Testament Greek Lexicon.* Accessed Oct. 13, 2022. www.biblestudytools.com/Lexicons/Greek/nas/pneuma.html.

Pollock, John, "Victory in 30 Seconds: How Castrated Hogs, Baseball, and Other Analogie Shape U.S. Elections." *Washington Monthly.* November 6, 2014. Accessed June 1, 2024). https://washingtonmonthly.com/2014/11/06/victory-in-30-seconds-how-castrated-hogs-baseball-and-other-analogies-shape-u-s-elections/

Pratt, Richard L. *I & II Corinthians, vol. 7. Holman New Testament Commentary.* Accessed LOGOS Sept 5, 2022. Nashville: Broadman & Holman Publishers, 2000.

Ramm, Bernard. "Bernard Ramm." *Wikipedia.* Accessed 17 March 2019. https://en.wikipedia.org/wiki/Bernard_Ramm.

"Remembering Anthony Bourdain," hosted by Christiane Amanpour on CNN, April 6, 2022. *A CNN Special Report, 2018,* posted on YouTube. https://video.search.yahoo.com/search/video?fr=mcafee&p=cnn+and+%E2%80%9CRemembering+Anthony+Bourdain%E2%80%9D+what+day+was+it+on+tv&type=E210US885G91826#id=2&vid=ebe24bfa40b1b0403be9f01d5bb892a3&action=click.

Rogers, Adrian, *Adrianisms: The Collected Wit and Wisdom of Adrian Rogers.* Collierville: Publishing, 2015.

Rogers, Adrian. "Daily Devotional: God's Point of View," October 16, 2022. Accessed March 11, 2023. https://www.lwf.org/daily-devotionals/gods-point-of-view.

Rogers, Adrian. "How to Make the Bible Come Alive." *Love Worth Finding. OnePlace.* Accessed March 18, 2019. https://www.oneplace.com/ministries/love-worth-finding/read/articles/how-to-make-your-bible-come-alive-15522.html.

Rogers, Adrian, "The Peril of Pride: Love Worth Finding." *One Place.* 15 Feb. 2011.

Rogers, Adrian. "The Problem of Pride." Accessed March 11, 2024. April 16, 2023. http://www.lwf.org/sermons/video/the-problem-with-pride-2223.

Rylant, Cynthia and Stephen Gammell, *The Relatives Came*. New York City: Aladdin, 1993.

Schreiner, Thomas R., "It All Depends upon Prophecy: A Brief Case for Nuanced Cessationism." *The Gospel Coalition*. *Themelios*, 44, no. 1., 2019.

Smith, Michael, *Becoming More like Jesus*. Colorado Springs: NavPress, 1999.

Spurgeon, Charles Haddon. August 12, "1888 Scripture: Joshua 1:10-11." *Metropolitan Tabernacle Pulpit Volume 34*. Accessed 1-31-2023. www.spurgeon.org/resource-library/sermons/crossing-the-jordan/#flipbook.

Spurgeon, Charles Haddon. "Pride and Humility." *The Spurgeon Center for Biblical Preaching at Midwestern Seminary*. August 17, 1856. Accessed March 11, 2024. https://www.spurgeon.org/resource-library/sermons/pride-and-humility/#flipbook.

Stanley, Charles, "The Path of Life," *In Touch Ministries*, January 3, 2023. https://www.intouch.org/read/daily-devotions/the-path-of-life.

Stanley, Charles. "Your Life is Your Time," *In Touch Ministries with Charles Stanley*. Oct. 17, 2022, www.crosswalk.com/devotionals/in-touch.

Stedman, Ray. "Nehemiah: Rebuilding the Walls." *Authentic Christianity*. June 21, 2015. Accessed March 15, 2024. http:www.raystedman.org/old-testament/Nehemiah.

Stefanacci, Richard. "Overview of Aging", *Merck Manual Consumer Version*. April 2024, https://www.merckmanuals.com/home/older-people-s-health-issues/the-aging-body/overview-of-aging.

Strong, James. *A Concise Dictionary of the Words in The Greek Testament and The Hebrew Testament: with their renderings in the Authorized English Version*. Logos Bible Software Accessed March 24, 2024).

"Taming the Crisis at Lagos Airport Cargo Terminal," *This Day*, November 28, 2014. https://www.pressreader.com/nigeria/thisday/20141128/281646778455906

Tarisai, Penman, "The Wisdom of Purah: Gideon's Mentor." *Blog*. October 16, 2011. https://writersfield.wordpress.com/2011/10/16/the-wisdom-of-purah.

"10 Tips to Manage Stress," WebMD Editorial Contributors, April 29, 2023. https://www.webmd.com/balance/tips-to-control-stress.

Thanedar, Neil, "15 Traits of a Terrible Leader," *Success Magazine,* 13 Jan. 2015. https://www.success.com/15-traits-of-a-terrible-leader.

Tolson, Jay, "Worst Presidents: Warren Harding (1921-1923)," *U.S. News and World Reports,*

16 Feb. 2007. https://www.usnews.com/news/special-reports/theworstpresidents/articles/2014/12/17/worst-presidents-warren-harding-1921-1923.

"Top ? People Want to Ask God: Why allow pain and suffering in this world," *Christianity Today,* n.d. https://www.christiantoday.com.au/news/top-question-people-want-to-ask-god-why-allow-pain-and-suffering-in-this-world.html.

Touch of Class. Touchofclass.com.

Tozer, A.W., *A Cloud by Day, A Fire by Night: Finding and Following God's Will for You,* Minneapolis: Bethany, 2021.

Tozer, A.W., *The Crucified Life: How to Live Out a Deeper Christian Experience.* Bloomington: Bethany, 2001.

Tozer, A.W., *Delighting in God.* Minneapolis: Bethany House, 2015.

Tozer, A.W., *Experiencing the Presence of God: Teachings from the Book of Hebrews.* Minneapolis: Bethany House, 2010.

Tozer, A.W., *God's Pursuit of Man: Tozer's Profound Sequel to The Pursuit of God.* Chicago: Moody, 2015.

Tozer, A.W., *The Knowledge of the Holy: The Attributes of God: Their Meaning in the Christian Christian Faith.* San Francisco: HarperOne, 2006.

Tozer, A.W., *Three Spiritual Classics in One Volume, The Knowledge of the Holy, The Pursuit of God, God's Pursuit of Man.* Chicago: Moody, 2006.

Treyz, Catherine, "Ohio Fugitive Who Sent Police a Selfie is Arrested," *CNN.* January 12, 2016. https://www.cnn.com/2016/01/12/us/ohio-fugitive-sends-selfie-to-police/index.html.

Trites, Allison, "Luke." Paul D. Gardner, ed. *Who's Who in the Bible.* Grand Rapids: Zondervan, 1995.

Unknown. Vice-President for Peas Please. Stories for Preaching. Accessed January 16, 2004. http://storiesforpreaching.com.au/sermonillustrations/vic-president-of-peas-please

Wallace, Wanda T. and David Creelman, "Leading people when they know more than you do," *Harvard Business Review,* 16 June 2015. Web. https://www.raystedman.org/oldtestament/nehemiah.

Weaver, C. Douglas, *Baptists and the Holy Spirit: The Contested History with Holiness Pentecostal Charismatic Movements,* Waco: Baptist University Press, 2019.

"What's a Spiritual Gift? – Arriving at a Biblical Definition," *Ministry Tools Resource Center.* Accessed March 12, 2023. https://mintools.com/spiritual-gifts-definition.htm.

Wiersbe, Warren, *The Bible Exposition Commentary.* 6 vols., Cook: Colorado Springs, 2002.

Wiersbe, Warren, *Real Worship: Playground, Battleground, or Holy Ground?* 2nd ed., Grand Rapids: Baker Books, 2004.

Wilkerson, David, *Brainy Quotes,* David Wilkerson's Quotes. Accessed March 12, 2024. https://www.brainyquote.com/quotes/david_wilkerson_296533.

Wilkes, C. Gene, *Jesus on Leadership: Timeless Wisdom on Servant Leadership.* Carol Stream: Tyndale, 1998.

Yerkes, Mary J., "When We Suffer: A Biblical Perspective on Chronic Pain and Illness." *Focus on the Family*, February 1, 2007. https://www.focusonthefamily.com/get-help/when-we-suffer-a-biblical-perspective-on-chronic-pain-and-illness.

Initial Chapter Quote Sources: Available upon request.

WHEN ALL IS SAID AND DONE: MOM'S NOTE TO HER KIDS

Jennifer Laura,

John Rodman, Jr.

James Charles

This book reflects your mom's deep love for each of you. It is a testament to my unwavering love and imperfect parenting journey. Guided by God's grace, this "legacy" book shares lessons and Christian principles, aiming to leave you a profound legacy beyond material wealth from me. I want to leave a legacy of myself, my thoughts, my writings, my experiences, and God's Words. When you want to hear what Mom (and God) says, turn to this book and find comfort in my words, guiding and uplifting you on your faith journey, and learn from my mistakes.

Dad and I intentionally nurtured your love for Christ, starting from each of your first church experiences at five weeks old and even today. The day each of you accepted Christ was significant to us beyond what some can imagine. And, I have the framed pics to remind me of that special time in your lives! As your parents, we treasured the responsibility of raising you, teaching you to make choices, and now letting you go. This legacy holds words of hope and encouragement for you and your families.

Acknowledging my perfections and imperfections, I recall moments, such as dropping the garage door on Jennifer's head, denying John permission to go to a coed slumber party, and being concerned when the police misidentified Jimmy. These examples, woven into our family narrative, highlight our humanity rather than showcase failure.

While *Unstoppable: Go the Distance with God* was initially my legacy book to all three of you, only to be written for your eyes, it has evolved to be a helpful guide for anyone desiring to know how to live the Christian life. We will all leave a legacy when we leave this earth and enter our heavenly home.

I entrust my thoughts, life's journey, and Biblical truths to you and others. I want you to reference them when you need them in your lives. It is a record of my faith—my way of passing on how I tried to live, knowing I failed many times. Jennifer, you were my guinea pig child. John, you were stuck in the middle to defend yourself, and Jimmy, your siblings think you beat the rap, and you probably did. Birth order counts, kids! And I am sure you are finding that out with your own children.

Always remember that you are who you are because God made you unique. He has a specific plan for you and gave you to Dad and me because He knew we were the "perfect fit" for you. The secret to finishing well is to keep focused on the Lord. Keep your eye on the reward and end well— it is your choice. You kids are our precious gifts from God.

I am filled with gratitude for all that has bonded our family together. Know that your presence in my life is a cherished blessing and testament to God's grace. May this legacy of faith and love endure throughout generations (especially to our awesome grandkids) as a testament to the enduring power of God's divine plan.

Kids, I wrote this "legacy" book for you and our family in mind, pouring my heart into it because I genuinely care about your spiritual journey. I hope that as you read these pages, you will come to understand the depth of Jesus' deep love for you. It is my prayer that these thoughts will inspire you, and both current and future generations to embrace God's love and the Holy Spirit's guidance. Keep the Lord at the center of your lives, even long after I'm gone.

I LOVE YOU.

Mom

—and may you be able to feel and understand, as all God's children should, how long, how wide, how deep, and how high His love really is; and to experience this love for yourselves, though it is so great that you will never see the end of it or fully know or understand it.

And so at last you will be filled up with God himself.

Ephesians 3:18-19 LB

—I have fought the good fight, I have finished the course, I have kept the faith; in the future there is reserved for me the crown of righteousness, which the Lord, the righteous Judge, will award to me on that day; and not only to me, but also to all who have loved His appearing.

2 Timothy 4:7-8

ABOUT THE AUTHOR

Patti Greene

Patti Greene has a diverse portfolio of self-published and published works Her books include three prayer journals, three Bible word search puzzle books, Baptist Standard articles, and a book on Christian caregiving. She is a trusted Bible reviewer for Thomas Nelson, a world leading publisher and provider of Christian content, and an occasional speaker.

Having earned a Bachelor of Arts from Baylor University, and a Master of Theological Studies from Dallas Baptist University, Greene also completed graduate classes at Southwestern Baptist Theological Seminary and the University of Missouri. She is a dedicated Bible study teacher and currently leads a weekly Bible study group.

Greene has held various positions throughout her career, including teaching 2nd grade, being a stay-at-home mom, and working as a school librarian—with high school being her favorite level! In her younger years, she worked as a grocery store clerk, waitress, accounting clerk, human resource clerk, secretary, and book buyer for the Baptist Bookstore (currently Lifeway) always believing that every person, job, or experience has prepared her for God's next step.

Greene trusted Jesus Christ while a first-year student at Baylor University. She has remained active in her faith ever since and currently is a member of the 1463 campus of Houston's Second Baptist Church in Katy, Texas.

Greene and her husband make their home in Weston Lakes, Texas, nestled within the greater Houston area. A devoted wife, mother, and grandmother, she cherishes time spent with her husband, their three children and their spouses, seven grandchildren, and a lovely circle of friends. Always eager to connect with others, she finds joy in meeting new people and sharing stories. A self-proclaimed book enthusiast, Greene embraces her love for reading.

Other Books by the Author

Prayer Journals

Awaken Me: A Devotional Prayer Journal

Anchor Me: Laying a Foundation in Bible Study and Prayer

Answer Me: Developing a Heart for Prayer

Bible Word Search Puzzles

Bible Word Search Puzzles: The Gospels

Bible Word Search Puzzles: Acts and Epistles

Bible Word Search Puzzles: Epistles and Revelation

Other

Christian Caregiving: Practical Advice for a Happy Ending

If you enjoyed ***Unstoppable: Go the Distance with God***
please spread the word by . . .

- Giving copies of this book as gifts.

- Writing a review of this book on your blog,
  favorite booksellers website, or store,
  including Amazon, Facebook, YouTube, and more.

- Recommending this book to your church, small group,
  or book club.

NOTES

www.ingramcontent.com/pod-product-compliance
Lightning Source LLC
Chambersburg PA
CBHW060900120626
46553CB00001B/155